Political Theory and the European Constitution

In June 2003, the Convention on the Future of Europe released the text intended as the Constitution of the European Union. This timely volume provides one of the first critical assessments of the draft Constitution from the vantage point of political theory.

The topic of constitutionalism in the EU challenges many of our standard political categories and conceptions, as well as raising immediate practical questions about European integration and the reform and development of EU institutions. Addressing the process of drawing up the Constitution as well as analysing and evaluating the text itself, the volume considers issues such as:

- should the EU have a Constitution at all, and how stable would one be?
- should it contain 'European values' and, if so, what are they?
- should there be a single Charter of Rights?
- what can be learned from the convention process that brought the draft Constitution into being?

This interdisciplinary collection draws on authors from a range of intellectual traditions and will be of especial interest to students and scholars in the fields of European studies, comparative politics, political philosophy, international politics and law.

Lynn Dobson is Lecturer in European Union and International Politics in the School of Social and Political Studies at the University of Edinburgh, UK. **Andreas Follesdal** is Professor of Philosophy at the ARENA Centre for European Studies and the Norwegian Centre for Human Rights, University of Oslo. He spent 2003 as a Fulbright New Century Scholar at Harvard University.

Routledge/ECPR studies in European political science

Edited by Thomas Poguntke,
Keele University, UK

Jan W. van Deth,

University of Mannheim, Germany on behalf of the European Consortium for Political Research

ecpr

The Routledge/ECPR Studies in European Political Science series is published in association with the European Consortium for Political Research – the leading organisation concerned with the growth and development of political science in Europe. The series presents high-quality edited volumes on topics at the leading edge of current interest in political science and related fields, with contributions from European scholars and others who have presented work at ECPR workshops or research groups.

1 **Regionalist Parties in Western Europe**
   Edited by Lieven de Winter and Huri Türsan

2 **Comparing Party System Change**
   Edited by Jan-Erik Lane and Paul Pennings

3 **Political Theory and European Union**
   Edited by Albert Weale and Michael Nentwich

4 **Politics of Sexuality**
   Edited by Terrell Carver and Véronique Mottier

5 **Autonomous Policy Making by International Organizations**
   Edited by Bob Reinalda and Bertjan Verbeek

6 **Social Capital and European Democracy**
   Edited by Jan W. van Deth, Marco Maraffi, Ken Newton and Paul Whiteley

7 **Party Elites in Divided Societies**
   Edited by Kurt Richard Luther and Kris Deschouwer

8 **Citizenship and Welfare State Reform in Europe**
   Edited by Jet Bussemaker

9 **Democratic Governance and New Technology**
   Technologically mediated innovations in political practice in Western Europe
   Edited by Ivan Horrocks, Jens Hoff and Pieter Tops

10 **Democracy without Borders**
Transnationalisation and conditionality in new democracies
Edited by Jean Grugel

11 **Cultural Theory as Political Science**
Edited by Michael Thompson, Gunnar Grendstad and Per Selle

12 **The Transformation of Governance in the European Union**
Edited by Beate Kohler-Koch and Rainer Eising

13 **Parliamentary Party Groups in European Democracies**
Political parties behind closed doors
Edited by Knut Heidar and Ruud Koole

14 **Survival of the European Welfare State**
Edited by Stein Kuhnle

15 **Private Organisations in Global Politics**
Edited by Karsten Ronit and Volker Schneider

16 **Federalism and Political Performance**
Edited by Ute Wachendorfer-Schmidt

17 **Democratic Innovation**
Deliberation, representation and association
Edited by Michael Saward

18 **Public Opinion and the International Use of Force**
Edited by Philip Everts and Pierangelo Isernia

19 **Religion and Mass Electoral Behaviour in Europe**
Edited by David Broughton and Hans-Martien ten Napel

20 **Estimating the Policy Position of Political Actors**
Edited by Michael Laver

21 **Democracy and Political Change in the 'Third World'**
Edited by Jeff Haynes

22 **Politicians, Bureaucrats and Administrative Reform**
Edited by B. Guy Peters and Jon Pierre

23 **Social Capital and Participation in Everyday Life**
Edited by Paul Dekker and Eric M. Uslaner

24 **Development and Democracy**
What do we know and how?
Edited by Ole Elgström and Goran Hyden

25 **Do Political Campaigns Matter?**
Campaign effects in elections and referendums
Edited by David M. Farrell and Rüdiger Schmitt-Beck

26 **Political Journalism**
New challenges, new practices
Edited by Raymond Kuhn and Erik Neveu

27 **Economic Voting**
Edited by Han Dorussen and Michaell Taylor

28 **Organized Crime and the Challenge to Democracy**
Edited by Felia Allum and Renate Siebert

29 **Understanding the European Union's External Relations**
Edited by Michèle Knodt and Sebastiaan Princen

30 **Social Democratic Party Policies in Contemporary Europe**
Edited by Giuliano Bonoli and Martin Powell

31 **Decision Making Within International Organisations**
Edited by Bob Reinalda and Bertjan Verbeek

32 **Comparative Biomedical Policy**
Governing assisted reproductive technologies
Edited by Ivar Bleiklie, Malcolm L. Goggin and Christine Rothmayr

33 **Electronic Democracy**
Mobilisation, organisation and participation via new ICTs
Edited by Rachel K. Gibson, Andrea Römmele and Stephen J. Ward

34 **Liberal Democracy and Environmentalism**
The end of environmentalism?
Edited by Marcel Wissenburg and Yoram Levy

35 **Political Theory and the European Constitution**
Edited by Lynn Dobson and Andreas Follesdal

Also available from Routledge in association with the ECPR:
Sex Equality Policy in Western Europe, *Edited by Frances Gardiner;*
Democracy and Green Poltical Thought, *Edited by Brian Doherty and Marius de Geus;* **The New Politics of Unemployment**, *Edited by Hugh Compston;*
Citizenship, Democracy and Justice in the New Europe, *Edited by Percy B. Lehning and Albert Weale;* **Private Groups and Public Life**, *Edited by Jan W. van Deth;* **The Political Context of Collective Action**, *Edited by Ricca Edmondson;* **Theories of Secession**, *Edited by Percy Lehning;* **Regionalism Across the North/South Divide**, *Edited by Jean Grugel and Wil Hout.*

Political Theory and the European Constitution

Edited by Lynn Dobson and
Andreas Follesdal

Routledge
Taylor & Francis Group
LONDON AND NEW YORK

ecpr

First published 2004
by Routledge
2 Park Square, Milton Park, Abingdon, Oxon OX14 4RN

Simultaneously published in the USA and Canada
by Routledge
270 Madison Ave, New York, NY 10016

Routledge is an imprint of the Taylor & Francis Group

Transferred to Digital Printing 2006

Typeset in Baskerville by Wearset Ltd, Boldon, Tyne and Wear

British Library Cataloguing in Publication Data
A catalogue record for this book is available from the British Library

Library of Congress Cataloging in Publication Data
Political theory and the European constitution / edited by Lynn
Dobson and Andreas Follesdal.
     p. cm.
Includes bibliographical references and index.
1. Constitutional law—European Union countries. I. Dobson, Lynn.
II. Follesdal, Andreas.
KJE4445.P65 2004
342.4—dc22

                                                                      2003026360

ISBN10: 0-415-34067-5 (hbk)
ISBN10: 0-415-40674-9 (pbk)

ISBN13: 978-0-415-34067-0 (hbk)
ISBN13: 978-0-415-40674-1 (pbk)

Contents

Notes on contributors   ix
Series editor's preface   xi
Preface   xiv
List of abbreviations and acronyms   xv

Introduction   1
LYNN DOBSON AND ANDREAS FOLLESDAL

1 **Is Euro-federalism a solution or a problem? Tocqueville
   inverted, perverted or subverted?**   10
   PHILIPPE C. SCHMITTER

2 **The EU as a self-sustaining federation: specifying the
   constitutional conditions**   23
   DAVID McKAY

3 **A union of peoples? Diversity and the predicaments of a
   multinational polity**   40
   PETER A. KRAUS

4 **The Good, the Bad and the Ugly: the need for constitutional
   compromise and the drafting of the EU Constitution**   56
   RICHARD BELLAMY AND JUSTUS SCHÖNLAU

5 **Europe: united under God? Or not?**   75
   TORE VINCENTS OLSEN

6 **The open method of co-ordination in the European
   Convention: an opportunity lost?**   91
   MYRTO TSAKATIKA

 7 **Conceptions of freedom and the European Constitution**   103
    LYNN DOBSON

 8 **The constitutional labelling of 'The democratic life of the
    EU': representative and participatory democracy**   122
    STIJN SMISMANS

 9 **Transparency and legitimacy**   139
    DANIEL NAURIN

10 **An institutional dialogue on common principles: reflections
    on the significance of the EU Charter of Fundamental Rights**   151
    CLAUDIA ATTUCCI

11 **Motivating judges: democracy, judicial discretion, and the
    European Court of Human Rights**   164
    ROBERTO GARGARELLA

    Conclusion   175
    ANDREAS FOLLESDAL AND LYNN DOBSON

    Notes   185
    Bibliography   194
    Index   215

Contributors

Claudia Attucci is PhD candidate at the European University Institute, Florence, and works on fundamental rights in the EU. During 2003 and 2004 she held fellowships at the Department of International Politics, Aberystwyth, University of Wales, and Columbia University, New York.

Richard Bellamy FRSA is Professor in the Department of Government, University of Essex. His research interests include democratic theory and the application of legal and political theory to the EU. He has directed a number of ESRC, Leverhulme and EC-funded research projects on these topics, and co-edits the *Critical Review of International Social and Political Philosophy*.

Lynn Dobson lectures at the University of Edinburgh, and holds postgraduate degrees from the London School of Economics and Political Science and the University of Essex. Her publications in political philosophy and international affairs include *Supranational Citizenship* (in press, Manchester University Press). In 2003 she was awarded the UK Political Studies Association's Sir Ernest Barker prize for best dissertation in political theory.

Andreas Follesdal is Professor at ARENA and at the Norwegian Centre for Human Rights, University of Oslo, and Founding Series Editor of *Themes in European Governance*, Cambridge University Press. He holds his PhD from Harvard and has published numerous articles and books, especially in international political theory.

Roberto Gargarella holds J.D. and LL.M (University of Chicago). The author of many books, he teaches Constitutional Theory at the Universidad Di Tella (Buenos Aires). He is Visiting Professor at the Universities of Pompeu Fabra (Barcelona) and Bergen (Norway), and has held two Guggenheim Fellowships.

Peter A. Kraus is Professor pro tempore of Political Science at Humboldt University, Berlin, and publishes on democratic transition and consolidation, politics in Southern Europe, cultural diversity and identity politics, and European integration. Recent work focuses on the implications of cultural pluralism and multilingualism for European polity-building.

David McKay is Professor of Government, University of Essex. Author and co-author of 15 books, most recently *Designing Europe: Comparative Lessons from the Federal Experience*, Oxford University Press, 2001 (winner of WJM Mackenzie Prize for the best book published in political science, 2001).

Daniel Naurin is PhD candidate in Political Science at Goteborg University. He holds a Swedish Research Council Fellowship and has held a fellowship at the European Institute, University of Sussex. He is a member of the board of the Swedish Network for European Studies in Political Science.

Tore Vincents Olsen is PhD candidate in Political Science at the University of Copenhagen, currently working on concepts of political philosophy and the European Convention. He has been a visiting scholar at the University of Essex and the European University Institute, Florence.

Philippe C. Schmitter has been Professor in Political and Social Sciences at the European University Institute since 1996. Educated at Dartmouth College, the National Autonomous University of Mexico, and the University of Geneva, he received his PhD from the University of California, Berkeley. He taught for many years at the Universities of Chicago and Stanford.

Justus Schönlau has degrees from the University of Edinburgh and Central European University, Budapest, gaining his PhD from Reading University in 2001. He is currently researcher to Jo Leinen MEP and Post-Doctoral Fellow at the University of Exeter, working on the European Convention.

Stijn Smismans is Jean Monnet Fellow at the European University Institute, where he gained his PhD (Law), and has been Fellow at the Institut d'Etudes Politiques, Paris. He has acted as expert for the EU's Economic and Social Committee and currently researches the participation of civil society in 'new modes of governance'.

Myrto Tsakatika holds PhD in Government from the University of Essex and teaches European politics at the Athens University of Economics and Business, having held a Research Fellowship of the Italian Ministry of Foreign Affairs at the University of Trieste. She works on European governance.

Series editor's preface

In view of the fact that it has become almost commonplace to refer to the European Union as a political system *sui generis*, it can come as little surprise that reflections on the draft Constitution are confronted with very specific theoretical problems. After all, the Convention, which was convoked as a result of the Laeken European Council meeting of December 2001, and which first met in February 2002, faced a task substantially different from that normally associated with constitutional assemblies. The convocation of the Assembly did not arise from one of the 'standard' situations that normally call for writing or fundamentally revising the basic rules of the game of a polity. There was no fundamental crisis of the institutions, or even a regime change; there was neither a secession of a member state nor the foundation of a new political entity. However, there was a decided awareness that the imminent accession of ten or more new member states required some streamlining of existing decision-making rules and procedures. There was an agreement that ideally, the complex web of existing treaties should be rationalized and simplified, the competencies between different levels and actors within the European system of multi-level governance should be clarified, and its democratic legitimacy should be enhanced.

Obviously constitutions rarely represent an entirely new beginning, as they normally build on previous constitutional traditions. Yet the Convention was clearly far more constrained than most other constitutional assemblies in that it was confronted with the task of re-configuring the rules of the game without fundamentally re-writing them. After all, a subsequent intergovernmental conference would have to approve the draft Constitution, which effectively meant a shifting back 'from democracy to diplomacy' or, put more bluntly, a move from the constitutional assembly's deliberative spirit to the logic of intergovernmental bargaining.

This is one of the reasons which led some of the contributors to this volume to express scepticism as to whether a constitution was really needed. Was there not a danger of unduly constraining an ongoing evolutionary process of institution-building? However, political theory, like other sub-disciplines of political science, struggles with the considerable challenge of understanding and explaining the very specific problems posed by the process of European integration in general and, in this case, the drafting of a European constitution. Is it appropriate to refer to the European Union as a 'federation'? After all, the controversial reference to federalism was removed from the final draft of the Constitution and the sovereignty of member states is safeguarded, including a codified right to secession. What exactly is the status of the European Charter of Human Rights which forms part of the draft Constitution? And which conceptions of freedom need to be considered in the European context where one important aspect of liberty is the protection of member states against undue encroachment from the supranational centre?

Those are only a few of the questions discussed in this volume. Like many others, they tend to engage with problems that arise, at least partially, from the specific nature of the EU as a political system *sui generis*: not a federal state, yet a system characterized by elements of statehood; a political system where sovereign governments interact, yet where they accept majority decisions in important policy arenas; a political entity that elects an increasingly powerful parliament, yet one that violates the arch-democratic principle of 'one man, one vote'.

Consequently, the question of the 'democratic deficit' looms large in several contributions, and authors differ considerably as regards their evaluation of the obstacles on the path towards a more democratic and accountable European political process. If communicative integration is an essential precondition for a meaningful democratic process, Europe still has a long way to go, and the present absence of a European community of communication may severely limit the effectiveness of strategies of institutional reform intended to reduce the democratic deficit. Even the (late) inclusion of a citizens' initiative in the draft Constitution may be of little political effect, given that European issues still attract comparatively little attention in European mass publics.

Naturally, this timely book provides not only new, if necessarily tentative answers to some of these questions, it also draws attention to new problems and challenges. This includes the role of Courts of Justice in a constitutionalized European Union or a somewhat peculiar conceptualization of 'participatory democracy' embodied in the draft Constitution which seems to reserve participation mainly to civil society organizations rather than individuals.

At the time of writing, sceptics seem to have been vindicated as the Brussels summit of December 2003 failed to reach an agreement on the revision of the decision rules. As a result, the entire process of accepting the Constitution has been delayed, and even if it seems likely that a compromise will eventually be found through the usual mode of intergovernmental bargaining there are many more pitfalls to come. A large number of member states will have to put the Constitution to a referendum and, in the absence of a European collective identity, it is far from certain that approval will be forthcoming in all cases. However, even if the draft Constitution should fail to be enacted in the end, it will remain, as the editors write, 'an important landmark in the journey'. As such, the draft European Constitution is worthy of our attention and academic reflection, and this volume makes an important contribution to helping us understand it.

Thomas Poguntke, Series Editor
Keele, February 2004

Preface

It is fitting that early versions of this volume's chapters were read at a workshop on EU federalism at the University of Edinburgh. Adam Smith taught here; David Hume studied here. Both Scots enjoyed European reputations in their own lifetimes and worldwide renown thereafter; and their thoughts on federalism informed the greatest political experiment of their time, created at the 1787 US Constitutional Convention. Smith, who later held a chair in moral philosophy, championed free trade while insisting that a fair political order must regulate and supplement the market and, as an early biographer (Rae 1895) noted, held that where they clashed public morals should override private profit. The sceptical Hume, a working diplomat as well as a political and moral philosopher of the first rank, warned against an easy identification of human motivation and political project. Yet his 'Idea of a Perfect Commonwealth' (1754) reveals his interest in constitutional design: 'The subject is surely the most worth curiosity of any the wit of man can possibly devise. And ... it must be advantageous to know what is most perfect in the kind, that we may be able to bring any real constitution or form of government as near it as possible, by such gentle alterations and innovations as may not give too great disturbance to society.'

Both men would have had much to say about the European Union's Constitutional Treaty. Our authors offer their contributions to scholarship and to the public debate on the EU in the spirit of Smith and Hume, seeking the interdisciplinary enquiry, critical rigour, and mutual empathy that both stood for.

Acknowledgements are due. As editors, we thank first our contributors for responding to our absurdly tight deadlines with grace and alacrity, and also series editor Thomas Poguntke for his speedy despatch of our mutual business. We are indebted to Børge Romsloe for invaluable last-minute research assistance. Finally, we are grateful for the sterling efforts of the ECPR Joint Sessions organizing committee in the Department of Politics at Edinburgh: Elizabeth Bomberg, Antonia Dodds, Luke March, and Charles Raab. Andreas Follesdal also thanks ARENA, the Norwegian Centre for Human Rights, and the Fulbright New Century Scholar Program.

Lynn Dobson, Edinburgh and Andreas Follesdal, Oslo
February 2004

Abbreviations and acronyms

CDU	Christian Democratic Union, a German political party
CFSP	Common Foreign and Security Policy, one of the Union's three 'pillars'
COR	Committee of the Regions
CZ	the Czech Republic
DE	Germany
DK	Denmark
EC	European Community/European Communities, one of the Union's three 'pillars'
ECB	European Central Bank
ECHR	European Convention on Human Rights, an international legal agreement under the auspices of the Council of Europe and the European Court of Human Rights
ECJ	European Court of Justice
EE	Estonia
EESC	European Economic and Social Committee
ELDR	European Liberal Democrat and Reform Group, a party group in the European Parliament
EMU	Economic and Monetary Union
EP	European Parliament
EPP	European Peoples' Party, the 'Conservative' party group in the European Parliament
ES	Spain
ESCB	European System of Central Banks
EU	European Union
FI	Finland
FR	France
HU	Hungary
IE	Ireland
IGC	Intergovernmental Conference
IT	Italy
JHA	Justice and Home Affairs, one of the Union's three 'pillars'
LU	Luxembourg
LV	Latvia

MEP	Member of the European Parliament
NGO	Non-Governmental Organization
OMC	Open Method of Coordination
PES	Party of European Socialists, a party group in the European Parliament
QMV	Qualified Majority Voting
SE	Sweden
SGP	Stability and Growth Pact, an agreement between the members of EMU
SI	Slovenia
SK	Slovakia
SPD	Social Democratic Party (of Germany)
TEC	Consolidated Treaty Establishing the European Community, 1997 [1957]
TEU	Treaty on European Union, 1992 (the Maastricht Treaty)
UK	United Kingdom
UNICE	Union of Industrial and Employers' Confederations of Europe
WG	Convention Working Group

Official EU documents: citation conventions used

Citation in text	*Bibliographical entry*
COR year, Cdr number	Committee of the Regions
EESC, year	European Economic and Social Committee
CEC year, COM number	Commission of the European Communities
CONV year, number	European Convention
European Council, year	European Council
EP, year	European Parliament

Introduction

Lynn Dobson and Andreas Follesdal

The Constitutional Treaty: how did we get here?

Much of the impetus to European unification grew out of the Cold War, but the European Constitution resulted from its demise. The disintegration of the USSR from the late 1980s sparked tumultuous changes throughout the international system. In Europe the shock waves were felt immediately. The 1992 Treaty on European Union ('Maastricht') was, in part, a stopgap solution by the Community's twelve member states to these strains and the alterations in member state relationships they portended. As the Union accommodated Austria, Finland, and Sweden (in 1995) and it became increasingly apparent through the 1990s that the westernmost successor states of the former Eastern Bloc were likely to accede to the European Union in due course, questions of the EU's institutional coordination, external relations, and internal freedoms of passage became central to its development – and the limitations of the Maastricht settlement for a Union of 25 or more states ever more evident. Though the Treaties of Amsterdam (1997) and Nice (2000) attempted to address these issues, they were widely recognized to have failed.

With the accession date for the candidate states looming, the December 2001 European Council meeting in Laeken called for attention to structural issues of European integration, including the allocation of policy responsibilities – 'competences' – over levels of political authority, the role of national parliaments, the status of the Charter of Fundamental Rights, the rationalization and simplification of the treaties, and new forms of multi-level governance. Most adventurously it laid out what we now know as the convention method for the fulfilment of these tasks, though it was the Convention itself that decided to do so in the form of a 'constitutional treaty'. Previous treaties had been prepared by intergovernmental conferences (IGCs), held behind closed doors, with participants restricted to member state ministers and functionaries. While the Laeken Declaration mandated an IGC to negotiate and contract the eventual treaty, it was to do so having been prepared by a thoroughgoing constitutional convention and on the basis of its draft. This convention was born

out of the success of a first, convoked to produce the Charter of Fundamental Rights and greeted enthusiastically by commentators eager to see
it as signalling a shift from diplomacy toward democracy. Its warm reception perhaps recommended the convention method to a political elite
mindful of past ratification difficulties.

Indeed, the significance of the Convention and its draft Constitution
can scarcely be grasped without an appreciation of how it fits into larger
empirical and normative contexts: the widening and deepening of the EU
just as the so-called Monnet method passed from senescence to obsol-
escence, and increasing public dissent over the EU's presumed deficits of
democracy and legitimacy. Enlargement – 'widening' – has been mentioned already. As for 'deepening', one cause arose between the Convention's convocation on 28 February 2002 and its closing on 10 July 2003.
The US-led war in Iraq revealed divisions between the European states on
core matters of foreign policy, reinforcing the resolve of some to carve out
a more independent and unitary role for the EU in global affairs. Sharper
definition of the EU in its international environment demanded greater
unity of purpose within the EU. It also required more public legitimacy
and support than the effective performance of bureaucrats and tech-
nocrats in the duller reaches of economic policy could provide.

Why normative political theory?

Normative theoretical questions about the justification of power in the
Union – who ought to have it, under what conditions, how and when it
should be exercised, and for what purposes – have refracted into numerous debates about legitimacy, citizenship, democracy, and representation
in the EU. The Convention was asked to arrive at what amounts to a normative order for the EU. Its members, representing both the governments
and the parliaments of member and future member states and also supra-
national institutions, working under the leadership of Valéry Giscard
d'Estaing, presented a draft constitutional text in three parts to the European Council at Thessaloniki on 18 July 2003. That draft became the basis
for the intergovernmental negotiations that began on 4 October 2003.

So stood matters as our chapters were written. On 18 June 2004, as
we went to press, the European Council reached final agreement, and
the constitutional treaty coming into force – assuming it does not fall at
the ratification stage – differs in some details from the draft produced
by the Convention and analysed here. The draft itself nonetheless merits
scrutiny: it was an avowedly normative project, demanding theoretical
explication. It emerged from the IGC surprisingly well, and changes made
to it mostly relate to important but narrow issues of institutional balance.
As our analyses take longer and larger views, their arguments have force
for the final Constitution as well as for its draft. Besides, initiatives and
ideas not adopted may be filed away now but taken out and dusted off

many years hence as more opportune times present themselves. Even paths not taken are important topics for reflection, as well as possible guides to future EU development.

For political theorists the draft Constitution of July 2003 has one inestimable advantage over what eventually emerged from the intergovernmental discussions: it was precisely not the outcome of straightforward member state bargaining along settled behavioural tracks. Instead, it emerged from a process slightly nearer to the regulative ideals of political theorists: the Habermasian 'ideal speech community' or the Rawlsian 'original position'. We do not, of course, suggest these devices are sensibly regarded as organizational aspirations realizable in real-world contexts. On the contrary, we would argue for the need to distinguish, at least for theoretical purposes, criteria for the normative assessment of standards of legitimacy for institutions on the one hand, and characteristics of the normatively preferable institutions on the other. It is doubtful that a wholesale ambition on the part of any representative toward a common European good, entirely disengaged from more confined commitments, would be normatively appetising (Follesdal 2002). And of course we know the *conventionnels* could not hope to escape bounded rationality, unintended consequences, institutional loyalties, propensities to unduly conflate the common good with one's own, nor the usual clutch of human fallibilities, foibles, and partialities.

Less excusably, the Convention's participants were also extremely unrepresentative of Europe's social diversity. Only 42 of the 231 participants were women and only one of its members was manifestly of colour. As to members of other (standardly self-defined) minorities, they either lay low or were completely absent. In June 2003, representational 'roles' included member, alternate member, guest, observer, substitute observer. The total number of 'roles' was 239: Praesidium 15 (12 members, 2 Commission substitutes, 1 'guest' representing candidate states); European Parliament 32; participating states 168 (28 states[1] × 6); other EU 'institutions' 24 (Economic & Social Committee, social partners, Ombudsman, Committee of Regions). There were 8 persons who occupied 2 roles, so the number of *persons* participating was 231. Of 239 roles, 43 were occupied by 42 women, of whom 23 were alternates or substitutes rather than full members or observers. The Praesidium included 1 woman, the European Parliament 12, and the other EU institutions 4. Of the 28 states, (a) 9 fielded no women out of 6, (b) 13 fielded 1, (c) 5 fielded 2, and (d) 1 state fielded 3 women (making it the sole state out of 28 to reach 50 per cent female representation). They are, respectively, (a) Denmark, Germany, Hungary, Ireland, Italy, Lithuania, Netherlands, Slovenia, Turkey; (b) Austria, Belgium, Czech Republic, Estonia, Finland, France, Greece, Luxembourg, Malta, Portugal, Romania, Spain, Sweden; (c) Bulgaria, Cyprus, Latvia, Slovakia, UK; (d) Poland. (The Praesidium member features twice as she also represented the UK.) The Convention's sole member of colour represented the UK. Tellingly, no EU institution monitored diversity of representation. [2] But we should bear in mind this was representation as found in early-modern *parlements*, convened not to represent EU citizens but to represent EU political elites. Convention members represented institutional interests, nearly all state interests, and this circumstance in itself goes a long way to explaining the Convention's very poor reflection of the European citizenry at large.

Nonetheless, with all its flaws, the convention was more open, accessible, and transparent than other methods yet ventured in EU decision-making, and also manifested more elements of consensual deliberation by and large oriented to (no doubt plural) views of the common EU good. For sure the Praesidium, particularly its President, had some latitude in gathering, interpreting, and assembling the various reports and amendments generated within the larger Convention. But its discretion was far from absolute. We may reasonably see the eventual document as the production of the Convention as a whole. It should be judged, with all its confusions and lacunae, as an attempt to arrive at a collectively acceptable normative order in the EU, and an attempt infused with other, and perhaps fewer, strategic calculations than is habitual in EU politics.

More prosaically, it may be wondered whether the actual text is worth the theoretical firepower we loose upon it. Of course, should it turn out to be the Constitution by which the EU is ordered for the next several decades, that worry – in hindsight – will look unduly timorous. But, even if the text fails to survive the ratification marathon, the EU will still have had a constitutional moment (Craig 2003: 27) – and the fact that we are close enough to know the Constitution was not produced by Olympians ought not to deter us from bringing as much theoretical perspicuity as we can to bear on its analysis. It is interesting to see exactly what a broad sample of European flesh-and-blood political elites would, when given the chance, propose as a justifiable constitutional order. And, regardless of what we surmise of actors' motivations or the extent to which those motivations factored into outcomes, we should in any case be prepared to normatively evaluate the outcome of the Convention since the constitutional treaty based on its deliberations will – if adopted – affect the configuration of power, its limits and its potentials, across the EU for some time to come.

Our rationale and contribution

European integration has provoked political philosophers and theorists to consider the EU in the light of central concepts of political theory, including sovereignty, democracy and legitimacy, and to reconsider our standard conceptions of these in the light of the EU (e.g. Weale and Nentwich 1998). The Constitution has added urgency to these concerns and widens the audience who are perplexed by them. The present volume addresses some of these core issues, shedding light on normative themes in the Convention's proposals. We do not seek to offer particular constitutional blueprints against which the Constitution ought to be compared, and certainly no normative stance – deliberative, contractualist, libertarian, republican – has been imposed. Instead, authors identify – or provide – and scrutinize the normative frameworks within which the draft Constitution answers salient questions of institutional design. Our contributors' backgrounds are in normative political theory, political science, and law, and each has undertaken their enquiry with methodological fidelity to their discipline and their subject. Just as the Convention's draft Constitution brought together normative problems and empirical practice, so each chapter addresses a normative problem in ways both empirically and theoretically informed.

The EU poses at least two challenges to a traditional conception of sovereignty as unitary, centralized public political authority: vertical, and horizontal, multi-level governance. First, the EU involves multiple territorial levels of decision-making, reminiscent – and perhaps prescient – of federal political orders of a kind known as 'coming together federations' (Stepan 2001: 320; Linz 1999). Second, EU institutions often include private actors in public decision-making in order to increase responsiveness and proximity to affected parties. Our chapters consider these 'new modes of governance' together with other institutional features, but engage the issues from a fresh perspective. Attentive to but moving beyond important technical discussions of institutional effectiveness, we grapple with the major philosophical questions: what kind of polity? And with what moral right, if any, do European politicians now rule, and claim citizens' compliance?

Besides matters on which the Convention was invited to deliberate, we explore topics already well established in the EU literature: subsidiarity, diversity, democratic and legitimacy deficits, and institutional balances of power. And we address these issues in the context of our larger philosophical questions through a number of themes that play out differently in federal or confederal than in unitary political orders:

- Constitutionalism: should the Union have a Constitution? If so what should it contain? How was the draft text arrived at and what does that process tell us? Does the Constitution mark a *finalité?* Is constitutional politics any different to IGC or day-to-day politics in the EU? How might a constitution be sustainable?
- European values: are there any common values, and, if so, what are they? How might they co-exist with particular (e.g. national) values? What is meant by the values proclaimed by the draft Constitution or embedded in institutional arrangements it establishes or affirms? Should the convention be perfectionist, mentioning values beyond those required for minimal civic functionality? In particular, should religious heritage(s) be mentioned in the Constitution?

- Liberty and power(s): different actors, ideologies, and states pursue different forms of liberty, with resulting theoretical and political tensions – between sovereignty as freedom to act, and immunity understood as non-domination; and differing imperatives for centre, large states, and small states; for majorities and minorities. How does the draft Constitution address these competing imperatives?
- Common or European interest: lofty sentiments regarding common European objectives are often muddled or conflated, different actors intending quite different things. What clarifications of the different senses of these terms can we offer?

The editors advance an ongoing research agenda, sharpening understanding of challenges confronting the EU. We highlight the need to clarify requirements for, and proper roles of, common values over and beyond mere acquiescence in the Constitution; we identify some of the tensions between partly conflicting values, and we note the difficulties of adequately specifying democratic imperatives and which roles and procedures should be subject to them. Taking it as read that the EU is not yet another statist political order to which received standards of legitimacy apply *simpliciter*, these essays contribute towards a systematic understanding of the sometimes profound differences in conceptions of what legitimacy requires, and what political power is for, in the European Union.

Constitutionalizing a multinational (con)federation

Should the Union have a Constitution emerging from a constitutional convention at all? Our first three chapters take the broadest view. Philippe Schmitter argues that this is the wrong initiative at the wrong time; David McKay and Peter Kraus look rather to specifying the challenges of establishing the EU as a federal order and evaluating how they may be met. McKay examines institutional, and Kraus sociological, conditions for success. McKay finds that the EU generally appears to meet those conditions, except for EMU arrangements. Kraus believes the EU may be able to generate a 'post-sovereign' politics of recognition, allowing processes of intercultural mediation between diverse collective identities.

Philippe Schmitter casts a sceptical eye on the prospects of a constitutional federal EU. Federalism in its current meaning, he argues, may not be a good solution in the quest for a definitive, stable, and legitimate set of EU institutions, especially at this moment in its evolution. We need to arrive at a more adequate concept than federalism to accurately capture what kind of polity the EU may become. Moreover, the EU's new mode of de-concentrated governance can only be accomplished incrementally, rather than achieved by the drafting of an entirely new Constitution. David McKay explores the challenges of stability for federal orders. They require institutional mechanisms preventing both steady centralization toward a unitary state and the unrelenting decentralization that leads to secession. Constitutional principles, modes of representation, constitutional design rules, and the structure of the party system are all relevant to assessing the stability of the emerging European order, regarded as a federal system. Peter Kraus addresses the problem of ensuring cultural diversity and political equality: the EU requires institutions providing and maintaining both overarching loyalty and an asymmetric allocation of competences. Institutional interpretations of 'diversity' and 'recognition' assume the relevant identities to be those of nation-states. What are the prospects for a politics of recognition offering a less imbalanced perspective? Reflecting on subsidiarity might help to reactivate and re-orient the constitutional debate.

The Convention process

How was the draft Constitution arrived at and what does that process tell us about its legitimacy? Our next three chapters incorporate case studies of the Convention process: Bellamy and Schönlau looking at the extent to which it did or did not conform – and should or should not have conformed – to norms of constitutional political behaviour, and Olsen and Tsakatika following in detail the Convention's work in particular areas where the notion of common values was tested. All three chapters show how 'politics as usual' dominated what had been expected to be unusual political activity.

Richard Bellamy and Justus Schönlau challenge the common justifications for constitutions and constitutional rights as providing the preconditions for politics and protecting non-political areas of life from undue political interference. Drawing on the processes of drafting the Constitution, they dispute idealized accounts of constitutional politics, instead claiming that varieties of reasonable compromise may be better suited for addressing 'constitutional' issues in the many areas where deliberation cannot be expected to produce consensus. They warn that reifying the compromises achievable at a particular time within a constitutional settlement may hinder future incremental reforms needed for changing circumstances and views. Instead, the challenge is to devise structures allowing for fair compromises in the future. Tore Vincents Olsen addresses the contested public philosophy of the Union: the defining values and principles discussed in the Convention. Does the draft Constitution, in the end, answer the Laeken Declaration's call for a vision of the Union able to enjoy legitimacy in the eyes of its citizens? Olsen argues that the Convention was unable to develop an understanding on the proper role of religion as a source of legitimacy. This inability to reach a common perspective on the nature of the Union's values suggests severe difficulties for the Constitution in serving as common ground for the European Union. Myrto Tsakatika examines the open method of coordination, where national bodies have leading roles, exploring how it may best be specified to secure the important values of legitimacy, efficiency, and respect for diversity. These matters were aired in a number of working groups during the Convention, but parallel and conflicting discourses resulted in the non-appearance of OMC in the eventual draft Constitution.

The Union's values: liberty, democracy, transparency, and rights

Since the Constitution declares the Union a normative power at home and abroad, conceptions of its values, means by which they are to be secured, and their compatibility with each other, are worth investigating. Our next five chapters probe the underlying assumptions of particular values or principles adopted within the draft Constitution. Dobson discusses three different conceptions of *liberty*, Smismans looks at (two modes of) *democracy*, Naurin identifies some self-defeating aspects of *transparency*, and Attucci and Gargarella consider the question of *rights*.

Lynn Dobson identifies three competing visions of political order springing from different conceptions of, and accounts of the interplay between, freedom and power, and discusses some of the constitutional and institutional features thought to flow from these distinct approaches. Examining provisions of the draft Constitution in their light, she finds that decisive shifts in underlying patterns of freedom and order are implied by it: the EU may have enhanced its capabilities, but heightened risks of domination. Several authors note the difficulties attending democratic imperatives. Stijn Smismans addresses two distinct versions of democracy now included in the Constitution: representative and participatory. Dealt with in several separate Articles of the draft Constitution, the precise interrelation between the two principles remains unclear, and Smismans explores these tensions. The recent focus on horizontal multi-level governance explains the inclusion of participatory democracy and the weakly developed delineation of the civil society organizations expected to participate. Participatory democracy has a strongly efficiency-driven flavour, and representative democracy remains poorly defined in its multi-level context. Among the democratic deficiencies of the EU, lack of transparency is much mentioned. The Convention suggests that both the European Parliament and the European Council ought to meet in public when discussing and adopting a legislative proposal. While generally beneficial, the gains may not be large, and there are also costs to these changes. Daniel Naurin argues that transparency as a tool for achieving legitimate outcomes is very much dependent on institutions and structures on the input side, such as European parties acting within a European public sphere. There are therefore clear limits to the extent which transparency may substitute for other reforms in the search for democratic legitimacy. Further, while transparency may strengthen output-legitimacy by preventing wrongdoing, effective problem-solving may be weakened.

Claudia Attucci explores how the EU Charter of Fundamental Rights (now incorporated into the Constitution) may contribute to the legitimacy of the EU, arguing that the Charter's worth and function lies in its enabling an institutional dialogue. Actors' normative choices on fundamental values can and ought to be justified, to other actors, against a background of common principles. The Charter underscores the legitimacy, and the limits, of different normative stands between the member states. Roberto Gargarella identifies institutional challenges regarding the courts' roles in the EU. The inclusion of the Charter and the prospect of the EU's accession to the European Convention on Human Rights (provided for by the draft Constitution) prompts a sharper look at judges' interpretive discretion on matters of individual rights. Rejecting both general optimism and general pessimism concerning the likely benefits of an independent judiciary, he insists that institutional means of motivating judges to make certain types of decision are needed.

1 Is Euro-federalism a solution or a problem?

Tocqueville inverted, perverted or subverted?

Philippe C. Schmitter

Federalism seems to be creeping onto the agenda of the European Union (EU), largely under the auspices of 'the Convention on the Future of Europe.' Although its final draft of a 'constitutional treaty' avoids an explicit reference to the concept, its declared principles of 'conferral,' 'subsidiarity,' and 'proportionality' (Title III, Art. 9) literally reek of federalist inspiration. Most observers of this process of reforming EU institutions find it difficult to imagine that 'the peoples of Europe' [could be] 'united ever more closely' [and manage to] 'forge a common destiny' (Preamble) by political means without resorting to this venerable form of state structure. We do not yet know whether this draft document will pass substantially unaltered through the Intergovernmental Conference (IGC) that began to meet in October 2003,[1] and there is even greater uncertainty about its eventual ratification by the member states. Nevertheless, the mere convocation of the Convention and the subsequent discussions surrounding it have definitely (and probably irrevocably) triggered a flood of attention concerning the meaning and the implications of federalism.

Alexis de Tocqueville, frequently extolled as one of the Godfathers of federalism, would have been surprised at this development. Although a lifelong advocate of political decentralization, he always regarded federalism as a *rara avis* – suitable for the 'exceptional' conditions of North America, but definitely not for the 'normal' conditions that (then) prevailed in Europe. Only because the United States was so isolated from international threats and had such a low intensity of class conflict due to its post-feudal origins and its open frontier could it get away with such a dispersed system of public authority. As for Switzerland, the one country in Europe that came closest to the American model at that time, Tocqueville was categorical and scornful in denying it either democratic or federalist credentials.[2]

This brings me to Tocqueville's generic message: the same rules or institutions do not produce the same results when inserted into different social structures and mores (*moeurs*). To which I would add, they also do not produce the same effect when applied to polities of different size, complexity and diversity. The well-received notion that federalism is uniquely capable of making socio-cultural and even ethno-linguistic cleavages compatible with democracy and, therefore, the 'natural' solution for the institutional design of the EU is far removed from Tocqueville's thought on the subject – no matter how frequently he may be invoked by the (self-proclaimed) 'founding fathers' (*les conventionnels*) of the constitutional treaty. In fact, what Tocqueville most admired about American federalism (and found lacking in the Swiss version) was precisely what is not likely to be enshrined in an eventual EU treaty, namely, its more statist and centralized aspects. He pointed out that, in the US Constitution, the central government had its own fiscal basis and capacity for direct intervention upon individual citizens (with force if necessary) – independent of its member states. He was especially appreciative of the role of the Supreme Court in its capability to declare state laws incompatible with federal ones (in this regard, the EU does not need a constitution). And he was not well-impressed by the fact that the ordinary policing of citizen behaviour was so variable from one state to another, considering this as no better than a necessary evil. By contrast, he considered the more 'confederal' systems of the early 1800s in Switzerland and Germany were so markedly inferior that he doubted they could survive – and, I suspect, he would have arrived at the same judgement about whatever 'federal' solution emerges from the IGC.

If and when they agree upon a definitive 'constitutional treaty,' its proponents are going to have to mount an effort similar to that of the authors of *The Federalist Papers* to convince the citizens of Europe to ratify their product. It is not going to be easy to find advocates of the intellectual quality of Madison, Hamilton and Jay (and skilled translators who will be able to transform their essays into the elegant prose of the EU's many official and unofficial languages). However, I have no doubt that there will certainly be a plethora of candidates who will volunteer for the job. But will they have a good case to argue? Should the EU become 'federal,' at least, in the same sense as existing self-declared federal polities?

Some anti-federalist thoughts

With this chapter, I am in effect applying for the eventual job of 'anti-Euro-Federalist,' i.e. for explaining (even before I have the definitive text in hand) why federalism in its prevailing meaning may not be such a good solution for the EU in its quest for a definitive-stable-legitimate set of institutions, especially at this moment in time and stage of its evolution. For, as we shall see, the political issue is not just what the meta-rules of the game should be, but also when specific rules are apposite and likely to generate consensus.

Before laying out some prospective arguments, let us first try to reach an agreement on what federalism is. The literature is notoriously 'slippery' on this matter. At one end of the spectrum are those who consider that any polity based on a 'covenant' must be, at least, partly federalist. At the other end are most American theorists who take the US model for granted as 'the' prototype and simply ask how close any other polity comes to resembling it. Nor is it conceptually acceptable to take a middle position and equate federalism with any form or degree of de-centralization or de-concentration of government. These are 'probably' related to each other along some continuum based on the territorial distribution of political authority, but how, to what degree and where to draw the line is not easy to discern, and there is more than a suspicion that the differences are qualitative and not just quantitative.

For my purpose, I will assume that a state is 'federal' if it has the following properties:

- Territorially defined political sub-units;
- Whose continued existence and decisional autonomy are constitutionally guaranteed;
- Whose participation in decisions taken by the central government is formally established, usually (but not always) as constituencies in one assembly of a bicameral legislature;
- Whose domains of policy action (*compétences*) are established and protected by statute and cannot be altered without voluntary consent;[3] and
- Whose secession or expulsion from the above arrangement cannot be accomplished unilaterally.

In other words, a federal state is considerably more than a polity that is de-centralized in its territorial structure or de-concentrated in its functional administration, but whose subordinate units can be ignored, combined or eliminated at the convenience of the central authorities. Federal sub-units have a distinct status in public law and capacity for exercising legitimate coercion within their respective domains; hence, they are not equivalent to the fluctuating multitude of private or semi-public units in civil society that may also perform important territorially or functionally based tasks within modern democracies. It should be noted, however, that this definition leaves room for a considerable range of variation within federal systems and, therefore, the issue for the EU may be not whether it should be 'federal,' but, if so, how 'federal' or, if not, what could be put in its place.

In the absence of a definitive text, my anti-federalist protestations bear a serious risk of being either vacuous or irrelevant. Once we have a final constitutional text in hand, it may turn out not to be federalist at all or to have anticipated all of my objections. All I can do at this point is 'flag' prospectively some of the controversial issues that may have to be addressed in the future.

Constitutionalization

All federal systems depend on a set of meta-rules that are established (usually by consensus among drafters and ratification by citizens). These should be considered 'sacred' by the public and inviolable or inalterable without some formal and elaborate amendment procedure. The EU presently does not have such a single and consistent set of meta-rules, just an accumulated set of treaties that are unknown and unintelligible to the public and that are periodically being altered (by unanimous consent of the member states) through new treaties. Is it desirable or feasible for the EU at this moment in time to constitutionalize its meta-rules? At a minimum, this would have to involve sequential processes of consent-formation, first by the Convention, then by the member governments in an IGC and, finally, by the citizens of each member state.

Stateness

All federal systems have at their core a political unit with the minimal properties of a state, i.e. a super-ordinate polity capable of administering legal norms and controlling the behaviour of a unique population within a specific territory through the use of a legitimate and organized mon-opoly of violence to ensure compliance. The EU is not presently a state by these criteria. Should it or could it acquire this centralized capability to impose a standard (if restricted) set of norms and behaviours, and what concentrated means of legitimate force would be necessary to make its stateness credible? It would seem that this can not be accomplished without depriving its member-states of at least some of their existing capa-bility to apply independently legitimate violence and without creating a new Europe-wide judicial and police system. Since neither of these accom-plishments seem to be presently feasible and are very unlikely to be pro-duced just by ratifying a document, my inference is that the eventual 'constitutional treaty' will neither be federal nor constitutional in conven-tional terms – and that this would be a desirable outcome.

Defined territoriality

Federations are supposed to have prescribed territorial boundaries, both external and internal – although the example of the USA demonstrates that rules can be specifically provided for a re-definition of those bound-aries. The USA also demonstrates that such extensions can be perilous for federal unity. Disagreement between North and South over the rules and consequences of 'enlargement' was a major contributor to the outbreak of the Civil War. Is it conceivable as of this moment that the founders of a federal EU will be able to fix definitively the outer and the inner bound-aries of the units that will compose it and come up with a fixed set of rules for governing such an extended polity? Given the large number of plausible candidates for membership and the practical difficulty of excluding many of them, the original members will very soon find themselves in a minority, unless they deliberately discriminate against new entrants – which would be 'anti-federal.'

Distinctive population

Each federation is presumed to have its own population that identifies predominantly, if not exclusively, with it. Moreover, if democratic, this population has to be accorded the equal rights and obligations of 'its' federal citizenship. This does not preclude simultaneous identification with one or more of its sub-units and variations in rights and obligations for different sub-units, but some overarching common identity is usually presumed to be a necessity for any federation to survive. Is it possible that, at least initially, an EU-Federation could have a population that does not identify with it and that this pseudo-*demos* could have quite different rights and obligations? Obviously, the gamble would be that, despite such an unfavourable point of departure, 'the peoples of Europe' are willing to overlook considerable discrimination in the way in which their votes are 'weighed' and are sufficiently committed to a convergence in standards and achievements that they will eventually acquire an overarching identity.

Policy compétences

According to the much-cited definition of William Riker, all federations rest upon the bedrock of a distribution of authority between central and regional governments in which each have prescribed and protected rights to make final decisions.[4] Needless to say, the formal distribution can be skewed to favour one or the other level and the actual practice can evolve over time (presumably in some consensual fashion), but at any given moment the units in a federation are supposed to have distinctive and significant policy *compétences*. This is not presently the case with the EU where, with some exceptions, very few are assigned exclusively to the supra-national level and very many are shared by more than one level. Is it either possible or desirable in a polity that is still emerging, i.e. manifestly not yet reached the functional scope demanded by its members, to attempt to fix this distribution, and is it not precisely the absence of such an effort that gives the EU significant flexibility in order to overcome differences in member preferences? Not only is it likely that, at this 'unfinished' point in the process of regional integration, the participants will be unable to agree upon such a rigid *Kompetenz-katalog*, but in order to do so they are likely to opt for some minimal common denominator solution that would prove unsatisfactory to everyone in the longer run.

Formal symmetry

Federations tend to be composed of sub-units that have the same legal status and are subject to the same rules of representation. Granted that informal distinctions in 'policy clout' do develop and that institutions such as political parties do emerge 'alongside' the constitution that can be very asymmetrically distributed across the territory, but de-centralized polities where these features are prevalent usually prefer to describe themselves differently, e.g. Spain. Despite the famous *acquis communautaire*, the EU has evolved in the direction of a polity whose members have different functional obligations and whose institutions have different territorial composition. Would it be possible for the EU to federalize itself and, at the same time, recognize formally the existence of such asymmetries? In my previous work on alternative futures for the Euro-polity, I have stressed the tendency toward what I called a *consortio* or even a *condominio* in which differences in functionally and territorially based authority might become institutionalized for some period of time.[5] A Federal Constitution *in strictu sensu* would preclude recourse to such interim solutions.

Democracy

Although many federalist theorists take it for granted, Euro-federalism would have to be made explicitly democratic. Its founding document – constitution, treaty or constitutional treaty – would have to convince the publics eventually called upon to ratify it that these rules embody adequate mechanisms so that the rulers of the federation would be held accountable to citizens of Europe for their actions in the public domain. As is already the case in the 'domestic' democracies of its member states, the actual work of accountability is done by representatives – politicians acting through parties, associations and movements. The EU may already be surrounded by lots of representatives (if rather skewed in their distribution of interests and passions), but its rulers are not accountable to them. Given the larger scale of authority and greater variety of preferences – and, hence, the more acute need to rely upon mechanisms of representation, will the usual institutions of federalism be sufficient to convince citizens that the rulers at the centre of the EU are being held accountable to them – and not to unrepresentative intermediaries or over-represented member states? My hunch is that, unless some new formula for legitimation can be found, there will always be a marked tendency to apply 'national' standards to the performance of the EU, even 'national-federal' standards, and it will inevitably be found deficient.[6]

Some thoughts on 'multi-level, poly-centric governance'

For better or worse, the present EU is not a federation or a confederation, nor is it even a state, but a 'system of multi-level, poly-centric governance,' i.e. a unique combination of the following properties:

Governance A method/mechanism for dealing with a broad range of problems/conflicts in which actors regularly arrive at mutually satisfactory and binding decisions by negotiating and deliberating with each other and co-operating in the implementation of these decisions.

Multi-level governance (MLG) An arrangement for making binding decisions that engages a multiplicity of politically independent but otherwise interdependent actors – private and public – at different levels of territorial aggregation in more-or-less continuous negotiation/deliberation/implementation, and that does not assign exclusive policy *compétences* or assert a stable hierarchy of political authority to any of these levels.

Poly-centric governance (PCG) An arrangement for making binding decisions over a multiplicity of actors that delegates authority over functional tasks to a set of dispersed and relatively autonomous agencies that are not controlled – *de jure* or *de facto* – by a single collective institution.

Moreover, I am convinced that this is likely to be the case for the foreseeable future and that efforts to 'improve' its status as either a federation or a state are likely to be counter-productive – *pace* the exaggerated expectations about what the Convention and its subsequent IGC is going to produce. This conviction rests on a *pastiche* of reasons drawn from the major contending (and, in some cases, complementing) theories of European integration.

- The EU is the product of successive treaties between formally (and formerly) sovereign national-states.
- *Ergo*, it is the outcome of a gradual and incremental process whose institutions were not modelled on any previous polity and, hence, whose eventual configuration could not be imagined in advance.
- *Ergo*, since formal revision of treaties requires unanimity, their provisions are virtually impossible to change and tend to accumulate over time – creating overlaps and inconsistencies that can only be revised by informal negotiations and that, in turn, reinforces both MLG and PCG.
- *Ergo*, if it were to be 'constitutionalized' and, thereby, its *finalité politique* defined, the EU would have to transform its MLG and PCG properties and become a polity more similar to an orthodox federal state with a democratic government – probably of the parliamentary/consociational *genus*.

- The actors/principals (i.e. the member states) that form the EU do not trust each other to respect mutual agreements faithfully and accurately.
- *Ergo*, they require an authoritative and independent agent to monitor and, when necessary, enforce these agreements – hence, the intrinsic

role for a supra-national secretariat and judiciary, i.e. the Commission and the European Court of Justice (ECJ).

- *But*, they are wary of delegating too much authority to this supra-national agent, hence, the dispersion of these monitoring and enforcing tasks to multiple sites (and the reluctance to provide it with the two key independent powers of any state, namely, taxation and security).
- *And*, even when they delegate this authority, they surround it with mechanisms of 'inter-level' representation/accountability that restrict its autonomy.
- *But*, the actors/principals do trust that none of the others will use force or the threat of force to impose an arrangement/outcome, hence, they are less concerned with relative benefits than in a traditional inter-governmental system.

- The actors/principals that form the EU do not have a common identity or politico-administrative culture.
- *Ergo*, these actors will be unwilling/unable to impose a single *modus operandi* on their common institutions and, therefore, will tend to disperse them to multiple sites.
- *Ergo*, the principals will only be capable of exercising a limited amount of solidarity among themselves, i.e. redistributing wealth from the more to the less well-endowed, and this leads to *lottizzazione* (proportional sharing out) of benefits across both territories and functions.
- *Ergo*, the member states will reciprocally defend each other's distinctive identity (out of fear of losing their own) and, therefore, prefer institutions that 'build-in' multi-level accountability – even at the cost of lower efficacy/efficiency.

- The tasks/functions independently assigned to the set of common EU institutions are sufficiently interdependent in their effects that they cannot be performed alone without incurring increasing costs or diminishing returns.
- *Ergo*, whatever the initial intentions, there will be a tendency to 'spill-over' within each function, as well as across them, and, hence, an (uneven) trend toward task expansion in both scope and level of authority.
- *Ergo*, the principals will resist this trend as much as they can, at least until awareness of the unintended and unwanted consequences begins to affect key domestic publics or the wider national citizenry who will mobilize collectively – both for and against the integration process – and, thereby, threaten what has already been accomplished.
- *When* this politicization reaches the level that it jeopardizes their tenure in office, the national governments as principals will prefer greater task expansion to contraction, but will seek to disperse its effects across a multiplicity of EU institutions – each with its surrounding system of inter-level negotiation.

- The member states of the EU were of uneven size, varying capability and different socio-economic composition at its point of departure and, thanks to successive enlargements, this diversity has increased over time – despite considerable convergence in macro-economic performances.
- *Ergo*, their initial governance arrangements reflected this diversity, as have subsequent ones – only more so.
- *Ergo*, the main consequence of this is the systematic over-representation of smaller member states – and the average member state has tended to get even smaller over time.
- *Ergo*, smaller (and, to a lesser extent, less developed) member states tend to prefer greater delegation of authority to common institutions in general (and the Commission, in particular), but they also insist on their (disproportionately) 'fair share' of voting weights, structural funds, institution sites, etc.

- The integration strategy initially chosen (the so-called Monnet Method and the only viable one at the time) was based on segmented interaction between a privileged set of actors – mostly, upper-level national bureaucrats, Commission officials and business interest representatives.
- *Ergo*, those institutions that might have represented larger numbers of citizens and a wider range of their interests were excluded from the process and have subsequently found it difficult to gain access.
- *Ergo*, those most closely involved tended to represent highly specialized (and relatively less visible) constituencies and this was reflected in a highly compartmentalized decision-making structure within and across EU institutions.
- *Ergo*, those political mechanisms that led to the break-up of MLG and PCG in previous federations or confederations – namely, the formation of national party systems and comprehensive nationalist ideologies – have had little opportunity to emerge in the EU.
- *Also*, the non-decision to include security issues from the initial (and, so far, subsequent) stages of the integration process, deprived the emerging EU-polity of the coercive mechanisms that elsewhere promoted greater administrative uniformity and concentration of governmental authority at the national level – namely, military mobilization and centralized taxation.

- The EU may be unique as a polity – precisely, because of its extreme reliance on MLG and PCG – but it is sensitive to broader trends in government and governance that are affecting the 'domestic democracies' of its member states. Indeed, one could describe the EU as the *reductio ad absurdum* of such trends.
- *Ergo*, the trend toward delegating tasks to 'guardian institutions' (central banks, regulatory commissions, autonomous agencies, etc.) at

the national and sub-national levels of member states will be imitated at the supra-national level.

- *Ergo*, the observed decline in partisan identification and electoral turnout in its member states will make it even more difficult to create a viable party system in the EU.
- *Ergo*, the national trends toward decline in political trust, loyalty to traditional institutions and symbols of legitimacy will not only be reflected at the supra-national level but magnified – given that the EU has never had a historical 'stock' of these properties to draw upon.
- *Ergo*, the collapse of several (admittedly, non-democratic) federations in the course of recent regime changes – *vide* Yugoslavia, the USSR and Czechoslovakia – and the difficulties experienced by existing democratic federations (Belgium and Canada) suggest that the *patina* of success attached to the very concept of federalism has tarnished and may be giving rise to thoughts of alternative arrangements for de-centralized and de-concentrated governance.

The prospects in Europe

The one place on earth where the issue of democratization and federalism will be most clearly and unavoidably conjoined is in the future evolution of the Euro-polity. For better or worse, the institutions of the European Union (EU) seem destined to determine whether this emerging polity will manage to combine the two elements – a democratic regime and a federal state structure – that Tocqueville regarded as crucial for the success of large-scale governance in the United States. If they are to do this, however, they will have to subvert, invert, or pervert Tocqueville's argument.

For, as we have seen, Tocqueville did not regard federalism as an appropriate solution to the problems of political order in Europe. He saw neither virtue nor survivability in the repeated efforts of European countries to establish 'leagues,' 'confederacies' or 'federations.'[7] A much more precarious international environment, sharper class conflicts rooted in the tumultuous transition from aristocratic-feudal societies, stronger historical, religious and linguistic differences between its component states and a persistent political culture (those *moeurs* that he was so fond of invoking) of dependence upon central state authority – all these things made it unlikely that the precarious American mixture that he called 'incomplete national government' could be sustained, especially at the level of the continent as a whole. The idea would never have occurred to him that a 'United States of Europe' was either possible or desirable.

But could Tocqueville be wrong for the right reasons? What if Europe today is closer to the context that favours federal/democratic solutions than it was in the past – even closer today than the United States itself?

First and foremost, the countries of Western Europe (and, perhaps, their closest Eastern neighbours) enjoy for the first time in their history a 'security community' in which it is inconceivable for one of its members even to threaten the use of force to impose its will on another. Military expenditures and the size of standing armies, navies and air forces are lower than ever before – much lower than in the United States. Even conscription, historically a very delicate task for central governments, has almost disappeared (or been largely converted into a civilian service). It is the United States, now, that has so many enemies and repeatedly demonstrated its willingness to use military might to achieve its national objectives.

Second, class conflict has quite remarkably declined in Europe and inequalities in income and access to public goods are now (with the notable exception of Great Britain) much less than in America. Linguistic differentiation remains, but it has been attenuated by the burgeoning use of English. Cultural and life-style differences between the peoples of Europe, especially among youths, are a mere shadow of what they once were.[8] Religious schisms are almost politically irrelevant – unlike the United States, where fundamentalist Christian sects now provide some of the most intractable issues before the polity.

Finally, thanks in part to the neo-liberal revolution in public policy, Europeans no longer have such exaggerated expectations about what their government should do for them, especially at the level of Europe as a whole, where progress toward harmonizing the provisions of the welfare state has been very modest. Despite all the complaints about 'social dumping' and 'free-riding,' the member states of the EU seem reconciled to tolerating substantial differences in their provision of social services and their extraction of taxes at the national level.

How, then, can this 'synergy' between federalism and democracy be brought about? Resistance to the very word, *federalism*, is surprisingly strong, especially in Great Britain and Denmark, considering the high esteem it enjoys in America, and one suspects that its complexities are not well understood elsewhere.[9] Pro-integration politicians in Europe could never get away with the sort of *coup constitutionnel* that their forerunners pulled off in Philadelphia in 1787. The recent experience of the Inter-Governmental Conference that culminated in the Treaty of Nice demonstrates that no committee of the whole will be given a mandate for minor reforms and come back with a wholesale re-founding of the institutional order. Its every move will be monitored closely and the agreements reached will be subject to the *liberum veto* of every member government – long before the issue of parliamentary approval or popular ratification comes up.[10]

Moreover, the timing for federalizing/constitutionalizing is simply wrong. In the absence of revolution, *coup d'état*, liberation from foreign occupation, defeat or victory in international war, armed conflict between domestic opponents, sustained mobilization of urban populations against the *ancien régime* and/or impending political collapse, no EU member state has been able to find the 'political opportunity space' for a major overhaul of their ruling institutions. Many drafts of a potential Euro-constitution, all impeccably federalist in form, have been produced, circulated and promoted over the past decades, but none of them have been taken seriously. I suspect that the reason for this may be due less to the quality of the politico-legal talent that went into assembling these impressive documents than to the way they were discussed and drafted.

Thanks, I suspect, to the awesome shadow cast by the Philadelphia Convention, the reigning assumption seems to have been that anything as important as federalizing and democratizing the European Union must be treated as a momentous and concentrated *event* – not a gradual and fitful *process*. Above all, this task must be accomplished by experts (constitutional lawyers, for the most part) and protected from the pleading of special interests and the scrutiny of mass publics. Only specialists, it is presumed, can be trusted to produce a coherent and consistent draft that will not reflect the self-serving aims of politicians and their surrounding clienteles.[11] Although this strategy may have worked relatively well when some type of national emergency or founding moment provided the context for deliberation and choice, it will not work in the case of the EU where there is no foreseeable emergency and the founding moment occurred more than forty years ago.

What is needed is an entirely new strategy that adopts a much longer timeframe and seeks to involve special interests and mass publics at various stages of the process. Only by deliberately politicizing the issues involved at the level of Europe as a whole and by gradually building up expectations with regard to a more definitive set of rules of citizenship, representation and decision-making can one imagine a successful constitutionalization of the EU. Admittedly, this is not the way the member states went about accomplishing this task, but one of my major assumptions is that the EU is not a mere repetition of previous nation, state and regime-building processes and it may well lead to an unprecedented outcome.

And here is where the potential perversion of Tocqueville comes in. He took it as axiomatic that federalism and its felicitous connection to democracy in large scale units required two things: *stateness* and *nationhood* – both of which are missing in the case of the Euro-polity and are not likely to emerge in the immediate future. The novelty of the EU lies in the growing dissociation between territorial constituencies, functional *compé-tences* and collective identities. The changes in scale that have occurred over the past four decades tend to overlap and do not reinforce each other within a congruent society/economy/polity as happened in the making of the classic sovereign national state. The exercise of public authority in different functional domains is not coincident or congruent with a specific and unique territory; nor is it contained within a distinctive and unique identity.

In the emergent Euro-polity, these domains have become *less* rather than *more* congruent over time. What seems to be asserting, and even consolidating, itself is a plurality of polities at different levels of aggregation – national, sub-national and supra-national – that overlap in a multitude of domains. Moreover, the EU authorities have few exclusive *compétences*, and have yet to assert their hierarchical control over member states – except through the limited jurisprudence of the European Court of Justice and in such restricted functional domains as competition and agricultural policy. Instead, multiple levels of government continuously negotiate with each other to perform common tasks and resolve common problems across an expanding range of issues. Without sovereignty – without a definitive centre for the resolution of conflicts or for the allocation of public goods – there is only a process and, hence, no definite person or body that can be held accountable for its actions in the public realm. Moreover, the participants in this process are not just a fixed number of national states, but an enormous variety of sub-national units and networks, supra-national associations and transnational firms.

Tocqueville would have been horrified at the prospect of federalizing such a polity and would, no doubt, have predicted a bleak future for it – unless he came to agree with me that the historical context has changed significantly and, therefore, what he regarded as a *prerequisite* for federal democratization could be converted into an eventual *product* of that same process. If so, and if its democratization cannot be indefinitely postponed, then it seems reasonable (to me) to presume that the Euro-polity will have to invent new forms of ruler accountability, new rights and obligations for citizens and new channels for territorial and functional representation. The concept of 'federalism' may not adequately capture these novel properties and it might be better if a different one were invented and applied to avoid misunderstandings. Moreover, it may be necessary to implement these reforms in a radically different fashion. When the moment comes – and I for one am not convinced that it has arrived – this new mode of decentralized and de-concentrated governance can only be accomplished gradually by building upon existing institutions rather than in the classic American manner that Tocqueville so admired, i.e. by drafting an entirely new constitution.[12] The gamble would be that, by so proceeding, Europeans could acquire through protracted experimentation what history has denied them in practice, namely, a viable continental state and a common political identity.[13]

2 The EU as a self-sustaining federation

Specifying the constitutional conditions

David McKay

Introduction

The extension of powers implicit in recent European Union (EU) treaties, and especially the Treaty on European Union (Maastricht), have led a number of scholars to view the EU as a nascent federation and to draw comparisons with existing federations (see, for example, Burgess 2000; McKay 2001; Nicolaidis and Howse 2001). As with the established literature on federalism, much of this opus dwells on questions of definition. Deleting the word 'federal' from Article 1 of the final draft of the EU Constitution and replacing it with the words 'a union of European states' might suggest that the EU is something other than a federal state, and indeed no one claims that the EU is a fully developed federation such as the USA or Switzerland. However the EU does meet the minimal definition of a species of federal-like state as elaborated by Riker and others. Hence Riker argues that federalism is a 'political organisation in which the activities of government are divided between regional governments and a central government in such a way that each kind of government has some activities in which it makes final decisions' (Riker 1975: 101; see also McKay 2001, Chapter 2). Riker also accepts that some federations are 'peripheralized' because the powers of the central government are temporally or functionally limited in such a way that can give individual states an incentive to secede. Such was sometimes the case with the early Swiss confederation or with the USA under the Articles of Confederation. Hence at certain points in Swiss history when the external threat to the confederation was low, some cantons calculated that the costs of contributing to the national defence were not worth paying. No federal sanctions were in place to punish secessionists, nor could the federation reward cantons with relevant collective defence (see the discussion in Bonjour *et al.* 1952).

Although it could be argued that the EU was, in this sense, 'peripheralized' for much of its history, this is clearly no longer the case.[1] The areas of exclusive federal competence – competition rules, customs union, common commercial policy and, especially, monetary policy – carry with them high exit costs. And according to most economists, the benefits of allocating these tasks to the federal level – increased trade, reduced transaction costs, greater transparency – are considerable (Calmfors *et al.*, 2003). In addition, like other federations the EU shares a number of responsibilities with the member states, although with few exceptions national governments rather than the EU take the lead decisions in most of these areas (for a discussion see Schmitter 1996; EU Draft Constitution 2003). As with other federations, therefore, the most important question for the development of the EU is the balance of central power in relation to state power. More specifically, how does the design of federal institutions prevent either the 'peripheralization' – or possibly the secession – of a state or states, or, alternatively, moves towards a centralized, unitary state? While it is possible to provide adequate answers to these questions by studying the historical development of individual polities (many millions of words have been written on the development of American federalism alone) building theory in a way that specifies the likely conditions for success among the universe of federal systems is much more problematical.

So far the most ambitious work in this direction involves attempts to use game and rational choice theory (RT theory) to establish the constitutional conditions that would encourage a self-sustaining federation (Ordeshook and Shvetsova 1997; Filippov *et al.* forthcoming; Bednar *et al.* 2001). This chapter strives to synthesize these perspectives with more traditional approaches in a way that facilitates an analytically useful way of applying federal theory to the European Union. The argument will proceed in three parts. Part One summarizes the RT position in the context of EU institutional arrangements. Part Two assesses this position in terms of its relevance for the EU Constitution. Part Three develops this theme with respect to the implications for federal stability of one especially problematical area of EU responsibility, that of monetary policy.

Part One: rational choice perspectives on the self-sustainability of federations

The most distinctive aspect of the RT perspective is the assumption that political stability depends on the ways in which particular constitutional and institutional arrangements provide elites with incentives to stick to the rules of the game. Political elites make up the dominant coalition that sustains equilibrium over time. This coalition will prevail so long as no alternative coalition emerges to challenge the *status quo*. In contrast to pluralists who assume that mass public opinion is the central dynamic in political change, RT theorists see the world in terms of elites manipulating the myopic self-interest of the voters in ways that, in the longer term, will ensure that they are net gainers from the democratic process. So, until some new coalition emerges in opposition to existing constitutional and political arrangements, all members of a dominant coalition (that might include a variety of political parties and interests) will have an incentive to uphold existing arrangements. They may lose particular elections or offices, but will gain from office-related success in the future.

This reasoning has typically been applied to mature democracies with little reference to the territorial dimension. Yet in an increasing number of countries, the coincidence of national, ethnic, linguistic or religious loyalties with territorial divisions represents the major challenge to the viability of democratic regimes. Federal political arrangements are often viewed as a means to accommodate these differences, and indeed to pre-empt moves towards territorially defined political extremism (Riker 1975; Lijphart 1977; Filippov *et al.* forthcoming, Chapters 1 and 2 and sources cited). If we view the accumulation of EU treaties and regulations, and especially the Maastricht Treaty, as an EU 'constitution' binding member states together in a federal regime, what are the theoretical conditions that will facilitate the self-sustainability of this regime? Three sets of conditions are relevant: *constitutional design rules, constitutional principles and modes of representation.* Although space limitations do not permit a full elaboration here, applying these conditions to the EU would look something like the following.

Constitutional design rules

These are elaborated by Filippov *et al.* as general design principles applicable to all political systems, federal and unitary.

1 Constitutional provisions ought to be simple and concise, unencumbered by legal complexity.
2 If society has a democratic tradition – even one that lies in the distant past – then any constitution ought to make as few changes in those traditions as possible and link itself to that past as much as possible.
3 A constitution should focus on those institutions minimally necessary to ensure society's ability to coordinate to those policy goals identified through such mechanisms as democratic elections.
4 As essentially a coordinating device a constitution's design should be based on the presumption that any need for greater specificity will be attended to by the legislative and judicial institutions it established and by the evolutionary development of subsidiary norms and conventions.
(Filippov *et al.* forthcoming: 205–7)

For the purposes of the present discussion, (1) and (2) need little elaboration. One purpose of the current EU Constitutional Convention is to codify in simple language what is enumerated at great length in the successive EU treaties. And no one doubts the democratic credentials of existing EU members. (3) too has obvious implications: constitutions should reflect the culture and societies that they serve. In the case of the EU, the key elections are at the national rather than federal level and constitutional arrangements should naturally reflect this. (4) is also basic to good constitutional design. The constitution should establish the basics of the relations between institutions, both horizontal and vertical, but the detail of how these relationships work out over time has to be left to judicial and legislative interpretation and to the evolution of union-wide norms and conventions. Great specificity discourages the bargaining and coalition building that allows the polity to develop and evolve through time without challenges to fundamental principles. A highly codified document is also likely to encourage frequent amendment attempts which could result in even greater specificity and leave even less room for bargaining and compromise (as is often said of the Indian Constitution, see Rudolph and Rudolph 2001).

Federal constitutional principles

With respect to federations, special rules should apply that have a specifically territorial dimension. These are:

1   'A system of individual level incentives designed to ensure federal stability should apply not to individual citizens but to political elites, since it is they, even in a democracy, who lead society from one equilibrium to another' (Filippov *et al.* forthcoming: 6). All parties to the federal bargain must subscribe to what Filippov *et al.* call Level 1 constraints, or an acceptance of the provisions of the constitutional settlement. In our example this means the accumulation of EU treaties. They must also agree to abide by Level 2 constraints or the rules of the game inherent in the constitutional settlement that govern day-to-day bargaining and negotiation (Filippov *et al.* forthcoming: 8). In the EU this would mean abiding both by the formal rules of behaviour in the Commission, Council of Ministers and other EU institutions, and the informal *norms* that govern behaviour in these institutions. An example of a failure to fulfil the first condition could be the reluctance of British elites to support EMU, and of the second, De Gaulle's 'empty chair' strategy during the 1960s.

2   The constitution should provide for 'effective co-ordination devices [that] must give local and regional political elites an incentive to uphold federative constraints even when their constituents prefer otherwise'. In other words individual level incentives (what Filippov *et al.* call level three rules) must operate in such a way as to legitimize the constraints inherent in federal arrangements (forthcoming: 9). Numerous examples of this can be found: for example the

Common Agricultural Policy and the meeting of the convergence criteria in the run up to EMU. In both cases, elites told voters that short-term pain (high food prices, some element of economic retrenchment) would be worth paying given the long-term gains of self-sufficiency and relative economic gains from EMU. Presumably both policy goals were achieved because the EU 'constitution' encouraged inter-elite bargaining that resulted in ubiquitously acceptable compromises.

3 In addition the federal constitution 'must create (office related) rewards for national [federal] elites that dissuade them from overstepping their constitutionally prescribed authority and to acquiesce in the legitimate authority of the regional governments' (Filippov *et al.* forthcoming: 9). Or as Bednar *et al.* put it, in a viable federation 'national [federal] forces must be structurally constrained from infringing on the federal bargain' (2001: 226).

4 The final constitutional principle is 'federal stability requires that regional and national elites maintain some (possibly evolving) consensus over the definitions of 'constitutionally prescribed' and 'legitimate authority'' (Filippov *et al.* forthcoming: 10). This seems to be a re-working of level one constraints to the effect that the constitution should be built on a consensus on the allocation of functions between levels of government, and this consensus should persist through time. So far the EU seems to have proceeded on this basis with successive intergovernmental conferences working according to consensus principles. However as EU responsibilities have become more extensive, so the potential for a breakdown in implementation of agreed policies increases. As will be argued later, just such a possibility is possible in the area of monetary policy.

Modes of representation

It is easy to infer which modes of representation are most likely to uphold these constitutional principles. They include *within* as opposed to *without* representation. Within representation refers to the formal incorporation of the states into national decision-making bodies such as upper chambers, which serve as 'houses of the states.' The assumption is that the careful delineation of upper house powers – for example over all matters that effect the states, as with the German Bundesrat – will provide an effective forum for mediation between different levels of government elites by specifying the parameters of state and federal power. In addition parliamentary procedures, by encouraging the developments of procedural norms, typically limit debate and facilitate the building of coalitions (Filippov *et al.* forthcoming: 148). 'Without' representation refers to informal devices such as first ministers' conferences that have no constitutional status and thus leave undefined what is 'constitutionally prescribed' and what is a 'legitimate authority.' Such arrangements can lead to disputes both over level one and level two rules – although they also can have the advantage of great flexibility. The classic example here is Canada, where intergovernmental conferences have been used by provincial elites to question the fundamentals as well as the interpretation of the Canadian constitution (McKay 2001, Chapter 4 and sources cited). In the case of the EU, the Council of Ministers, which is the functional equivalent of the upper house, is the ultimate exemplar of a 'house of the states,' operating as it does on territorially based supermajoritarian or unanimity decision rules (although the supermajoritarian rule will be weakened somewhat if the recommendations of the Convention's draft Constitution are adopted). Any change in what is constitutionally prescribed is, moreover, subject to unanimous approval. And in contrast to all other federations, the lower house has no agenda setting power over the constitutional architecture of the union.

The EU also conforms nicely to Filippov *et al.*'s (and implicitly Bednar *et al.*'s) injunction that delegated representation is preferable to direct representation (Filippov *et al.* forthcoming: 161–5, Bednar *et al.* 2001: 233–6). With the former, the danger that legislators will 'go national' is reduced because delegated representatives can be recalled by the states should they fail to represent state interests. Going national can, of course, become the equivalent of state or regional elites transmuting into national figures championing the extension of national power. Just this has happened with most directly elected upper house members in a number of countries including the USA and Australia (on the US, see Riker 1955, on Australia, see Holmes and Sharman, 1977). The extent to which this can happen depends on a number of factors including the 'representational mix' between upper and lower houses and the length of term served by legislators. By whatever measure however, EU constitutional design more than adequately serves state interests. The lower house is weak even if directly elected, and members of the Council of Ministers usually act as delegates for national governments. Proposals at the Constitutional Convention that national parliaments should be more closely involved in EU decision-making would actually strengthen within representation, assuming that national legislatures operated as delegated proxies for national governments.[2]

The third representational mode concerns the relationship between executive and legislature. In sum, the separation of powers will encourage within representation while parliamentary arrangements will facilitate without representation. A chief executive checked by state representation in the upper house of the national legislature will more likely preserve the union in a way that protects each level of government's sphere of authority than a chief executive drawn from the lower house, especially if the upper house is politically subservient as is the case in Australia (for most of its history) and Canada. Interestingly, it is difficult to find a real world example of the separation of powers working in quite the way that Filippov *et al.* suggest. As noted, US Senators have long since ceased to be state champions, although the separation of powers has almost certainly prevented further accretion of authority to the centre (and also at the centre). The EU has no chief executive, of course, although proposals for the creation of an EU President have been discussed at the Constitutional Convention. In any event, the non-parliamentary arrangements of the upper house certainly encourage within representation. As a number of scholars have noted, both in the EU context and elsewhere, parliamentary arrangements are probably incompatible with federalism (see for example, Bednar *et al.* 1996). Finally, both Filippov *et al.* and Bednar *et al.* (2001) are sensitive to the ways in which these representational modes interact with political parties. Institutions such as parliamentary government, simple plurality electoral rules, and actual or *de facto* unicameralism are more likely to encourage the development of highly disciplined and centralized parties that will increase the freedom of federal elected officials to overstep their constitutionally prescribed authority. Just this has happened in two federations (Canada and India) who display all of these 'bad' institutional features (on Canada, see McRoberts 1997; on India see Jayal 2001). In reaction state interests may develop socially, religiously or ethnically inclusive parties who will have an incentive to use without representational modes to combat federal power or even to champion secession. In contrast, institutional features such as the separation of powers, proportional representation, power sharing and bicameralism are more likely to encourage the growth of decentralized 'bottom-up' parties, which are also spatially and socially inclusive. Both the United States and Switzerland have developed party systems that approximate to this type.

Of course social divisions may be such that some federations acquire the 'wrong sort' of parties whatever the institutional arrangements. The point, however, is not that institutions are all-determining, but that they do help shape incentives in ways making the growth of top down or bottom up parties more or less likely. Hence it is clear that EU institutions – notably the primacy of the Council of Ministers and the weakness of the European Parliament – have helped prevent the development of centralized parties. Instead, via national governments, national parties dominate decision-making. Because no European parties worthy of the name operate at the supra-national level, it is difficult to classify the EU as having a 'properly configured' party system. However, in functional terms national parties are supportive of the EU project if only because they are essentially unmobilized on the issue. At both the EU (EP) and national levels, very few overtly centralist or decentralist (specifically pro- or anti-EU) parties have emerged.[3] Perhaps this is because until recently the scope of exclusively EU powers was limited. However, with the coming of EMU the potential for some mobilization by anti-EU parties exists. We will return to this point later.

It is important to stress that though they focus on elite decision-making in particular institutional contexts, the rational choice theorists are not blind to the importance of history, identity and culture – although it is sometimes easy to infer that they are. The extent to which the federal settlement involves the ceding of state power to the centre will primarily depend on the unique historical development of the states involved. In some cases (for example Switzerland) strong regional identities will limit the scope of federal power, while in others (Australia) where regional identities are weak, federal governments can do much more. The point is, rather, that the constitutional compact should be established on the basis of consensus on the allocation of functions between different levels of government, and that institutional arrangements should prevent illegitimate incursions by one level into the domain of another. In some systems this may result in a centralized federation and in others in a decentralized or even peripheralized system. Clearly the EU is at the latter extreme of this particular dimension.

Part Two: the RT theory of federalism and the EU, how relevant?

While it might easily be inferred from the brief discussion above that institutional arrangements in the EU encourage self-sustainability, the use of RT theory in this context does raise a number of conceptual and empirical problems. Some of these relate to elite–mass linkages and in particular to the imperfect way in which, according to the theory, elites serve mass publics. According to RT theorists the core intellectual problem in designing successful federalism is not, as with conventional principal-agent theory, how to construct institutions that will ensure that elected representatives faithfully serve the interests of their constituents, but rather the opposite: how can institutions be designed in such a way that the politicians become imperfect agents of the voters? For if the federation is to evolve into a stable polity, state-level elected representatives must persuade their voters that their interests must be put to one side, at least in the shorter term, because of the sacrifices involved in ceding power to the federal government. Moreover, Filippov *et al.* are insistent that this exercise must be conducted openly and honestly. The voters should not be tricked into compliance, but genuinely believe that it is in their interest to comply. Similarly, the politicians must somehow represent constituents other than their own (Filippov *et al.* forthcoming: 20–5). The preferred solution to this problem involves assuming that politicians act *as if* they represent constituencies in addition to the ones they currently represent. More specifically:

> We can, however, begin to see a solution . . . if we assume, as a starting point, that politicians act *as if* they care not only for the constituency

they currently represent but also about other constituencies, including but not necessarily limited to those they hope to represent in the
future ... elected elites can be led to serve the interests of a constituency different from the one they currently represent, and voters
can be induced to act *as if* they approve of such action.

(Filippov *et al.* forthcoming: 20, emphasis in original)

A 'properly configured party system' along the lines discussed above
will facilitate such an outcome by providing both elected officials and
voters with opportunities for future office- and policy-related benefits
resulting from participation in a larger political unit. One obvious
problem with this schema is that irrespective of the institutional context
party systems cannot be created from scratch. They depend on already
established identities grounded in culture, economy and society. As such,
party systems are often not amenable to institutional manipulation, as the
examples of Northern Ireland and Belgium show.[4] In the EU case,
although it could be argued that the extreme decentralization characteristic of the ways in which parties operate undermines the opportunities for
mediation between different levels of government, this would be greatly
aggravated if party systems reflected strong national (member state) identities opposed to the extension of federal power. But they do not. Instead
most national parties appeal to voters on grounds of ideology, interest or,
more rarely, region, none of which have a specifically EU territorial
dimension.

In fact, it is all too easy to re-interpret the *as if* assumption as an ideological commitment to the *idea* of federation. Ideological commitment
may not sit comfortably with rational choice theory, but it does seem to
have played a major role in the evolution of the EU (on ideology as an
impulse to federation, see Franck 1968; on the role of ideology in the EU,
see Elazar 2001). Whatever the case, focusing on the ways in which elites
in emerging federations are required to persuade voters that it is in their
interest to vote for politicians who may not be acting directly in their
interests, does have analytical utility, even in the EU case. We will return
to this point later.

A further problem with the RT approach is the insistence that federal
sustainability has to be facilitated by the individual incentives of elected
officials. Only elected officials have a monopoly of coercive power and
only elected officials depend for their political survival on the voters'
approval. Other elites, including business interests and intellectuals,
cannot be shown to have such a direct stake in federal political arrangements, although they may claim some (often vague) ideological commitment to or economic interest in the idea. Indeed this is a main point of
dispute between the RT theorists and the consociationalists, with the latter
insisting that institutional arrangements have to be tailored to the interests of elected and un-elected elites. It is the dominant *interests* in society

that have to be persuaded of the need for novel institutional devices such as federalism and power sharing. This is especially so in divided societies, where the intra-elite connections in any one community are typically strong (see for example Lijphart 1996 on the Indian case).

In the EU it is national rather than community difference that is relevant and a small mountain of research shows the crucial influence of unelected elites in the European integration process, from academic economists, bank officials, EU bureaucrats to organized economic interests (for a summary of this literature, see Verdun 2002, part 1). And while, for much of EU history, this process may not have qualified as 'federation building' but as neo-functionalism (or something else), this argument cannot be invoked for the period immediately up to and following Maastricht. We also know that decision-making at Maastricht was dominated by bankers, economists and finance ministry officials rather than elected politicians (Dyson and Featherstone 1999). However, none of this negates the need for elected politicians eventually to put this extension of federal power to the vote, which they did either directly or indirectly during the ratification process. And whatever the source of new policies, federal institutional arrangements remain important determinants of the ways in which state actors and interests interact with those at the federal level.

This brings us to another potential problem with the RT schema. It is premised on the assumption that the main danger to the stability of federal unions comes from overweening federal level politicians and especially chief executives. Perhaps this is because in recent years some of the richest empirical material relating to the viability of federal unions comes from such countries as Yugoslavia, the Soviet Union, Russia (post 1991) and (to a lesser extent) Canada where chief executives and their parties have acted – and have been given the institutional freedom to act – in an imperious manner.[5] Putting to one side the fact that only the latter of these qualify as democracies; it would be difficult to argue that the danger to EU stability comes from this source. Proposals for the introduction of a longer-term president of the Council of Ministers to replace the rotating presidency in the draft constitution (Article 15) hardly add up to the creation of a strong chief executive. Indeed the draft Constitution continues the resolutely decentralist nature of the EU that has been its hallmark from the outset. This accepted, threats to the viability of federations whether decentralized or not usually derive from the exercise of some variety of central power regarded by one or more of the states as illegitimate. This may come via executive power, judicial interpretation (crucial at various points in US and Canadian history, see Bednar *et al.* 2001: 231–62), or (probably uniquely) policy led 'technocratism' such as has often dominated the accretion of power at the centre in the EU.

What then is the utility of applying RT theory to the developing European Union? As stated, much of the EU institutional and constitutional architecture appears roughly to conform to the principles, design rules and modes of representation elaborated by Filippov *et al.* and others. And rather than weaken these rules and principles, the codification of the draft treaty tends to strengthen rather than weaken them. In particular:

1   The 2003 draft is concise and largely avoids specificities, thus by implication leaves much of the detail to be decided by legislative and judicial authorities or to the accumulation of norms and conventions over time.

2   Codification formalizes the 'constitutionally prescribed authority of the EU' which continues to be constrained by the unanimity decision rule in the Council of Ministers, applicable to those areas that are most jealously guarded by the member states – enlargement, taxation, revision of treaties, social security, defence and foreign affairs. In this sense the 'federal government' is indeed structurally constrained in ways that prevent it from impinging on the prerogatives of state governments. Indeed, by identifying the areas to be protected by the unanimity rule and specifying that any extension of QMV would have to be approved by all 25 member states, the Constitution actually strengthens 'state' control over some aspects of the federal agenda.

3   This said, the areas where the QMV rule applies would be extended to include justice, asylum and immigration and the rule itself would be weakened to a simple majority as long as this represented at least 60 per cent of the EU population. Whether this represents an 'illegitimate' extension of federal authority remains to be seen – although if the worry by some member states is that this will result in a more liberal immigration regime, then they should look at the experience of other federations where the 'nationalization' of immigration law typically results in more restrictive immigration controls. The 60 per cent rule is potentially more problematical as it over-represents the larger states. Whether this will be viewed by the smaller states as sufficient for them to support 'federative constraints' remains to be seen. Although, as with all provisions of the treaty, a consensus may emerge during the ratification period.

4   The changes to the representational structure of the EU proposed by the Constitution also largely conform to the RT theorists' admonitions. The creation of a Council President elected by the member states changes little in formal Constitutional terms. And, assuming that Council decisions will typically extend rather than limit the federal authority, the extension of the 'co-decision' mechanism by the European Parliament to a range of new areas actually adds an additional veto point that potentially constrains rather than expands the federal power.

5   Incorporation of a Charter of Fundamental Rights into EU law might

look like an extension of federal power, but the exact meaning of the change will be decided only by judicial interpretation over time.

6   Article 59 permits any state to withdraw from the Union in accordance with its own constitutional requirements. Although this provision has been criticized as too generous, its inclusion strongly suggests that the framers see the EU as a peripheralized rather than a centralized federation. At least in democratic federations, secession clauses tend to have real force. In the EU case it is difficult to imagine the Council and Parliament denying any secession application. It is also difficult to envisage a member state rejecting all aspects of EU membership – although as will be discussed below, seceding from a particular aspect of federal authority, such as EMU, may be more plausible.

In sum, the draft Constitution is not a radical document in the manner of the US Constitution, which differed fundamentally from the Articles of Confederation that preceded it. Instead it reflects the evolutionary nature of the EU system of government – a development that has not thus far involved strains and stresses that threaten the viability of the project. In this sense it is possible to infer from the RT perspective that the EU does not suffer from a system-threatening democratic deficit (DD). Indeed, without raising the question of sustainability, scholars from other intellectual traditions have come to similar conclusions (see for example Moravcsik 2001). Yet this conclusion is premised on the assumption that with or without a new constitution, the highly decentralized decision-making system of the EU will always effectively constrain the extension of federal power in ways that are acceptable to member states. In fact, in addition to its decentralist – and indeed in some areas, peripheralized – status, the EU is different from other federations in two other important respects. First, its territorial limits have yet to be reached and as the controversies surrounding the acceptance of the draft Constitution showed, establishing constitutional conditions that suit all members, potential and existing, in ways that maintain a constitutional equilibrium raises new design challenges.

But there is a second issue on which the draft Constitution is curiously silent: the institutional design of arguably the main federal responsibility, monetary policy, is egregiously out of step with institutional design in other policy areas, economic and otherwise. The experience of EMU to date is such that we can make sensible inferences on the appropriateness of the institutional arrangements that are in place for monetary policy and whether these are compatible with the conditions necessary for a self-sustaining federation.

Part Three: policy asymmetry, legitimacy and institutional impasse: the case of monetary and fiscal policy

Perhaps the most important insight of RT theory is the need to build and, through institutional innovation, maintain support for the federal project among national and federal level elites. Federal actors must be structurally constrained from encroaching on areas constitutionally reserved to the states. When disputes arise, as inevitably they must, given that some ambiguity on the allocation of functions will always exist (for the classic statement on this subject, see Elazar 1987), they should be mediated through appropriate institutional mechanisms. In monetary policy, however, the preferred institutional design involved the creation of a central bank that is not only autonomous but also more insulated from political pressures than any other modern central bank. Unlike other central banks, however, the European Central Bank (ECB) operates in an economy characterized by extreme fiscal decentralization. In other words, uniquely among world economies, the EU has acquired a striking asymmetry between centralized monetary policy and decentralized fiscal policy – and also decentralized policy in most other important areas. This policy asymmetry is paralleled by decision-making asymmetry. For in monetary policy closed majority decision rules apply, while in almost all other areas, territorially-based open supermajoritarian or unanimity decision rules prevail at the federal level (on double asymmetry see Gustavsson 2002). As discussed earlier, the draft Constitution generally endorses rather than undermines these decision rules.

These gross asymmetries would raise few difficulties were monetary policy essentially a technical matter with few ramifications for other policy areas. But interconnections do exist. Monetary policy interacts with fiscal policy and thence most government functions. Closed decision-making in the ECB interacts with the more open decision-making of the Stability and Growth Pact (SGP), Ecofin and the Council of Ministers. These interconnections are all the more important because, unlike other federal economies, the states have provided no constitutional prescription for a system of fiscal federalism or for federal control of national taxes (see McKay 1999, and sources cited). Put another way, the sort of federal level interventions that are seen as a necessary concomitant to independent monetary policy in all other federations lack legitimacy among EU national elites (on the political economy of EMU, see Boyer 2000).

Interestingly, some of those economists who see this asymmetry as a potential problem, view it not in terms of elite preferences but in terms of the impact on mass publics. Hence Wilhelm Buiter notes:

> Monetary union involves a transfer of national sovereignty to the central or federal level. Unless this transfer of power is perceived as legitimate by the residents of Euroland, the authority of the

institutions of the ECB and the ESCB will be questioned and challenged by those who perceive themselves to be adversely affected by it. Generally in the past, central banks have been created when a stronger and more legitimate Federal governance structure was in place than is currently the case in the EU.

(Buiter 1998: 6; see also Buiter 1999)

Other economists share this assumption on the weakness of federal power but draw different conclusions. Instead of making ECB decision-making more democratic, they propose to make national fiscal policy-making less democratic. Or because they consider that national politicians are slaves to domestic electoral pressures and economic interests (witness recent failures of the Germans, Portuguese and French to abide by SGP rules), the key decisions over tax matters should be subject to central (federal level) controls (McKinnon 1997; Calmfors *et al.* 2003).[6] These are far from being counsels of despair. Pressures for fiscal harmonization and centralization are very much on the agenda among leading economists and some federal level (Commission) officials (see references in McKay 2002).

In terms of RT theory, the rules under which the ECB operates are constitutionally enshrined in the Maastricht Treaty. In other words, short of some sort of 'constitutional change' the 'national (federal) forces' (ECB) are set up in such a way that members have little incentive to respond to the pressures applied by national (member state) actors. Secrecy ensures that punishment (blame) cannot be visited on individual decision-makers. And while it was always intended that ECB members would not be structurally constrained from taking decisions in the monetary policy area, it was (presumably) not anticipated that this would have profound spillovers into areas where the EU has, in the past, been structurally constrained by others aspects of the EU constitution. What we have in the operation of the European Central Bank, therefore, is a federal authority whose extensive policy scope has powerful effects on the domestic economies and polities of the member states. The Constitutional design that informs the day-to-day operations of the ECB was based on a highly centralized decision-making system involving almost no mechanisms for the brokering of member state/ECB differences. As such the ECB violates the constitutional ground rules that are necessary for a self-sustaining federation. The system will work only if (a) the scope of its powers is limited, which is patently not the case; or (b) if an inordinately high degree of elite consensus on its operations exists.

The way in which the SGP operates is also inimical to effective self-sustainability, but in a rather different way. The rules are quite rigid, and allow only limited room for compromise. Either national governments comply with the rules (which are enforced by the Commission) or, as has happened with both Germany and Portugal, the rules are openly flouted.

Yet SGP rules have real legal force, and can only be overturned by a unanimous Council vote. In terms of federal theory these events demonstrate nicely the link between pluralist and rational choice perspectives. The working of the SGP to date appears to fit well with a pluralist position. Politicians in Germany – and potentially elsewhere – appear eager to please the short-term demands of voters and limit the spending cuts and tax hikes implied in SGP rules. They have, moreover, the means to do this via lobbying the Commission and Ecofin. Some doubts must exist, however, as to the longer-term sustainability of the SGP. In their present form SGP operating procedures have been questioned by economists (Buiter 1999 and sources cited; Eichengreen and Wyplosz 1998). Ultimately the application of the rules is a matter for the Council of Ministers, but it is unlikely that the Council will publicly condemn one of its own members for a failure to comply. Instead, national governments will (and indeed have) resorted to informal lobbying both of the Commission and Ecofin. In other words the way in which the SGP is developing encourages 'without' representation where the participants are not agreed on fundamental principles. Open and egregious flouting of the rules might establish a link in the minds of voters between fiscal rectitude and EMU. As such, the elite consensus on the status of the ECB under EMU might begin to break down with voters in one or more countries forcing the hands of politicians unable to deliver the goods even in the longer term. This may also induce changes in party systems. If EMU *per se* is blamed for fiscal retrenchment, political entrepreneurs in one or more countries may have an incentive to 'go local' by changing existing party programmes to an anti-EMU position, or by forming new, anti-EMU parties (on the role of political entrepreneurs in moving the policy agenda to a more extreme position, see Rabushka and Shepsle 1972). In the absence of member state/ECB mediating mechanisms this may produce a crisis in the monetary policy constitution and thus in the EU constitution. In the worst-case scenario it might induce departure from EMU, or even secession from the EU.

Conclusions

The trick in successful federal constitutional design is the creation of institutional arrangements optimizing opportunities for intra-elite bargaining and mediation, and in particular able to provide both national and federal politicians with an incentive to keep to the conditions of the federal bargain. Application of aspects of RT theory to the EU and to the draft Constitution suggests that in its fundamentals the constitutional design of the EU has thus far been compatible with self-sustainability. Highly decentralized decision-making structures reflect both strong regional (member state) identity and the limited scope of the federal government. Majoritarian parliamentarian decision-making is extremely limited, with decision-making dominated by an upper house operating according to unanimity or supermajoritarian rules informed by a clear constitutional mandate to represent the states through within representation. These arrangements might well be compromised by constitutional change that elevates the EP to a central decision making role and/or abandons unanimity voting on the fundamental allocation of powers between the states and the federal government. But the draft constitution proposes nothing remotely as centralist as this. The shift to a simple majority rule by Council members so long as they represent 60 per cent of the EU population maintains the territorial basis of Council voting, and while the areas covered by QMV will be expanded, unanimity continues to apply in the crucial areas of enlargement, taxation and foreign and defence policy. The EU party system is also 'appropriately configured' in the sense that it is highly decentralized and, with minor exceptions, made up of parties whose appeal to voters is not based on the assertion of anti-EU 'state rights' or support for the creation of a unitary EU.[7] None of this is to suggest that the EU has anything approaching an ideal constitutional system. For one thing this chapter has tested EU institutions on the basis of just one value, that of sustainability or stability. By other measures – efficiency, democracy, liberty – the present and proposed arrangements may be less than adequate, as some of the other chapters in this volume demonstrate.

Even by the measure of the conditions necessary for the maintenance of stability, however, present arrangements hold with some dangers. In the case of monetary policy, an attempt was made to show how the way in which EMU was designed displays a gross policy and decision-making asymmetry. The institutions of federal fiscal constraint are constitutionally fragile and subject to the vagaries of without representation. Monetary institutions are subject to closed majority decision-making rules that greatly reduce the scope for federal/state mediation. Given the interconnectedness between the two policy areas and their central importance to distributive politics in all member states, the result may be a breakdown in the elite consensus, probably precipitated by electoral pressures, that presently underpins the status of the Euro.

Providing greater specificity for both the monetary and fiscal constitutions need not violate the principle of constitutional simplicity elaborated earlier. The draft EU Constitution clarifies nothing in this regard. No substantive changes are proposed either to the ECB or to the SGP. QMV voting will be extended to a number of areas, but none that fundamentally alter the EU's role in monetary and fiscal policy. At the same time, Article 10.3 of the Constitution: 'The Union shall have competence to co-ordinate the economic policies of member states' (EU Draft Constitution 2003) is simply empty rhetoric given that nothing more is added to address the gross asymmetry between federal monetary and fiscal power. What is needed is a form of wording that both specifies the legitimate scope of federal level power in economic policy and also facilitates the involvement of the member states in EU level economic decision-making in ways encouraging the mediation of federal/state disputes. As can be inferred from the discussion to date, this should, at a minimum, involve a major reform of the SGP and the ECB. The failure of the draft Constitution to address this issue is remarkable given that this is an area that is already infused with federal state conflict of the sort that, under some circumstances, might present a real challenge to the sustainability of the EU project.

3 A union of peoples?

Diversity and the predicaments of a multinational polity

Peter A. Kraus

From Kakania to EUkania?

The issue of diversity involves one of the main challenges that the political integration of Europe has to confront at its present stage. One can reasonably argue that, up to now, a broad agreement on overcoming nested traditions of nationalist strife between states and between peoples has constituted an important normative rationale for the process of European integration. At the same time, according to the official approach to the making of the European Union (EU), this aim is to be pursued without threatening historically established cultural identities, at least as long as these correspond to the identities of member states. Thus, seen from the angle of those who have an optimistic view of the perspectives of European polity-building, the emerging EUkania may be able to fulfil a promise that a similarly Byzantine political order, Kakania, as Robert Musil called the Austro-Hungarian monarchy in his famous novel *The Man without Qualities*, was not able to keep.

According to the Hungarian political analyst Oscar Jászi (1961 [1929]: 3), the historical uniqueness of the Habsburg monarchy was based upon the effort to hold together a 'variegated mosaic of nations and people and to build up a kind of universal state, a supranational monarchy, and to fill it with the feeling of a common solidarity'. To be sure, Jászi had an utterly critical view of the disastrous institutional failures that culminated in the dissolution of the Austro-Hungarian empire at the end of the First World War. Nonetheless, he felt also compelled to express a sympathetic view of the attempts that were undertaken in Kakania in order to accommodate an extraordinarily high degree of diversity. For Jászi, these attempts had to be interpreted as one of the most ambitious political experiments in human history:

> For, if the Habsburgs had been able really to unite those ten nations through a supranational consciousness into an entirely free and spontaneous cooperation, the empire of the Habsburgs would have surpassed the narrow limits of the nation state and would have proved to

the world that it is possible to replace the consciousness of national unity by the consciousness of state community. It would have proved that the same problem which Switzerland and Belgium have solved on a smaller scale among highly civilized nations under particular historical conditions should not be regarded as a historical accident, but that the same problem is perfectly solvable even on a large scale and among very heterogeneous cultural and national standards.

It may seem exaggerated that a contribution to the debate on Europe's constitutional process begins by establishing a comparison between the European Union and the Habsburg monarchy. Obviously, there are substantial differences between the two types of political order. There are, however, a few interesting common elements as well. One element is the complex institutional architecture of the two polities; in both cases, it implies a great potential for institutional deadlocks. A second element may be discerned in the lack of a genuinely democratic legitimacy, even if this lack was certainly much more marked in the Kakanian than it is in the EUkanian case. Another comparable feature is that in the Austro-Hungarian monarchy as in the EU mass support for the properly supranational levels of rule remained or remains modest, due to the predominance of national patterns of identification. (One could speak of an emerging predominance in the first, of a continuing predominance in the second case.) Finally, one may well make the point that diversity and cultural heterogeneity are factors hardly less relevant in present-day European politics than in the late period of the Habsburg system.[1] While, to quote Jászi (1961 [1929]: 3) once again, the Austro-Hungarian empire comprised 'almost ten nations and twenty more or less divergent nationalities', cultural pluralism also is a salient feature of the EU, and bound to become even more significant in the course of the Union's Eastern enlargement.

The EU is often characterized as a polity of a new kind. In its system of multi-level governance (Hooghe and Marks 2001), different policy areas are regulated according to specific institutional logics at varying territorial and functional levels. At the same time, the EU can also be conceived as a new type of multinational polity. In this respect, its novelty would reside in the creation of a multinational order that lacks an internal hegemonic force and that has a culturally open or 'undetermined' constitutional structure. In view of this unprecedented multinational constellation, analyses of the problems experienced when the strengthening of Europe's political dimension is at stake frequently point at the weak sociocultural foundations available for constructing a European 'state'. From the corresponding angle, a common political will among Europeans is unlikely to materialize as long as collective loyalties manifest themselves primarily as national attachments. Ultimately, then, the legacy of European nationalism appears as a major obstacle on the way towards the making of a European *demos*.

Irrespective of the normative stance we may take regarding the prospects of democracy beyond the nation-state, the present situation in Europe must be considered particularly interesting from the point of view of modern constitutionalism, as normative presuppositions become inextricably intermingled with the sociological realities of democratic politics (Weiler 1999). In contrast with many previous historical experiences of nation-state formation, in which 'the people' had typically already been made before the age of democracy began, the *demos* can't be simply taken as given in the EU's constitutional setting; it must rather be seen as the potential outcome of a highly reflexive political process (Kraus 2003: 670–5). Without a fixed realm, without a shared past, without an unchallenged cultural identity and without a common language, the foundations of political unity in the EU may well look shaky, at least for those who regard the nation-state as the paradigmatic model of integration in the modern world.

Against this background, the problem of creating an overarching institutional frame that contributes to a voluntary association of diverse identities, a problem so cogently scrutinized by Jászi in the context of the demise of the Habsburg empire, has reappeared, though, fortunately, in far less dramatic terms than in the past, in the process of European constitution-making. At the same time, the issue at stake in EU politics touches upon a central question of contemporary democratic theory, a question that remains largely unresolved. The question is how political unity – be it conceptualized as a democratic collective subject or as an integrated frame of communication – is to be constituted under conditions of cultural diversity. As we will see, diversity has attained a very prominent status in Europe's constitutional discourse. At any rate, *United in diversity* has become the Union's official creed. Yet, unsurprisingly, the way the issue of diversity has been addressed by EU constitutional politics is to a great extent symptomatic of the contradictions inherent in European integration.

Diversity and political integration in liberal democratic theory

The debate on the implications cultural diversity has for the political integration of Europe seems to oscillate between two poles that can be related, if things are put in a bold and simple manner, to the names of John Stuart Mill and Walter Hallstein. On the one hand, contributions drawing their inspiration from 'grand' political theory often show a preference for creating or preserving political units with a high level of linguistic and cultural homogeneity. On the other hand, the pragmatically oriented 'official' discourse that underpins the process of European integration is typically eager to celebrate diversity, without, however, being too explicit about how such an approach is to be implemented in the political and institutional realm.

Let us cast a glance at democratic theory first. It generally assumes that a high level of communicative integration, often associated with the use of a common language, is a requirement for the functioning of an integrative public sphere. After having been made by John Stuart Mill (1972 [1861]: 392) in the *Considerations on Representative Government* this claim would soon attain an almost canonical status in modern liberal thinking. Mill wrote:

> Free institutions are next to impossible in a country made up of different nationalities. Among a people without fellow-feeling, especially if they read and speak different languages, the united public opinion, necessary to the working of representative government, cannot exist. The influences which form opinions and decide political acts are different in the different sections of the country. An altogether different set of leaders have the confidence of one part of the country and of another. The same books, newspapers, pamphlets, speeches, do not reach them. One section does not know what opinions, or what instigations, are circulating in another.

If one adopts such a perspective, the prospects of sustaining legitimate forms of rule depend widely on the degree of national and linguistic unification observable within a given political unit. Mill thinks that a collectively rooted 'fellow-feeling' is a crucial requisite if democratic institutions are to work appropriately in the long run. His view is grounded on the assumption that a liberal democracy will only be able to avoid its break-up in situations of intense political conflict as long as its citizens share some fundamental identity patterns, as manifested by language and culture. According to Mill, the extension of political citizenship rights will have undesirable institutional effects without previous communicative integration.

Mill's approach entails a clear normative preference for creating democracies that are homogeneous along linguistic and cultural lines, as cultural diversity is taken to be a major impediment to civic solidarity. During a long period of time, lasting way into the twentieth century, this preference remained a standard ideological orientation for liberal nationalists, who tended to adopt the maxim *one people, one state.* We should keep in mind, however, that in Mill's line of reasoning the preference has rather the quality of an empirically derived conclusion than the status of an *a priori* judgment. In other passages of the *Considerations* in which nationality issues are discussed, it becomes clear that one major focus of preoccupation for Mill is precisely the Austro-Hungarian domain of rule. Yet his argumentation does not really scrutinize whether there is general empirical evidence that gives the preference a robust analytical and empirical foundation.

Mill's scepticism seems to have impregnated the bulk of both normative and empirical theoretical work dealing with the capacity culturally diverse democracies have for political integration.[2] Unsurprisingly, Mill's legacy is also a palpable element in the current debate on Europe's political future. Here, the assumption is frequently made that the high degree of cultural heterogeneity within the EU acts as a factor obstructing the formation of a common civic identity among Europeans. In Germany, for example, this case has been made by Dieter Grimm, a prominent constitutional lawyer and former member of the Federal Constitutional Court. The constitutional expert doubts that there is a chance of creating a European community of participation without having previously created a European community of communication. According to Grimm, the Europeans face the problem that they are not yet able to develop a properly transnational political discourse, as they lack the communicative bond of a common language. For this reason, Grimm considers that, in spite of all well-intentioned constitutional plans aiming at higher levels of political integration, the structures of a European public sphere will remain precarious, at least within the foreseeable future. Linguistic differentiation is thus seen, in quite a Millian vein, as a particularly challenging form of cultural diversity if a democratic polity is to be institutionalized. In contrast to Grimm, Jürgen Habermas (2001a) is far more optimistic when assessing the perspectives for the formation of a European public sphere. In his eyes, the intensification of transnational political communication in Europe, up to a point at which a critical threshold is surpassed, is basically a matter of appropriate institutional provisions. He too endorses the view, however, that such a dynamics can only work if there is a common linguistic medium. For Habermas (2001a: 122), this medium will be English, which is assigned the role of a 'second first language' for Europeans.

Regardless of all differences concerning their specific understanding of the concept of the public sphere, Mill, Grimm and Habermas seem to agree on the basic assumption that a democratic public must be a linguistically integrated public. From the corresponding angle, processes of political communication that pretend to meet democratic criteria require the vehicle of a shared *lingua franca*. Language – in singular – thus becomes an essential means for constructing a public sphere. Yet languages – in plural – appear to be barriers to democratic integration, at least as long as they entail a markedly multilingual context of political communication, as is the case in the EU at present.

Consequently, linguistic manifestations of cultural diversity involve a serious dilemma for liberal democratic theory. While the separation of church and state was supposed to guarantee institutional neutrality towards particular types of religious identity, there is no analogous strategy that could be adopted in order to deal with linguistic pluralism: public institutions do not have to pray, but they have to rely on linguistic communication. Political theory has typically tended to circumvent the dilemma by linking the processes of public communication that articulate democratic sovereignty to the existence of culturally standardized units. To the extent that the historically dominant model of nation-state formation is taken as given, an implicit connection between democratic theory and state theory is established. Ultimately, the postulate is that a modern polity should have a uniform identity, a single source of sovereignty and a unitary conception of citizens' rights and duties; in short, political integration presupposes cultural homogeneity (Parekh 1997: 192).

All in all, since Mill, liberal democratic theory seems to have turned an empirically open question into a normative axiom. Against this background, it should be stressed that the evidence we have at our disposal when we want to examine which alternative mechanisms of integration may sustain democratic polities that are built upon 'weak' communicative foundations is still highly fragmentary. Sticking dogmatically to the Millian approach, therefore, does not seem to be an ideal starting point for those who want to formulate an innovative response to the challenge of diversity in present-day European politics – such as the Convention on the Future of Europe.

European identity and cultural diversity

Apparently untroubled by the verdicts uttered in the realm of political theory, the members of the Convention preparing the constitutional draft submitted to the European Council in summer 2003 seem to have leaned towards a fairly positive view of the role that diversity has to play in the process of creating a more democratic Union. The draft's preamble, which begins with a quotation taken from Thucydides that invokes the principle of democracy,[3] already contains a direct reference to the Union's official motto, speaking of a Europe 'united in its diversity'. Subsequently, several other sections of the draft emphasize the normative significance of the principle of diversity for the EU.

The draft thus takes up a normative guideline that has had a remarkable presence in European integration since the process was initiated in the 1950s. Let us bring into focus what one of the 'founding fathers' of the EC/EU, Walter Hallstein, the first President of the European Commission, had to say while reflecting on the relationship between diversity and integration:

> Europe is diversity. We want to preserve the wealth and the difference of characters, of talents, of beliefs, of habits, of customs, of taste. (. . .) The fact that the Europeans do not speak the same language cannot disturb us. Switzerland provides us with the classical example showing that linguistic variety does not constrain, but rather enrich, and we wish for our Belgian friends that they can soon be cited as another example. The multiplicity of languages is not an obstacle but an incentive. The experiences with our European officials in Brussels (. . .) prove this.[4]

With his diversity-oriented understanding of integration, Hallstein is a true spokesman of the generation of pioneers of European unification, who were determined to insulate the realm of *cultural* identities against the functional spillovers of the Common Market. While building Europe should imply giving up monolithic conceptions of national belonging and contribute to the formation of new patterns of *political* identification, Hallstein and his fellow travellers had no pretensions to work out common European standards in the domain of culture. Thus, from the beginning, the institutional approach to the uniting of Europe was to combine the objective of market integration with respect for those cultural differences embodied in nation-state identities. If we take linguistic pluralism as an example, it seems pretty obvious that the formal adoption of the principle of 'integral multilingualism' by most European institutions is to be interpreted as a tribute the EU pays to cultural diversity. In the area of language, so far, the EU's policy has largely been an attempt at formulating a consensual response to an intricate multinational constellation. Nonetheless, somewhat paradoxically, the dominant players in this constellation are nation-states; diverse communities that are not state-based are clearly relegated to a secondary rank. The intention of giving all state languages the same official status was to erect a symbolic barrier against setbacks provoked by nationalist resentments (Coulmas 1991). After the ratification of the Treaty of Rome, the elites devoted to securing a fragile European consensus were eager to keep away from the conflict potentially involved in raising language issues, as the quote taken from Hallstein indicates. However, if we leave aside the continuous declarations of good will and the need to respect the prerogatives of the member states, the EU has no proper programme that tells in which areas and in which ways cultural and linguistic diversity is ultimately to be protected (Kraus 2000).

Since the EC (European Community) began to engage in 'identity politics' by adopting a 'Declaration on European Identity' at a summit held in Copenhagen in December 1973, Europe's 'official' identity discourse has kept on turning around two main axes.[5] On the one hand, a set of common political values establishes the framework for European unity. On the other hand, cultural diversity retains a central normative status within this framework. Accordingly, up to now, the EC/EU's official approach to the question of cultural identity has been extremely cautious. One feels tempted to say that, in the meanwhile, the recurrent pledge to respect and to protect the diversity of cultures has almost developed into a ritual. Obviously, culture is a highly sensitive matter in European politics. It continues to be a competence primarily held by member states that are generally unwilling to expose their own 'identity affairs' to supranational supervision. Nonetheless, in the period since 1973, the cultural dimension has successively become a significant component of the efforts officially undertaken in order to define and strengthen Europe's identity, as a look at treaties, declarations and related documents shows. The evidence is particularly striking if one concentrates on the period that goes from the signing of the Treaty on European Union in 1992 to the submission of the draft of a Constitution for Europe in 2003.

The Treaties of Maastricht and Amsterdam (1997) included an amendment of the Treaty establishing the European Communities, signed in Rome in 1957. The modified version of the Treaty of Rome contained a specific title for culture, that has been incorporated in the constitutional draft.[6] The corresponding section reads:

1   The Community shall contribute to the flowering of the cultures of the Member States, while respecting their national and regional diversity and at the same time bringing the common cultural heritage to the fore.

2   Action by the Community shall be aimed at encouraging cooperation between Member States and, if necessary, supporting and supplementing their action in the following areas:

- improvement of the knowledge and dissemination of the culture and history of the European peoples;
- conservation and safeguarding of cultural heritage of European significance;
- non-commercial cultural exchanges;
- artistic and literary creation, including in the audiovisual sector.

(. . .)

4   The Community shall take cultural aspects into account in its action under other provisions of this Treaty, in particular in order to respect and to promote the diversity of its cultures.

It can be argued that, all in all, the texts of the Maastricht and Amsterdam Treaties already show a tendency that seems to have turned into a more or less stable pattern in the course of the drafting of the Charter of Fundamental Rights and the Constitution for Europe: the goal of establishing 'an ever closer union' based on common values and the goal of preserving the diversity of cultures – a diversity which has essentially to be seen as a diversity of the cultures of nation-states – are set next to each other, without the placing of major efforts on reconciling their potentially conflicting logics. The 'Charter of Fundamental Rights of the European Union', solemnly proclaimed by the European Parliament, the Council and the Commission in Nice in December 2000 may be read as a document that summarizes the main developments of the Union's official doctrine on diversity. As a result of the Convention's deliberations, the Charter is expected to be ratified as Part Two of the Constitutional Treaty. The following paragraphs are taken from the Charter's Preamble:

The peoples of Europe, in creating an ever closer union among them, are resolved to share a peaceful future based on common values.

Conscious of its spiritual and moral heritage, the Union is founded on the indivisible, universal values of human dignity, freedom, equality and solidarity; it is based on the principles of democracy and the rule of law. It places the individual at the heart of its activities, by establishing the citizenship of the Union and by creating an area of freedom, security and justice.

The Union contributes to the preservation and to the development of these common values while respecting the diversity of the cultures and traditions of the peoples of Europe as well as the national identities of the Member States and the organisation of their public authorities at national, regional and local levels; it seeks to promote balanced and sustainable development and ensures free movement of persons, goods, services and capital, and the freedom of establishment.

Article 22 of the Charter of Rights (Article II-22 of the Constitutional Treaty) consists of one short sentence that puts additional stress on the political significance of cultural diversity in the EU: 'The Union shall respect cultural, religious and linguistic diversity'. It should be noted that, as this Article is included in Title III of the Charter, the respect of diversity is directly connected to the purpose of promoting the principle of equality for all European citizens.

Finally, diversity has also figured as an important concept in the text that is the genuine outcome of the debates held in the Convention, i.e. in Part One of the Constitutional Treaty. The Constitution's Preamble has already been mentioned. Article I-3 of the Constitution lists the Union's objectives. In subsection 3 of this Article, two paragraphs may be understood as a specific reference to what it means to be 'united in diversity':

It [the Union] shall promote economic, social and territorial cohesion, and solidarity among Member States.

The Union shall respect its rich cultural and linguistic diversity, and shall ensure that Europe's cultural heritage is safeguarded and enhanced.

Against the background of these passages taken from the draft Treaty, the problem of constituting and constitutionalizing a European public sphere seems to lead back to the 'Kakanian' challenge faced by the EU: how can an institutional frame for transnational communication be created that allows the 'transcendence' of cultural differences without negating them? This question clearly touches upon central aspects of the political identity that shall sustain a constitutional community of a new kind. The making of such an identity will hardly be the exclusive result of a constitutional process in the strict legal sense. As a matter of fact, so far, official European actors who were eager to consolidate Europe as an 'identity project' did certainly not limit their efforts to the level of basic treaties and official declarations. This is especially true for the Commission under Delors in the period before and after Maastricht. The institutional outcomes of the policy initiatives set up to give European identity a graspable meaning must not be underestimated.[7] They comprise such measures as the introduction of Union citizenship, the proliferation of official European symbols in all realms of social life and the adoption of several important European programmes devoted to education and culture. To say that attempts at identity-building from above have been one of the main concerns of the EC/EU in the last two decades is hardly an exaggeration. Nonetheless, it seems that these attempts have only had limited success in resolving the contradictions built into the European project. With few exceptions, as far as the mass public is concerned, identification with 'Europeanness' lags well behind national or regional attachments. In some cases, there are even symptoms that the growing visibility of a 'Europeanization' of everyday politics is provoking an increase in anti-European sentiments.[8] At any rate, European identity does not necessarily imply the formation of a harmonious link between different levels of political and cultural loyalties. It should not be complacently taken for an efficient tranquillizer, to be prescribed whenever the dynamics of European integration seem to enter the field of contentious political issues. Often enough, in such cases, instead of concealing the tensions between different identity options, the medication rather ends up revealing them.

Nice and the aftermath

European institutions started their activities in the field of 'identity politics' well before this concept became a subject of intensely led and still continuing disputes in the social sciences and the humanities. Nonetheless, it seems that the appeals to foster European identity have only had limited success in constraining intergovernmental attempts at securing nation-state prerogatives in the Euro-polity. As is known, the central purpose of the EU summit held in Nice in December 2000 was to pave the way for a far-reaching reform of Europe's institutional framework, a reform that was unavoidable in order to give the EU a chance to manage the challenges associated with its Eastern enlargement.[9] Moreover, the pressures towards realizing major institutional changes were thought to offer a welcome opportunity for achieving higher levels of transparency and efficiency in the system of European decision-making. At any rate, this was the declared goal of the numerous voices that were claiming that widening and deepening the EU were in no way incompatible, but rather mutually reinforcing political objectives.[10] In more general terms, the main tasks of the Nice meeting consisted in discussing Europe's 'finality', in delineating the general interests uniting all Europeans, and perhaps even in defining a European 'common good'. In this respect, however, most observers would describe the results of the Nice conference as thoroughly disappointing. The 'all-European' perspective got virtually lost in the arena of tough intergovernmental bargaining. In the prolonged and difficult negotiations, the representatives of the member states seemed to focus almost exclusively on their respective national interests. In the end, the strategy of *sauve qui peut* threatened to displace the traditional European *on sàrrange et puis on voit* approach. Even the old cleavages characteristic of the European system of nation-states in a foregone period were apparently re-emerging. As a well-informed commentator (Neunreither 2001: 191) put it: 'For the historically minded, a shadow of the continent's troublesome past which was characterized by endless struggles about dominance became visible for a moment'.

In the press reports covering the Nice summit, the use of language drawing analogies to warlike situations was quite frequent indeed: commenting upon the re-weighing of power and the modifications affecting the use of qualified majority voting (QMV) in the EU, newspapers spoke of an intense and open confrontation between France and Germany as well as of a clash of the smaller and the larger countries. In the end, there was much speculation about the winners and losers at Nice and about the forces giving proper support to the tiny compromises reached at the conference. After all, it was plainly evident that the main players in Europe's institutional setting were still the nation-states. This became especially clear in the discussions concerning the redistribution of voting power in the Council. The procedure adopted in Nice and constitutionalized in the *Protocol on the Representation of Citizens in the European Parliament and the Weighting of Votes in the European Council and the Council of Ministers*, annexed to the Draft Treaty, requires that decisions made under QMV meet three conditions: they must be supported by a qualified majority of weighted votes, count on a majority of member states, and, finally, represent a demographic majority of 62 per cent of the EU's population. All in all, the entrenchment of intergovernmentalism in Europe's semi-constitutional structure implies that stateness receives a high premium with regard to political representation: in a European Union with 27 member states, Germany, with a population of approximately 82 million (17 per cent of the total), gets 29 votes in the Council (8.4 per cent); for Luxembourg, the corresponding figures are 429,000 (0.09 per cent) and 4 (1.16 per cent). Thus, when it comes to assign formal powers in Europe's political system, the principle of equality of states clearly predominates against all other principles that might be used in order to represent European constituencies in terms of their diversity. The 'statist' bias of representation is also at work in the context of the European Parliament: here, for example, a British parliamentarian represents roughly 823,000 citizens, whereas in the Irish case, the ratio is 312,000 citizens per MEP.

Of course, one has to be aware of the fact that formal procedures do not automatically translate into factual political weight in Europe's institutional system. Nevertheless, it is evident that the nation-states are not about to stop being the basic political units in the EU.[11] Hence, for the time being, political interests continue to be principally framed as national interests, in the sense of the interests of nation-states. In spite of the institutional discourses and structures focusing on 'other' Europes, such as the Europe of the citizens, the Europe of the regions or the Europe of organized interests represented in the Economic and Social Committee, the European Union has basically been constructed as a union of nation-states. This is reflected in its institutional architecture, which is permeated by a 'thin' nationalism. The commitment to protect cultural identities is not simply an exercise in rhetorics. Yet, in order to be eligible for a high level of protection, such identities must be framed as the national identities of the member states. Only in this sense is the commitment well embedded in the Union's constitutional structure. Thus, the making of the EU does not seem to have led to a thorough supersession of nationalism (at least, as far as its 'thin' versions are concerned). It has rather contributed to the reframing of nationalism in a new political setting. The institutional logics of the EU imply a more or less continuous reproduction of national structures. In the context of EU politics, this means basically that political interests are legitimized on the grounds of entrenched cultural identities, as long as these identities are those of nation-states.

Democratic interculturalism

In the course of its institutional development, the EC/EU has acquired more and more features of a polycentric multinational community. This community lacks a hegemonic force controlling the process of political integration. At the same time, the emergence of a European level of governance has strongly affected the sovereign character of the member states. Due to the steady Europeanization of decision-making structures, unilaterally conceived national initiatives have become obsolete in many important policy areas. Moreover, the dynamics of Europeanization are loosening up the traditional interconnection of cultural and political identities that constituted a typical feature of sovereign statehood. While EU member states show a growing disposition to give up rigid ways of interpreting old prerogatives regulating the institutional articulation of collective identities, the EU itself does not claim to acquire new prerogatives in that domain. Therefore, the EU may well be considered to constitute a post-sovereign order that implies a clear departure from former models of national rule.[12] The Union has few pretensions to create a close transnational fit between the realms of politics and culture; its aim is rather to protect the plurality of politically relevant cultural attachments that can be found in the sphere of its institutional activities.

Against this background, Europe seems to offer promising conditions for formulating an innovative political response to the challenges of diversity. However, creating an encompassing discursive frame for the definition of a common political identity is a very ambitious task, if linguistic and cultural diversity is to be promoted at the same time. At present, the bases for processes of *horizontal* political communication in the EU are still rather precarious. In contrast, there are significant tendencies that indicate a *vertical* shifting of political discussions into the specialized forums that constitute the universe of 'comitology'. This semi-public universe dominated by experts remains largely inaccessible for most citizens. While it provides a convenient setting for efficient decision-making, comitology is not likely to increase the normative appeal of EU politics for a broader public. The present situation raises important questions regarding the material fundamentals of democratic participation in an institutional environment that is undergoing a substantial transformation. It may be symptomatic that many contributions made in the field of political theory that deal with the problems of transnational governance do not really address these questions. Thus, advocates of deliberative politics in the EU have surprisingly little to say about the communicative modalities of deliberation in a culturally differentiated and multinational context.[13]

Integration has implied paving the way for a 'politics of recognition' (Taylor 1992) on a European scale. However, the enactment of cultural recognition in the EC/EU is not exempt from striking contradictions. On the one hand, recognition is biased towards the identities embodied by nation-states. Subnational, transnational or intercultural and 'hybrid' patterns of identification play a clearly subordinate role in the institutional approach taken by the Union when it confronts diversity. Thus, cultural identities often enter the political stage as mere tactical devices used to underpin the articulation of nation-state interests in the system of intergovernmental bargaining. On the other hand, the preponderance of nation-state based legitimation discourses in EU politics makes it extremely difficult to formulate a coherent response to the manifold challenges cultural diversity poses for the Union. Up to now, as far as cultural matters are concerned, respect for the national identities of the member states has the highest priority in the policy packages set up by the European Union.

The Union's institutions seem overwhelmed by the dilemma involved in finding a balance between the protection of diversity and the development of a common political framework for Europeans. Institutional inertia, however, will not provide for proper defence against the dynamics of 'negative' integration. The term has been coined in order to describe the tendency that, because of the lack of explicit political deliberation and regulation, matters of collective concern end up becoming the object of 'invisible' market forces. Culture should not be regarded as a domain that is immune to this kind of tendency. The way the language issue is dealt with in the realm of European institutions is a good case in point: the option for non-decision-making in the field of language policy offers no solid support for cultural pluralism; it will end up producing very specific and selective results. Instead of breeding an interplay of identities that is free of domination, negative integration in the field of culture will lead to standardization without a political debate.

What could a politics of recognition that offers a more balanced perspective for dealing with diversity in the EU look like? While observing general criteria of equality, as listed in the 'Charter of Fundamental Rights', the Union would have to show its respect for the diversity of cultures at the level of transnational institution-building. Diversity should not be reduced to the particular identities of homogeneous nation-states, nor should it be declared a matter of 'benign neglect' expressing a supposedly abstract cosmopolitanism. Subsidiarity might be a promising point of departure for implanting such an understanding of recognition in Europe's institutional setting. The Maastricht Treaty seemed to assign the concept a crucial role in the Union's political architecture. At the beginning of the 1990s, subsidiarity was apparently bound to become one of the basic principles in the further institutional development of the EU, especially in terms of offering a coherent response to Europe's diversity. In the meanwhile, it is rather evident that the harsh realities of EU politics have largely deprived the concept of any deeper meaning. Nevertheless, reflecting on subsidiarity may still offer important insights for those who want to reactivate and reorient the debate on civic identity and cultural diversity in an emerging European polity.

Both in normative and in empirical analyses of political integration, subsidiarity can be taken to entail an institutional logic that departs from the idea of a single and indivisible source of sovereignty. The dangers of experiencing dangerous clashes of different cultural identities in the European polity would be reduced by splitting up levels of identification according to the principle of subsidiarity, thereby allowing people to remain sovereign 'within their own circle'. An approach of this kind obviously has to avoid an *a priori* commitment to the sovereign territorial state as the only legitimate institutional setting for a political community. In consequence, it runs against the intergovernmental bias in the institutional architecture of the EU. In modern political thinking, such an understanding of subsidiarity can be traced back to Althusius's merging of consociational and federal ideas in the early seventeenth century (Hüglin 1991). The tensions between the principles of subsidiarity and sovereignty did not remain restricted to the realm of the history of political ideas; they were also reflected in the large-scale developments that shaped political structures in the real world. Thus, in the early modern period, city states and city leagues, sharing and dividing powers according to the principle of subsidiarity, were manifest expressions of possible institutional alternatives to the sovereign territorial state (Tilly 1990; Spruyt 1994; Le Galès 2002). Historically, subsidiarity had an important role to play in culturally heterogeneous polities, that used the guideline for distributing competences in a way that should take into account both the diversity of collective identifications and the state's obligation to foster group-transcending solidarity.[14]

In the sense described here, subsidiarity might serve as a mechanism that contributes to the breeding of a democratic interculturalism in EU politics. What does the concept of democratic interculturalism refer to? On the intercultural side, the concept takes into account that recognition is an indispensable component of any constitutional order that aims at accommodating diversity in all its forms and at allowing an articulation of identities in a way that counterbalances domination.[15] If Europe is to move towards an 'ever closer union' of its peoples, it will certainly need to rely on a political ethos nurtured by intercultural empathy. A political community that is able to cope with identity conflicts and that, 'united in diversity', is prepared to explore new paths of democratic integration depends substantially on citizens with a high level of intercultural competence. On the democratic side, the concept indicates that defining a 'common good' in the institutional context of the Union remains a primary political goal. This goal is a rationale needed if the variegated processes of political communication in the transnational public sphere are to be related to each other. Accordingly, interculturalism is introduced here as a concept that deliberately aims at avoiding the tendency to place different collectivities that are defined by cultural criteria statically beside one another in a given political setting, as essentializing multiculturalist approaches sometimes do. Cultural identities are phenomena that are socially produced and reproduced; they can be changed by political means and become the subject of processes of collective self-determination.

Recognition plays an elementary role in culturally differentiated political communities if group relations are to be permeated by a moment of reflexivity. Taking recognition seriously means to understand that the political freedom of citizens is a socially embedded freedom. The construction of the transnational order of the EU requires from all parties involved that they learn to see that the sociocultural dimension of political integration is a fundamental aspect in the institutional changes we are going through. Ultimately, the politics of recognition evidences that the citizens themselves can't be regarded as something 'given', as a factor that is exogenous to democratic processes. Rather, 'citizenization' (Tully 2001: 25) and its institutional regulation must be seen as constitutive aspects of democratic politics.[16]

It should have become clear that recognition is not a principle forged with the purpose to institutionalize a static politics of 'being'. Rather, it is a guideline for regulating a politics of 'becoming', a politics that frames identities in a way that does not exclude the possibility of transforming them. Seen in this light, recognition becomes an important precondition for a reflexive view of one's own identity, a view that is aware of the existence of other identities and tolerates their articulation in a shared democratic context. The politics of recognition has a great potential as a normative frame for processes of democratic innovation in the 21st century. At the present stage, considering the constitutional travail of the Convention, Europe certainly still has a long way to go in order to turn this potential into significant political realities.

4 The Good, the Bad and the Ugly

The need for constitutional compromise and the drafting of the EU Constitution

Richard Bellamy and Justus Schönlau

The Convention on the Future of Europe has provoked both cynicism and idealism. Cynics see it as a largely rhetorical exercise that consolidates but does not go beyond the achievements of recent intergovernmental conferences (IGCs) or greatly transforms the nature of the EU (Moravcsik 2003). Idealists view it as offering the potential for a new departure that replaces intergovernmental bargaining with deliberation to produce a genuine European consensus (Habermas 2001b). According to this interpretation, a constitution should take the form of a contract that all rational individuals possessing a sense of justice would approve. Discussion within a constitutional convention should serve to weed out self-serving arguments, leading people to converge on a position that reflects common interests as defined by the exacting standards of public reason. From this perspective, the inevitable elements of real political negotiation and compromise that arise in any convention, however well designed (Elster 1996), represent unfortunate impurities that inevitably involve a sacrifice of principle to pragmatism in order to accommodate the partial concerns of powerful groups. What the cynic sees as a confirmation of the basically instrumental motivations of political actors, the idealist regards as a lost opportunity (Eriksen *et al.* 2002, Ch. 1; Magnette 2003). In this chapter we wish to dispute certain aspects of both these positions.

Underlying the idealist's account is the belief that a well-ordered society requires that people agree on certain just principles that offer the rules of the game for how they handle conflicts stemming from their different interests or beliefs (Rawls 1993: 53). However, though the members of any political society will need to reach an agreement on how to settle their differences, the terms of that agreement may well involve making a decision over some of the very issues they disagree about – not least because their differences on many matters may be related to their holding different views of justice. These disagreements are often reasonable and so cannot always be ascribed to purely self-interested, myopic or other unworthy motives. Nevertheless, in such cases consensus in terms of a convergence on a single position as clearly the best proves impossible. Rather, some form of bargaining will be necessary to produce a mutually acceptable compromise of either a substantive or a procedural kind. Thus, the idealists are wrong to suppose a constitution based on compromise is a compromised constitution that has failed to achieve some putative ideal consensus on truth and justice. Yet, the cynics may be mistaken in believing it is just a self-interested bargain. It may represent the fairest and most appropriate agreement available given a plurality of equally reasonable, yet divergent and occasional conflicting, views.

There are deep and reasonable differences within the EU over the two basic purposes of any constitution. A constitution both establishes a polity, defining who the people subject to it are and within which functional and territorial spheres, and creates a form of regime, designating the procedures or styles of decision-making that need to be followed for arriving at and implementing common policies, authorizing who can rule and limiting the scope of any governmental intervention through devices such as judicially protected rights. On both counts, members of the convention were divided between those favouring keeping the largely intergovernmental and market-orientated character of the EU, and those looking to create a more federal and unitary structure with a broader remit. In addition, national and ideological differences cut across this divide. As a result, if the EU was to live up to its declared intention of preserving diversity in unity, a compromise of some kind was inevitable. The key issue is how satisfactory are the compromises that were achieved. As we shall argue, a pure bargain of the kind assumed as the norm by the cynics may often produce bad or ugly compromises. As the idealists hoped, the convention setting offered an improvement in this respect. But a more deliberative politics rarely leads to consensus so much as good compromises, the result of a more complex kind of negotiation that is principled yet sensitive to clashes of interests and ideals.

Our investigation proceeds as follows. We start by outlining why compromise can be necessary and the types of compromise available, and offer an analysis of when they are good, bad or simply ugly. We then turn to the convention, explore those features that promoted different sorts of compromise and provide examples and an assessment of the main forms that were agreed. We shall conclude that, within pluralist contexts, such as multinational associations, the role of a constitution is not to produce a deliberative consensus within which bargaining can occur but to facilitate an ongoing process of compromise similar in kind to that achieved in the convention itself.

Why compromise?

Compromise is sometimes portrayed as a shoddy capitulation, whereby principle gets sacrificed to self-interest and short-term advantages. For example, in the case of a constitution it might be supposed that it should be based on principles that ought to be embraced by all who endorse liberal and democratic values rather than simply balancing the particular interests of those currently affected. Such calculations, critics of compromise standardly argue, can only lead to incoherence and injustice, such as the initial endorsement of slavery in the US constitution. Yet, compromise can also indicate a laudable willingness to see another's point of view, thereby showing a decent respect for difference. If there are divergent and competing views and interests, each of which are well-founded, then, if a collective agreement is necessary, it seems both prudent and justified to seek an accommodation between them.

There are various circumstances that might render such compromises necessary (Bellamy 1999, Ch. 1). These range from contingent or logical conflicts in satisfying particular human goods, of not being able to fund, say, both libraries and swimming pools, differences between divergent conceptions of the good, such as the clash noted by Machiavelli between the Christian and the Pagan life, to the pull of different sorts of moral claim, such as the tension between consequential and deontological considerations. Not all goods and values can be accommodated in a given social space, and to the degree they are incommensurable as well as incompatible ranking them will prove a difficult task. Though certain philosophers believe that they can, at least in principle, resolve such dilemmas, no such proposed resolution commands universal assent. As John Rawls has pointed out, what he calls the 'burdens of judgement', defined as 'the many hazards involved in the correct (and conscientious) exercise of our powers of reason and judgement in the ordinary course of political life' (Rawls 1993: 53–6), place limits on what we can justify to others. Even the best argued case can meet with reasonable dissent due to such factors as the complex nature of much factual information and uncertainty over its bearing on any case, disagreement about the weighting of values, the vagueness of concepts, the diverse backgrounds and experiences of different people, and the variety of normative considerations involved in any issue and the difficulty of making an overall assessment of their relative weight (Rawls 1993: 56–7). As a result, 'many of our most important judgements are made under conditions where it is not to be expected that conscientious persons with full powers of reason, even after free discussion, will all arrive at the same conclusion' (Rawls 1993: 58).

Elsewhere we have argued that even the most basic of constitutional principles, namely fundamental rights, can be subject to disagreements resulting from these sources (Bellamy and Schönlau, forthcoming). For example, think of the debates over breaches of privacy. It is often difficult to identify these not just because the empirical details may be unclear but also (and most importantly) because people differ over the boundaries of the concept, hold different accounts of the public interest and where it overrides the right to privacy, view personal responsibility differently, and so on. As a result, they have different views of when a right exists to be breached in the first place. Indeed, the laws in many states differ on this point. For example, France and Germany protect the privacy of public figures more than Britain or the United States. Thus, although all EU member states share a commitment to human rights, when it came to drawing up the Charter of Fundamental Rights they frequently divided over the *substance* of rights, or which rights we have and why, the *subjects* of rights, or who may possess them, the *sphere* of rights, or where they apply, the *scope* of rights, or how they relate to other rights and values, and the *securing* and *specification* of rights, or the type of political or judicial intervention and the precise set of entitlements that are needed to protect them, both in general and in particular cases. Members of that convention disputed whether rights covered social and economic matters as well as civil and political issues, if they applied simply to EU institutions or the domestic arrangements of the member states as well, their impact on certain collective national interests, how far, if at all, they covered all persons residing within the EU territories as opposed to EU citizens alone, the ways they were to be framed – abstractly or very specifically, as policy goals or clear entitlements – and the extent to which the Charter was simply a declaratory statement or legally binding. These disagreements were largely overcome through various kinds of compromise. Our claim here is that much the same can be said for its successor convention when it came to debating other parts of the constitution.

How to compromise

In circumstances of reasonable disagreement, deliberation will not necessarily act as a funnel that leads the disputants to converge on a single position. There is no better argument none can reasonably reject and no compelling reason for anyone to transform their position to adopt another's. We submit that people overcome this impasse by dropping the search for a strong consensus (in the sense of all being converted to a particular view) and looking instead for mutually acceptable agreements. In this case, all the parties remain convinced that their own position would be the best, at least given their own concerns, but come to appreciate that reasonable alternative perspectives exist that ought to be acknowledged in some way as well. In other words, compromise need not be simply a matter of prudence but also of principle, reflecting a willingness to 'hear the other sides'. Here deliberation works more like a filter, weeding out purely self-interested moves in order to reveal those positions that ought to be accommodated and those that should not (Bohman 1996, Ch. 2). This process achieved, then different sorts of compromise may well be available, depending on the issue in dispute.

Roughly speaking there are three broad categories of compromise, each of which has a number of variations (Bellamy 1999, Ch. 4). The first kind seeks a direct compromise between the different viewpoints. One of the commonest methods consists of bargaining and arises in what Albert Hirschman has called 'more-or-less' conflicts (Hirschman 1994). In these cases, the disputants are either arguing over a single good whose meaning they share, or are able to conceive their various demands as being translatable into some common measure, such as money. Thus, when employees haggle over wages or house buyers over the price of their prospective home, they may have issues other than money in mind – such as the need to work late or the proximity of a railway line in these two examples – but they can nevertheless put a price on their concern that enables the parties to agree a mutually satisfactory deal. According to this model, democratic bargaining should yield partisan mutual adjustment in order to arrive at a mutually beneficial compromise on matters of collective concern. However, there are a number of problems with this approach. There is a danger that bargainers look out for themselves and seek to get as much of what they desire as they can. They only take account of the interests of others to the extent they are obliged to. Given that the strong and rich generally need concede less to the weak and poor than to other rich and strong groups, pure bargaining seems unlikely to produce equitable or stable compromises. Add to this weakness the problems of free-riding and selective defection in decisions over most public goods, and the likelihood of bad compromises resulting from the bargaining model increases. Finally, there are questions of integrity and the incommensurability and incompatibility of what different groups want. Certain values are integral to a given group's identity and could not be bargained away without a sense of deep loss. Particular goods are often simply different, and to seek to compare them would be as absurd as asking whether we should regard Mozart as better or worse an artist than Shakespeare.

These difficulties are what give compromise a bad name. However, fortunately more complex and deliberative forms of arranging compromises exist on those occasions when we need to make a decision and pure bargaining would be inappropriate. Thus, a more sophisticated style of negotiation goes beyond simply 'splitting the difference' and involves trading to mutual advantage, whereby each gets some if not all of what they want. For example, most political parties have to engage in a degree of logrolling to get elected. This procedure brings into a single party various groups who may disagree over many issues but prioritize them differently. If three groups are split over the possession of nuclear weapons, development aid, and a graduate tax, but each values a different one of these more than the others, it may be possible for them to agree to a package giving each the policy they value most while putting up with another they disagree with in an area that matters less to them. Of course, sometimes the result can be a programme that is too inconsistent to be tenable or attractive. Here, it might be better for the groups to shift to an agreed second best. A notion adapted from economics, the basic idea is that modifications to one's preferred option may be less desirable than obtaining one's next best or even lower ranked choice. A cheap sports car that pretends to be an expensive one may be less appealing than a solid family estate. Individuals and groups with conflicting first preferences may even have a shared second preference. Sometimes it may appear that people's concerns are simply incommensurable, irreconcilable or that they talk past each other. Appeals by religious groups for special treatment have sometimes been portrayed in such terms. Yet it may be possible to employ analogies to appeal to a shared norm or precedent and argue casuistically towards a common position. Within a largely secular political culture, say, it may be possible for a religious group to point to some humanist analogue to religious belief, such as state support for the arts, to justify protection of their religion on grounds of equity.

These more developed forms of compromise share a common desire not so much to compare different positions as to give each one its due and to seek reciprocal solutions. They adopt a problem solving approach to conflicts, rather than viewing them as a battle to be won or lost. The aim is an integrative rather than a distributive compromise, with the interests and values of others being matters to be met rather than constraints to be overcome through minimal, tactical concessions. Such compromises try to include the moral reasons of each side. Conflicts can often appear intractable at the level of abstract principle because radically under-described. Deliberation overcomes this problem by allowing the concerns of the parties involved to be fully articulated, so that the specific force of the various reasons involved can be appreciated. Thick description may help clarify the distinctive weight of different demands. Each party may agree that reasons of different weight or involving different sorts of consideration are involved. When described in detail, it may prove possible to address the main preoccupations of each party in a coherent way. The forms of compromise suggested above, such as log-rolling, second best and reasoning by analogy, represent attempts to put together a coherent package that finds a place for the views of all concerned.

Sometimes time constraints or the character of the differences dividing them prevent parties from agreeing a compromise on substance. A second kind of compromise often comes in here, which employs a procedural device to overcome deadlock. In these cases, the parties agree to defer to whatever outcome issues from the procedure, regardless of whether they agree to the decision or not. The acceptability of the procedure does not turn on its coming up with the 'right' answer, for that is what is in dispute. Nevertheless, there must be something about the procedure that inspires confidence that its decisions would not be so irrational or arbitrary that it would be preferable to live with the conflict. In general, the procedural virtue appealed to is that of fairness in the weighing of the different views – that all are shown equal consideration and have a chance to influence the outcome. Taking turns offers a simple form of procedural compromise, but risks becoming a nonsense if it means that decisions change with the decision-maker. A presidency that rotates between different groups is one thing, a rotating policy quite another. Ronald Dworkin calls compromises of the latter type 'checker board' solutions (Dworkin 1986: 179). He gives as an example of such a compromise a proposal that abortions be permitted amongst women born in odd but not in even years – after all, anti-abortionists would regard this as better than no ban and pro-abortionists as superior to a complete ban. Yet, compared to the integrative compromises discussed above it appears incoherent – a compromised form of justice rather than a just compromise. For example, it is in stark contrast to Dworkin's own attempt to address this issue by giving weight both to 'the intrinsic value of life' and the 'procreative autonomy' of women, which can be seen as an attempt at an integrative moral compromise (Bohman 1996: 92), even if he does not portray it in these terms himself.

To avoid such checker-board solutions, procedural compromises usually involve an agreement that a given decision process is fair for choosing a single collective outcome. Choosing by lot or tossing a coin offer pure procedures of this nature. However, these mechanisms also seem better adapted (and are more common) for choosing decision-makers than making decisions. Giving all views an identical chance to define the outcome can be at variance with showing everyone equal concern and respect. Collective political decisions usually affect very large numbers of people. To give the opinion of a single individual the same weight as a view supported by many thousands of people is to treat the latter unequally. Unanimous decision-making, which gives a veto to even very small minorities, suffers from a parallel failing. By contrast, as May famously showed (May 1952), majority voting alone satisfies certain basic criteria of fairness and rationality. In particular, it weighs each person's view equally, rendering all preferences equally (if minimally) decisive. Of course, this result assumes ideal conditions. In real politics, there are problems of consistent minorities and tyrannous majorities. Because of these problems, strict majoritarianism is rare.[1] Most legislatures are elected via systems that produce multiple parties and a degree of representativeness that makes coalition building necessary. The attempted compromise here is to give disadvantaged minorities a role in collective decision-making that ensures their views are not discounted entirely, but without undermining equality and effectiveness. In particular circumstances, animosity may run so high that people prefer to defer the decision to another. Third party arbitration, where trust is placed in the arbitrator to do the balancing in an impartial manner according to a fixed set of rules, likewise represents a procedure aimed at giving equal weight to all views.

At times even an acceptable procedural solution may seem unavailable. This situation can arise either when an issue is so divisive no common position would ever prove acceptable or when one or more of the parties involved do not recognize the right and/or the need for decisions on a given matter to be taken collectively (or at least by a given collectivity). In these circumstances, compromise can take the form of either trimming or segregation. Trimming arises when certain issues simply get taken off the agenda, most commonly through the employment of constitutional 'gag-rules' (Holmes 1998). The classic case is the strict separation of Church and state. The difficulty is that the 'method of avoidance', to use the Rawlsean term for this strategy, suggests a lowest common denominator that may favour the status quo and involve keeping quiet about a deep injustice. In this respect, trimmers resemble G. K. Chesterton's man of universal good will, ridiculed for saying 'Whatever the merits of torturing innocent children to death, and no doubt there is much to be said on both sides, I am sure we all agree that it should be done with sterilized instruments'. Moreover, trimming may be as controversial as a more positive policy, taking off the agenda the issues that most animate people and delegitimizing the political system in the process. For example, removing religion from politics will not be perceived as a neutral solution by those people whose deepest political convictions stem from religious beliefs. After all, this is the case not only for Christian fundamentalists, whose demands typically drive liberals towards the trimmer's position, but also for Abraham Lincoln and Martin Luther King. Allowing views, even extreme ones, to be publicly debated enables reasonable views to be distinguished from the irrational and bigoted.

Segregation similarly seeks to skirt around conflict by preserving the integrity of each value, culture or interest within its own domain. The private gets separated from the public, people placed into groups of the like minded and given autonomy to decide language, religious or other policies for themselves. Some segregation is vital for individual and group autonomy. However, the borders are rarely clear cut and can be as politically controversial as the issues they are meant to resolve. No matter how well drawn, they almost always include dissenting minorities in their turn, many of whom would belong to a majority given other arrangements and often were members of the majority prior to the new boundaries being drawn.

All three kinds of compromising, along with their variants, are standard political techniques and frequently combined. Each has its respective merits and demerits, according to the issue and the perspectives of the people concerned. Take, for example, religious education in a multicultural society. Trading might yield ecumenical solutions or concessions, such as special rights, in other areas that certain religious groups regard as more important, as in Britain's exemption of Sikhs from wearing crash helmets on motorcycles. Or it might be better to trim or establish as a shared second best that schools are strictly secular. Societies that are deeply segmented along religious lines have often adopted various forms of segregation, such as consociationalism (Lijphart 1968). Sometimes a minority group engages in negotiation to get accepted. For example, British Muslims have pointed to analogies with established liberal or Christian practices to get certain of their claims recognized as legitimate and to promote understanding of them (Modood 1993).

While consensus aspires to a fixed point above normal political divisions, compromises necessarily reflect them. They differ according to context and evolve as people's circumstances and views change. Nevertheless, the above discussion of compromise offers us certain guidelines for distinguishing the good from the bad and the ugly. Pure bargaining works well for issues working along a single dimension in which matters of principle and identity are not involved, but even then has potential problems of non-compliance, free riding and inequity that are only likely to be addressed by a more deliberative and negotiated strategy (Neyer 2003). As such, critics of compromise in the constitutional realm are right to object to pure bargaining on most occasions. However, a more deliberative approach can give rise to integrative compromises. The qualities evidenced by such compromises are a willingness to 'hear the other sides' and to reach mutually acceptable agreements. Similar virtues of equality of concern and respect and reciprocity characterize good procedural compromises. Indeed, a good procedure is likely to be one that is sufficiently inclusive as to lead to integrative compromises. By contrast, pure procedures have no filtering mechanisms, and let irrational and intolerant positions stand unchallenged. Equal weighting is different to identical weighting. The latter also often produces substantively incoherent or compromised decisions, such as checker-board solutions. When neither an integrative compromise of a substantive kind nor a fair procedural compromise proves possible, then segregation can offer the answer. After all, a checker-board involving different jurisdictions is both common and arguably fosters individual and group autonomy. However, sub-dividing existing units can often be ugly if not exactly bad, while trimming is invariably so. Table 4.1 summarizes the different forms of compromise.

With these considerations in mind, let us now turn to the Convention on the Future of Europe and address the issues of why compromise was necessary, whether it offered a context liable to promote good compromises, and the degree to which the agreements reached were indeed good.

A compromised Constitution?

The Convention on the Future of Europe was expected to overcome the 'pure bargaining' of the intergovernmental conferences traditionally entrusted with reforming the EU's primary laws. The use of the convention method to draft the EU Charter of Fundamental rights had produced a surprising degree of agreement on an array of controversial issues (Eriksen *et al.* 2003, Ch. 1). A convention was now seen as the appropriate tool to propose solutions for the 'left-overs' of Nice (i.e. those institutional

Table 4.1 Different forms of compromise

Quality of the compromise	Type of compromise					
	Bargaining	Negotiating (trading, log-rolling, second best etc.)	Procedural		Trimming	Segregation
			Pure (e.g. lottery or rotation)	Imperfect (e.g. majority – or qualified majority – decision-making)		
Good	In single dimensional, more or less disagreements	When integrative	When for decision-makers	When likely to give rise to integrative compromises	When mutually acceptable as the most integrative solution	To promote individual and group autonomy
Bad	In matters of principle	When involves irrational or intolerant views that do not accommodate positions of others	When for decisions	When leads to the tyranny of the majority	When produces injustice	When exchanges the oppression of one minority by another
Ugly	Results in mere modus vivendi, so unstable, because dependent on the bargaining power of those involved	When distributive	When for decisions	When the agreement is brokered by others	When drives dissent underground and gives irrational and intolerant views a spurious legitimacy	When the borders between groups or values are controversial

questions at the eve of EU enlargement which had been solved only partially with the Treaty of Nice) as well as for such long-standing problems of the Union as the division of competencies between the EU and the member states (European Council – Laeken Declaration, 2001). Though most governments were initially reluctant, they seem to have reasoned that this was potentially their last chance for major institutional reform, which many feared would become harder post-enlargement, and so they became willing to adopt alternative methods to break through the apparent deadlock of the IGCs. The role of governments as guardians of national interests, on the one hand, and the general taboo on questioning established arrangements lest all the extant bargains and agreements unravelled, on the other, were seen as inhibiting discussion of the radical changes needed to shape the integration process and either extend or constrain it. They hoped a convention would be freer to consider a wider range of options. A convention was also viewed as a mechanism for securing a degree of popular and especially parliamentary support for any decision (Magnette 2004).

Although the convention set up at the Laeken summit had a wide remit, it was not given the task of drafting a European Constitution but of studying the questions and presenting options for Treaty reform which would then be discussed and decided on by a subsequent Intergovernmental Conference. Prompted by the convention President, Valéry Giscard d'Estaing, it took on this constitutional role itself, believing the merging of the various treaties into a single, more coherent document offered the best solution to the various issues it had been asked to consider. There were a number of features of the convention that favoured its being more deliberative than an IGC, although as we shall see the result was not consensus in the strict sense so much as a better form of compromise.[2] First, it had more time. Originally the convention was given a year for its colossal task of examining the more than 800 articles of the current EU set-up, starting from 28 February 2002. In the event, the convention took more than 50 official meetings and a little more than 17 months to produce its draft, which was presented to the heads of state and government in June 2003. Thus, its deliberations took place over months rather than days. The need for quick decision-making almost always precipitates a tendency to bargain. Opponents get bought off or powerful groups simply cut a deal that ignores minority views. As we shall see, time pressures often had this effect in the convention too.

Second, it had a broad membership, bringing together representatives from the Commission and European Parliament, as well as the national parliaments and governments of both the then 15 member states and the ten candidate and three applicant countries.[3] With two members of each national Parliament and from the Commission, one from each national government and 16 from the European Parliament, the convention had 102 full members (shadowed by an equal number of substitutes), plus a president and two vice-presidents. The convention also included observers from other EU institutions like the Committee of the Regions, the social partners and the European Ombudsman, and aimed at consulting widely (though it was also criticized for not succeeding e.g. Shaw 2003). Bargaining typically took place among a small group of like-minded actors, who did not need to consult either experts or stakeholders, and for whom making a decision proved more important than getting it right. A larger group, involving a number of stakeholders and experts, was more likely to raise problems and divergent perspectives, all of which would need to be explicitly addressed. However, the convention was not so big that discussion between all the members of the convention could not take place, or individuals got tempted into playing to the gallery rather than making arguments. Nevertheless, smaller working groups frequently proved crucial for brokering agreements in sensitive areas.

Third, its deliberations were largely public without being in the glare of publicity. Bargaining is notoriously characteristic of 'smoke-filled rooms'. A degree of publicity forces people to make their case by appealing to public interest arguments and generally acceptable reasons rather than naked self-interest or purely partial concerns. Such public reasoning may often be employed hypocritically, but it nevertheless constrains what people can demand of others. However, too much publicity leads to grand-standing and populist attempts to palliate or appeal to influential interest groups outside the convention. To a degree, European IGCs suffer from both problems – their deliberations are private but so widely publicized that politicians will always want to claim that they have struck a 'tough bargain' for their constituents regardless of the justifiability of their demands.

Fourth, the convention was task-orientated, focused on producing workable, long-term arrangements. From his inaugural speech onwards, the convention's President was at pains to uphold the 'convention spirit'. He invited members to 'embark on our task without preconceived ideas, and form our vision of the new Europe by listening constantly and closely to all our partners'(cited in Magnette 2004). As a result, he urged that 'the members of the four components of our convention must not regard themselves simply as spokespersons for those who appointed them'. He made members sit in alphabetical order rather than in political or national groupings. Though not entirely successful, since these groupings met outside the plenary sessions, overt references to ideology or national interest were seen as breaches of convention etiquette.

Fifth, Giscard d'Estaing also decided (and was not seriously challenged on this by the convention) that the decision-making method would be 'by consensus' rather than by unanimity or majority vote (Magnette 2004). Unanimity could have allowed the tyranny of the minority, whereby a very small group – even one representative – could hold out against any agreement until their demands were met. However, given the diversity of interests involved, a bare majority risks a minority being unduly and consistently passed over. The decision to seek a 'consensus' could at one level be seen as itself a compromise between two of the positions the constitution sought to reconcile: namely unitary, 'pan-European' interests, where a simple majority of the European population could be sufficient to carry a policy, and the various distinct interests of the different member states, which are only likely to be satisfied by seeking an agreement acceptable to all. Nevertheless, the President's interpretation of this rule was at times both obscure and controversial.

Finally, the convention contained sufficient power holders or their trusted representatives to be realistic in its objectives and not be tempted into utopian schemes. A mere talking shop divorced from the realities of politics has no incentive to make its proposals either practical or popularly legitimate. Yet, the degree of government interest, which grew towards the end, was also a weakness. In general, rules should not be made by those likely to be subject to them. Once again, this will encourage a form of bargaining, where short-term considerations of immediate advantage will compete with a more deliberative desire to devise general rules that can be equally applied to all for the common benefit.

As Table 4.2 shows, the results of the convention's deliberations supply examples of many types of compromise, and more examples could easily have been added. While pure bargaining played a lesser role, because in the complex context of constitutional negotiations there are not many one-dimensional issues that lend themselves to more-or-less agreements, it was not entirely absent. Certain national governments attempted to force through concessions by using the threat of a veto – especially in the very last phase of the convention when time pressures meant that such tactics could be used without having to be justified before the convention as a whole. For example, Germany and France were each able to overturn a previously agreed extension of qualified majority voting to an area of particular sensitivity to them: namely, immigration and access to the labour market, and trade in cultural goods, respectively.

However, the commonest kind of compromise was based on negotiation. Examples of 'good' negotiated compromise include the involvement of national parliaments in monitoring subsidiarity. The debate about how to uphold the principle of subsidiarity without overly curtailing the EU's capacity to act or jeopardizing the efficiency of its law-making power, was initially polarized between those seeking the creation of a third chamber representing national parliaments and others advocating very little, if any, change to the current (weak) system of enforcement. The compromise solution integrated both points of view. Though national parliaments were not formerly involved in EU decision-making, their role is strengthened. They must now be kept informed of EU developments and have the possibility of issuing 'early warnings' when they believe the principle of subsidiarity to be under threat, supplemented with the ultimate sanction of

Table 4.2 Different forms of compromise within the Convention

| Quality of the compromise | Type of compromise | | | | | |
	Bargaining	Negotiating (trading, log-rolling, second best etc.)	Procedural — Pure (e.g. lottery or rotation)	Imperfect (e.g. majority – or qualified majority – decision-making)	Trimming	Segregation
Good		Early warning system on subsidiarity for national parliaments – protocol division of competencies: no rigid catalogue, but categories (Arts 11–17)	General principle of equal rotation for presidency of sectoral council formations (Art. 23.4)	Election of Commission president by majority of European Parliament on proposal by qualified majority of the Council (Art. 26.1)	No re-discussion of the Charter compromises	Strengthening of subsidiarity control via national parliaments; principle of enhanced cooperation of member states which want to go further (Art. 43)
Bad	Last minute exceptions to qualified majority voting introduced by individual powerful players – cultural trade (France), immigration (Germany)			Qualified majority threshold raised to majority of member states and 60% of population – risk of blockade by minority (Art. 24)	Economic governance – since no agreement could be reached in the working group, Constitution is weak on the subject	Possibly the institutionalisation of the Euro-group (Art. I-14, Arts III 88–96)
Ugly		Unclear job description of president of European Council (Art. 21)		Proposal of three candidates for Commissioner per country (Art. 26)	Ignoring an initiative of 200 convention members for a stronger transparency-clause (Bonde)	Decision about how each parliament exercises its right of appeal over subsidiarity left to national legislation

bringing cases before the European Court of Justice via the national governments.

Another successful integrative compromise resulted from the negotiations about the division of competencies between the European Union and its member states. A core question of the Laeken mandate, this issue provoked heated debate during the early stages. Some, notably the German Länder, wanted a fixed catalogue of competencies, others were wary of prematurely fixing EU structures in their current state. As with the agreement on national parliaments, a compromise was forged within a working group. The proposed solution was to introduce three basic categories of competencies (exclusive and shared competencies and a category of 'supporting, coordinating or complementary action', Arts 12, 13 and 16), as well as special provisions for specific policy areas (economic and employment policy, foreign and security policy, Arts 14–15) and a flexibility clause which allows the Union to adopt measures for which it does not have specific competencies, but which are necessary to obtain the objectives of the Union. The safeguard against excessive use of this latter provision is the unanimity requirement and the necessary consent of the European Parliament (Art. 17.1), the specific reference to the subsidiarity monitoring mechanism (Art. 17.2) and the exclusion of harmonization (Art. 17.3). This complex compromise seems to have satisfied most if not all convention members that the right balance had been struck.

However, while the convention method was successful in filtering out clearly unreasonable or irrational views during the deliberation process, and thus avoided really bad negotiated compromises, it did produce a couple of ugly negotiation results. Perhaps the ugliest of all (certainly from an aesthetic point of view) was the rather convoluted preamble, with its vague appeals to somewhat questionable European values. Another, more serious, example is the vagueness of the article on the role of the Chair of the European Council, which had been a very contentious issue from the beginning. Due to extensive negotiation and various rounds of compromise, the article in its current form tries to accommodate opposing views (those who thought an elected president of the European Council would be the key solution to the EU's effectiveness and legitimacy problems, versus those who saw it as the end of European integration because of its strengthening of the intergovernmental aspect of the EU). The result is a weak compromise, which is at best a lesser evil for both sides.

Procedural compromises were naturally crucial to the Union's institutional arrangements. The principle of equality of member states was frequently invoked in the debates about them, with equal rotation promoted as its clearest expression. This was introduced at Treaty level in its basic form in the article on the rotation of the Presidency of the Council of Ministers (Art. 23), even though various proposals had been made for elected Chairs of these bodies. Nevertheless, the specifics of the 'equal rotation' are left for the European Council to decide, '... taking into account European political and geographical balance and the diversity of Member States' (Art. 23.4). Similarly, the equal rotation of Commissioners proposed in Article 25 mentions special 'principles' that need to be followed when establishing the details – a reflection of the difficulties attending the adoption of this particular procedural compromise.

On the whole, however, the need to develop coherent policy-making structures meant that more complex procedural solutions were adopted. The system for the election of the President of the European Commission as introduced by Article 26 represents a good compromise in this respect. It combines the two logics (the intergovernmental and the supranational) of European integration: the European Council proposes a candidate by a qualified majority, for the EP to elect by a majority. The somewhat vague formula that in choosing the candidate the European Council should take 'into account the elections to the European Parliament' is a compromise solution that allows room for some flexibility until a more stable European party system has emerged.

By contrast, the system for the definition of the qualified majority (Art. 24) represents a bad procedural compromise. The system agreed at Nice had been a classic case of the dangers of hurried bargaining. It had exacerbated existing disproportionalities in the number of votes per country, made the voting system far too complex and raised the threshold of a qualified majority (Maurer 2003). The originally proposed solution of a double majority based on a majority of member states representing a majority of the EU population would have been a clear, simple and fair solution. Yet, in the negotiations bargaining once again came to the fore and the threshold of the population requirement was raised to 60 per cent, thereby increasing the relative weight of large member states. While some rebalancing seemed necessary of the hitherto disproportionately represented small member states, the compromise here seems to go too far in the other direction. Paradoxically, it had appeared the IGC following the convention would hinge on this point because of the intransigence of two member states (Spain and Poland) who wanted to maintain the favourable position offered by the Nice system.

A merely ugly compromise is the procedure for the choice of the members of the Commission (independently of the question of how many members the Commission will ultimately have): for Article 26.2 stipulates that 'each Member State determined by the system of rotation shall establish a list of three persons in which both genders shall be represented, whom it considers qualified to be a European Commissioner'. It seems difficult to imagine that this will lead to a genuine competition between equally qualified persons as opposed to political game-playing with a list of one real candidate and two bogeyman/woman candidates. This compromise can only be explained as an attempt to placate fears that the appointment of the Commission members would otherwise be taken over by the elected Commission President and thus be completely out of the hands of national governments.

As far as trimming is concerned, it is difficult to establish in many cases which issues could have been debated by the convention, but were not included as a matter of choice or reasoned decision. On the whole, the convention sought to avoid the vagueness and deliberate ambiguities that were often employed to reach agreements at IGCs. From this point of view, trimming was seen as a failure. However, one issue which was consciously (and largely successfully) removed from debate was the contents of the EU Charter of Fundamental Rights. While the Laeken mandate had clearly indicated that a solution had to be found on the questions of if and how the Charter should become part of the constitutional treaty, it did not mention the contents of the Charter. Yet there were voices in the second convention's early debates that criticized certain aspects of the Charter and seemed to imply the need to re-open the issues decided by the first convention. Nevertheless, the working group on the Charter very clearly stated that '. . . the content of the Charter represented a consensus reached by the previous convention . . . The whole Charter – including its statements of rights and principles, its preamble, and, as a crucial element, its "general provisions" – should be respected by this convention and not be re-opened by it'. (CONV 354/02:4). Given that it is unclear that the decisions of the second convention could have been any different to the first in this regard, trimming on this issue was probably the best solution. Nevertheless, a certain 'ugliness' resulted from this compromise. Two far from elegant preambles is arguably at least one too many within any constitution. Moreover, the inclusion of the explanatory notes of the first convention's Praesidium, requested by Britain since they believed these clearly restricted the scope of the Charter to EU institutions, arguably creates more rather than fewer ambiguities. The status of the notes was in any case unclear, given that they were not discussed by the Charter convention.

Other areas of trimming were rather less felicitous. The convention's failure to reach agreement on the issue of economic governance (working group final report: CONV 357/02) meant that the draft constitution is largely silent on some crucial matters in this area. In the fields of taxation and monetary policy, for example, the working group could only agree to recommend that the EU's existing limited competencies should be maintained. And while it recommended that other issues (for example social dialogue) should be discussed in the convention as a whole, because these issues went beyond its mandate, the failure to reach a compromise in the working group also led to a curtailment of debate on these apparently divisive issues in the convention. How far these lacunae will lead to injustices remains to be seen, though problems in this area are bound to resurface sooner rather than later.

Segregation was also a tool employed by the convention in the search for agreement. Clearly, to reserve certain decisions within the EU context for member states or even sub-national actors is a form of segregation. To some degree, a clearer demarcation of state competences in certain areas was employed to allow greater integration in others. In this regard, the new arrangements for protecting subsidiarity represented a compromise between the groups in the convention who clearly pushed for further centralization of competencies, and those who wanted to roll back integration and give powers to the national level. This sort of compromise was not possible in all issue areas, however, with foreign affairs and common defence and security policy proving particularly tricky. Various forms of flexible integration have been offered as ways of getting round this problem. The idea of enhanced cooperation, for example, allows those countries wishing to embark on further integration in certain areas to do so without waiting for the agreement of those member states that are unwilling or unable to participate. The challenge is to balance such a clause against the danger of an overall dissolution of the European Union or the creation of a two-tier system if the mechanism is used too often. The procedure for enhanced cooperation in Article 43 of the draft constitution therefore introduces a large number of safeguards (such as non-exclusivity of the groups forging ahead, the rule that enhanced cooperation be used as a 'last resort', only upon authorization by the Council and with a minimum of one third of member states as participants, etc.) to ensure it does not lead to the development of permanent parallel groups of member states. Once again, it represents a fair balancing between the demand for unity and consistency, on the one hand, and for diversity and autonomy, on the other.

Similar reasoning lies behind the institutionalization of the Euro-group, where different speeds of integration are already established. By adopting specific provisions for those countries which have adopted the Euro (Art. I-14.3 and Arts III 88–90), decisions about monetary issues are to a certain extent segregated. While it seems obvious that EU members belonging to the Euro naturally have to take certain decisions together without those who do not belong to the single currency, the inclusion of such specific provisions at the constitutional level raises the question of whether a permanent closure might be established of the Euro-group *vis-à-vis* a minority of non-Euro member states. This impression is exacerbated by the fact that the Constitution also contains a section on 'transitional provisions' (Arts III 91–96) on member states that do not (yet) fulfil the criteria for Euro-membership, but it does not seem to provide for member states to decide not to join the single currency at all. How these provisions will interact with political reality is a matter for future analysis, but there is at least the danger of segregation being imposed by the majority on the minority.

Another instance of segregation, which reflects the provisions on subsidiarity mentioned above, is the referral of the decision on how each national parliament can exercise its rights under the new subsidiarity surveillance system to national legislation. For legal reasons this solution is probably the only one possible, but it risks internalizing the potential conflicts between national parliaments and the European level (which is the necessary arena to find an agreement on subsidiarity issues) to one between national parliaments and their national governments, especially in cases where a second chamber has a different political majority to the national government. Moreover, this arrangement weakens the overall effectiveness of the subsidiarity check because it might lead to an uneven application of the sanctioning mechanism envisaged by the compromise. Therefore, this provision is an ugly part of an otherwise good compromise.

Conclusion

The convention represented a successful departure from the intergovernmental bargaining of the IGCs, and managed to produce integrative rather than merely distributive compromises. However, these compromises should not be regarded in their turn as falling short of some ideal consensus, the result of continuing elements of pure, self-interested bargaining. A reasonable difference of opinion exists as to how far the EU serves the interests of citizens within the member states better than their national governments. These debates involve both normative as well as empirical considerations. Moreover, citizens within each member state are divided on this issue to a greater or lesser degree. A very broad spectrum of opinion exists between Eurosceptics and Eurofederalists, with people being more pro-Europe on some issues than others and differing over which ones. Compromise is inevitable therefore. From this perspective, the key successes of the convention do not lie in having fixed those issues that are EU matters and those that are not. Views on this subject are likely to change over time and vary according to the issue. Rather, its main achievement lies in devising workable structures of governance that reflect the spirit of compromise and that will allow further compromises to be negotiated in the future.

5 Europe

United under God? Or not?

Tore Vincents Olsen

Introduction

One of the major concerns in the academic and political debate about the European Union from the 1990s to the present has been the Union's legitimacy deficit. This concern was voiced in the Laeken Declaration convening the Convention on the Future of Europe, and in the Convention's subsequent debate about the Union's defining values, principles, and other sources of authority. The Declaration and the Convention debates sought to clarify the basis and nature of the Union to make it more comprehensible and to bring it closer to the citizens, as direct or indirect subjects. This chapter explores different approaches in the Convention to the legitimacy basis, or the 'public philosophy' of the Union, and traces how these different approaches found their way into the final draft Constitution. The draft Constitution does not provide the clarification requested by the authors of the Laeken Declaration, so citizens will likely remain confused about the basis and nature of the Union. This confusion may in turn contribute to the Union's legitimacy deficit. So, while the Convention process merits praise for its contribution to basing future European integration on democratic dialogue rather than diplomatic negotiations, its end result requires continued debate about the constitution of Europe. Exploring the various approaches present in the Convention can qualify this debate.

Three elements were central in the Convention's debate about the legitimacy bases of the Union: the constituents of the Union, the Union's values, and its objectives. This chapter analyses the Union's values, and particularly attends to the debate about their nature. The debate came about because a substantial part of the Convention sought to introduce a reference to God in the draft Constitution, and to give special recognition to the Christian tradition and the work of the churches as essential contributions to European moral and societal life. Before turning to the substantive analysis, a theoretical introduction to different approaches to the concept of a public philosophy is needed.

Public philosophy and the constitution

For the purposes of this analysis, a public philosophy is understood as a set of values and principles that functions as a common ground for a political community. It provides a language through which conflicts can be addressed and resolved. In order to function as such common ground, the public philosophy has to be equally acceptable to all citizens. This is a general criterion for justification or legitimacy (Barry 1989: 8; Habermas 1990: 66). A constitution can be seen as a legal embodiment of this public philosophy, which serves as an interpretive guideline for the constitution itself.[1] In this sense, the constitution provides a common ground on both a symbolic and institutional level. On the symbolic level, it contains values and principles seen as common by all members of the community. On the institutional level, a constitution coordinates political and social action, and organizes the pursuit of collective goals.

Without public recognition and reciprocal assurances that institutions and citizens adhere to the same critical standards of legitimacy and feel bound to act in accordance with them, the trust necessary for continued cooperation and willingness to comply with institutions and rules is endangered (Follesdal 2001). Therefore, even if the constitution is most likely destined to be the subject of continual contention, both at the symbolic and at the institutional level, there are limits beyond which the constitution stops functioning as common ground. This may happen in two cases. The legitimacy of the constitution may be directly denied by large sections of society, or it may become public knowledge that different groups and actors support the constitution on the basis of radically conflicting sets of reasons.[2] The Union may have been at this critical limit for some time.

The notion of producing a common ground points towards a deliberative political process where argumentative speech plays a predominant role and supplements bargaining and other ways of aggregating pre-given preferences such as voting. Deliberation implies an approximation of worldviews, while bargaining might not have the same integrating effect. Bargaining may result in compromises based on very conflicting reasons (Elster 1997, 1998). Furthermore, those not directly involved in the bargaining process may not feel that they benefited from the bargain. In the absence of a coherent set of reasons for the agreement, they are unlikely to be convinced of its general acceptability.

In its initial stages, the Convention officially adhered to norms of deliberation, strongly concerned to create a Constitution that could be understood and accepted by the citizenry at large. Later the focus shifted towards bargaining between the various interests represented in the Convention. At this point the Convention members may have lost sight of the citizenry, relying too much on their own ability to represent Europe as such. It remains to be seen whether their proposed Constitution, as mediated by the ensuing intergovernmental talks, will meet with the approval of the European population.

Different approaches to producing a common ground

The task of forming a common ground for Europe and identifying the Constitution's sources of legitimacy may be based on different views concerning the feasibility of reaching consensus in political processes like the Convention. Consensus here means an agreement in which all parties agree for the same (identical) reasons. The different conceptions of feasibility influenced both the prescribed political action and the standards for evaluating the result.

Statists

At one end of the spectrum, statists would see the task of the Convention as being to strike or facilitate a Pareto-optimal bargain between various interests in the Convention, primarily the member state governments' interests. The strongest version holds that the common principles that would and should be reconfirmed are those of member states' national identity and sovereignty. A common ground based otherwise would appear unnecessary. Bonde (EP, DK, Group for a Europe of Democracies and Diversities) asked of the Praesidium's first proposal regarding Union values: 'Do we need values in an international treaty?'[3] Common values would thus not be the centre point for legitimacy. Rather, the legitimacy of a Union constituted through a treaty rests on respect for member state sovereignty, including national democratic and constitutional rules and procedures; on the 'outcomes' the Union produces; and on the ways they fit the goals otherwise pursued by the individual states.

Liberals

At the other end of the spectrum there is a universalistic approach based on equal concern and respect for all individuals. In this case, the goal is to find principles that are impartial and fair. The common ground should be neutral towards particular conceptions of the good, and exclude controversial values. This is the only way to find a common ground in modern pluralist societies, if the principle of equal concern and respect for all individuals is to be met (Arneson 1992: xviii; Rawls 1972; Barry 1995). It is to 'work by reduction, and look for more general views', to borrow Zieleniec's phrase in the Convention plenary on Union values.[4] This is the essence of the liberal approach. In the European Union it may not lead to the complete rejection of member state sovereignty as long as sovereignty does not conflict with the principle of equal concern and respect for individuals (Follesdal 1997). However, for present purposes the liberal approach is thought of more in terms of a European Union entailing a 'model of unitary republican citizenship, in which all citizens share the identical set of common citizens' rights' (Barry 2001: 7, 8–17) within the framework of a federal European state (Mancini 1998; Habermas 2001b).[5]

Liberals are sometimes said to base the legitimacy of the constitution on pre-political moral principles or 'natural law' (Castiglione 1996). These principles are often thought to include the fundamental rights charter of the constitution, that limits government policies and points to the fundamental task of government in protecting the equal freedom of all in coordinating (and facilitating) their private action plans. However, most liberals would argue that the constitution, in order to respect the principle of autonomy, ought to be authorized or at least authorizable by the people understood as a collective of individual citizens.

Communitarians

Communitarians share the idea that consensus about common values is possible, but disagree with some liberal views of the constitution. First, they claim that the principles that liberals say are universal are in fact based on a particular and only contextually valid conception of the good, which in turn is only a part of 'what we value' as a community (Taylor 1989a). Second, they fault the liberal priority of individual rights insofar as it overlooks the need to confirm and regenerate shared values and common identity through common political practices. This need is at risk by a rights-oriented 'possessive individualism' (Taylor 1985, 1995). Only through reciprocal affirmation that we share values and pursue certain goals in a common enterprise will we be willing to show solidarity with one another (Taylor 1989a; Avineri and De-Shalit 1992). At the same time, a shared cultural and political identity provides for possible democratic decisions based on majority rule. In this approach, the 'thin' liberal approach to the common ground should be replaced by a more 'thick' conception of the common good.

In this view, the legitimacy of the constitution is based on the traditions and the common values of the community as an ethical community. The traditions and roots of our strong evaluations may be retrieved by thorough and sincere collective analysis of our common history. This was indicated by Fini (Govt, IT, Alleanza Nazionale) in the Convention: 'authentic' defenders of laicism would know that 'l'identità europea' and the connected value of 'il primato della persona' can be understood only poorly if they are separated from the religious tradition.[6] Therefore, the constitution reflects the normative *telos* or *teloi* of the community. Again, the individual rights in the constitution may play a significant role in making explicit 'who we are' and what we see as valuable goals to pursue in common. Further, the constitution is meant to specify the goals of government and outlaw certain practices by government and individuals that are not consonant with 'who we are'.[7] In this view, the constitution should be established by the people, but understood not only as a collection of individual citizens but also in terms of a collective subject.

Pluralists

Pluralists, placed somewhere in the middle of the spectrum, reject the idea that a common ground can be based on consensus about either a thin set of principles or a thick set of shared values. Such 'monistic' approaches are mistaken and harmful. First, conflict and incommensurability among our many values prevent their full reconciliation within the same single framework, and some values must be excluded for the sake of others (Berlin 1990; Bellamy 1999: 1–13; Parekh 2000: Ch. 1). Second, a liberal approach seeking common ground by abstraction is oppressive in terms of alienation and self-denial for certain groups within the political community (Bellamy 1999: Ch. 3; Young 1990: Ch. 2). The communitarian approach has even more homogenizing and oppressive effects. Further, pluralists also reject the view of (international) politics held by some statists. Ethical issues and questions about identity are not appropriately dealt with through just any kind of bargaining, since in these areas one cannot just 'split the difference'.

Good politics in the pluralist view consist of deliberative negotiating processes in which 'all parties [in a spirit of reciprocity] moderate and in part transform their preferences by placing them in the context of the claims and needs of the rest of the society'. By trying to see the moral values of others as also a part of the common ground, and taking into consideration their reasons as public reasons, the parties aim for 'collective agreements embodying the highest degree of mutual recognition attainable' (Bellamy 1999: 111). Out of two (or more) conflicting sets of values and beliefs a new alternative set is constructed (Bohman 1996: 93). Pluralists primarily base the legitimacy of the constitution on its ability to structure such democratic negotiating processes, and through its recognition of various groups (and thus their values) as equal partners in political dialogue (Bellamy 1999: Ch. 5). This pluralist approach might be illustrated by Haenel (Parl., FR,) who stated that in order to give Europe an identity we would have to 'accepter et reconnaître l'influence des héritages culturels, humanistes et religieux de l'Europe sur son identité profonde' without giving a privileged position to one particular belief or another.[8] Pluralists envision 'a civic Europe made up of different nations' involving the acknowledgement of 'the validity of certain general norms and obligations, . . . without insisting that such acknowledgement needs to be the same kind for all parties or requires the adoption of a totally unified political system' (Bellamy and Castiglione 1999: 179; Parekh 2000: Ch. 7). They emphasize respect for diversity. Pluralists insist on the democratic pedigree of the constitution, but because they do not accept the notion of the people as either a collective of abstract individuals nor as a monolithic collective subject, the constitution is conceived of as a basic treaty between several groups of society (Tully 1995: Chs 4 and 5).

The Convention debate

Naturally, neither theorists nor the world ever fall neatly into analytical categories, and the actors in the Convention did not identify themselves as statists, liberals, communitarians or pluralists. But, given the varying conceptions, we may identify some normative sources perceived as bestowing putative legitimacy on the Union.

First draft

The Convention Praesidium's first draft (hereafter FD) Articles 1 to 16 (CONV 2003, 528/03) set the scene for much of the subsequent discussion about the public philosophy of the Union. These articles concern the definition and objectives of the Union, fundamental rights and citizenship of the Union, and Union competences. Other articles such as the articles on the democratic life of the Union (now Articles 44 to 51), as well as the rules for Union membership (now Articles 57 to 59), also played a part, as did most articles in the first part of the present draft Constitution (CONV 648/03, CONV 650/03). The focus is mainly on the discussion pertaining to Articles 1 to 3 concerning the constituents, the values, and the objectives of the Union, because this discussion reflects the general discussion about the legitimacy of the Union.

In FD 1–16, the legitimacy of the Union constitution rests on the *constituents*, but also on the Union's *values*, and in particular on the *objectives* of the Union. In this draft there is a relatively clear communitarian approach to the legitimacy of the Union Constitution. In addition, the wording implies that the constituents (re-) constitute themselves through the constitution, thereby leaving the concept of an international treaty behind:

> *Reflecting the will of the peoples and the States of Europe* to build a common future, this Constitution establishes a Union [entitled ...], within which the policies of the member states shall be coordinated, and which shall administer certain common competences on a *federal* basis.
> (CONV 2003, 528/03: 2, italics added)

The wording was meant to 'express the dual dimension of a Union of States and of peoples of Europe' (CONV 2003, 528/03: 11). FD 1(3) and 2 specifically address the question of producing a common ground for the Union and introduced the second source of legitimacy for the Union, its values. FD 1(3) reads:

The Union shall be open to all European States whose peoples share the same values, respect them and are committed to promoting them together.

Several criticisms were levelled against this formulation. One of them was that the states (not the peoples) should be the main interlocutors: the states should do the sharing (e.g. Hain (Govt, UK, Labour) 2003, Hjelm-Wallen (Govt, SE, Social Democratic Party) *et al.* 2003, and partly Bonde *et al.* 2003). However, an 'important point' behind this formulation was that these values 'have to be rooted in society' and not just in official state documents.[9] According to FD 2 the Union was to be

founded on the values of respect for human dignity, liberty, democracy, the rule of law and respect for human rights, values which are common to the member states. Its aim is a society at peace, through the practice of tolerance, justice and solidarity.

These are 'the basic values which make the peoples of Europe feel part of the same "union" and makes up the substantial part of the 'Union's "ethic"' (CONV 2003, 528/03: 12). A European identity is envisaged as built around certain shared values promoted in a common enterprise. Consequently, those states that do not respect these values will be subject to sanction.[10] While the broad values mentioned would also be endorsed by other theoretical approaches, the conception in the Praesidium's explanation to FD 2 is predominantly communitarian. This communitarian and teleological approach to the Union fits well with the third source of the Union's legitimacy, namely its objectives. The objectives set out by FD 3 'justify [...] the very existence of the Union and its action for its citizens' and 'the creation of the Union for the exercise of certain powers in common at [the] European level' (CONV 2003, 528/03: 12). In general it should 'promote peace, its values and the well-being of its peoples' (FD 3(1)). FD 3(2) in general restated the objectives contained in Article 2 of the TEU and Article 2 TEC, excluding those concerning CFSP and JHA. The main objective was thus to 'work for a Europe of sustainable development based on balanced economic growth and social justice.' In relation to the JHA and CFSP, the Union should *inter alia* 'constitute an area of freedom, security and justice' in respect of the richness of its cultural diversity. In addition it should 'seek to advance its values in the wider world', including 'sustainable development', 'peace', 'eradication of poverty' and 'protection of children's rights' (FD 3(3–4)). In the debate that followed, the FD 1–3 was criticized on all three issues: its conceptions of the constituents, of the values, and of the objectives. It is worth noting, however, that the FD presents a fairly coherent, communitarian view of the sources of legitimacy of the Union.

Constituents: the debate

Regarding the constituents, statists objected that the FD included the word 'federal', giving the impression that the states were no longer sovereign and that the Union Constitution gave powers to the member states, not the other way around.[11] On the other hand, pluralists, liberals and communitarians were in favour of giving more weight to constituents other than states. The pluralists argued that the formulation should consider that peoples and states are not necessarily congruent entities, especially since there are national or ethnic minorities in many member states (Szajer 2003). Liberals and communitarians emphasized the need to put the individual citizens at the heart of Union activities.[12] The different proposals were generally based on the need to take into account the autonomy of the different types of subjects, whose interests the Union should respect or pursue.

In the following debate, the Praesidium conceded that the FD 1 had given the wrong impression about the source of the Union's powers.[13] In addition, and in order to underline the continued autonomy of the member states, the Convention Praesidium introduced a new article (now Art. 59) to clarify that a member state would be free to withdraw from the Union should it decide to do so (CONV 2003, 648/03: 2). Some liberals and communitarians lamented this new article. Liberals underscored the rights that the Union bestows on legal and natural persons. For the sake of these rights, a state should not be allowed to leave without further ado.[14] Communitarians complained that an exit clause would give the wrong impression of the nature of the commitment that a state assumes by becoming a member of the Union. According to some, this introduced a 'utilitarian' understanding of the Union and weakened the mutual confirmation that the Union is a common enterprise moving towards 'an ever closer union'.[15] Once a member of the Union, there should be a 'duty to belong' (see Taylor 1985).

Constituents: the end-result

In the Convention's final draft of the Union Constitution the statist approach prevailed. The word 'federal' was removed and replaced by the expression 'Community way'. Further, even if double legitimacy was maintained through the mention of the citizens as co-constituents (instead of peoples), it is clear that it is member states that confer competences on the Union in order to pursue objectives that they share as member states. Though this article does not alter the institutional powers and the internal workings of the Union as such, it gives a rather different symbolic meaning to the Union than did the first draft. Interestingly, the idea that the peoples of the Union feel part of the same union because they share the same values also was left behind in the final Constitution. According to Article 1(2) the Union is open to 'all European *States*, which respect its values and are committed to promoting them together' (emphasis added). This is only a restatement of the old membership criteria in TEU Art. 49, but nevertheless the more openly stated proclamation of a European common ground shared by its peoples was pushed back.

Objectives: the debate

In the Convention debate about Union objectives very few criticized the objectives listed in the FD 1–16. In general, most accepted the teleological approach taken by the FD. Only a few were critical towards the teleology. In an earlier debate on Union policies, Zieleniec had made the liberal-democratic argument that the constitution should be neutral towards specific goals: 'the most important question is whether the new constitutional framework should already predetermine a political solution. Our aim is to create a level playing field and rules of the game, not to decide how many goals each team will score.'[16] And, as has been observed, he still favoured 'working by reduction'. Other liberals did not take this approach, probably because none of the objectives were illiberal in the sense that they necessarily would go against the aim to create equal opportunities for all and improve the value of individual rights.

Only the discovery of space, which was listed as an objective in FD 3(2), was scheduled for deletion. There were many suggestions for the introduction of additional objectives. Some were in favour of tipping the balance more towards the social dimension by mentioning the European social model or social market economy based on the recommendations of the Working Group on Social Europe.[17] There were also suggestions for strengthening the formulations about the protection of the environment, and of consumers. Others wanted mention of the linguistic, religious, historical and legal diversity of Europe. Finally, quite a few stressed that the formulations dealing with the Union's external relations should more strongly indicate that the Union has an open and justice- and peace-seeking approach to the rest of the world (CONV 2003, 574/1/03 Rev 1; CONV 2003 601/03; CONV 2003 674/03).

The debate about Union objectives seemed less to be about the objectives mentioned, and more about the competences, the decision procedures and the legal instruments of the Union in areas such as economic governance; social policy; freedom, security, and justice; and foreign policy. It is beyond the scope of this chapter to make a detailed analysis of the many different positions. Generally, however, statists and pluralists favoured keeping national or regional control over substantive policy areas such as economic and social policy, as well as over justice and home affairs. Alternatively, liberals and some communitarians advocated Union legislative competence, community method, qualified majority voting (QMV), co-decision, and harmonization or approximation to common rules and standards. For liberals, this was most likely due to the need to safeguard the equal treatment of individuals within the Union. Some communitarians also wanted to confirm that Europe is a common project moving towards an 'ever closer union'.

Objectives: the end-result

In general, the wishes of the communitarians and the liberals have prevailed in the final Constitutional Draft when considering the simplification of the decision procedures, the introduction of QMV and co-decision on an increasing number of policies, as well as the establishment of Union legislative competence in a number of new areas.[18] This of course relates to the other very significant motive for establishing the Convention, to make the decision procedures more efficient and workable in an enlarged Union of 25-plus members. Although the debate about the *constituents* of the Union seems to have gone in the statists' favour, the list of Union *objectives* has favoured the liberal and communitarian stances. This weakens the coherence of the overall vision of the Union, partly undermining the original purpose of the Convention's work.

Values: the debate

The debate about the definition of Union values had two main elements: the values of FD 2, and the conception of these values. Many convention-eers criticized the FD 2 for not mentioning equality, especially equality between the sexes and social justice. Others pleaded for values such as pluralism, cultural and linguistic diversity and respect for national and regional identities. Advocates for equality were plentiful, the majority apparently from the centre-left side of the political spectrum. Many also supported 'diversity' as a value, albeit with different conceptions of what diversity meant. The statist version meant 'respect for the diversity of member states' and was closely associated with national sovereignty.[19] The more pluralist version was based on the special attachment that people have to certain values and activities, for example the value of being able to speak and to express themselves through their own language, especially urged by small nations and minorities.[20] This pluralist approach also sought to safeguard regional and local self-government, and include the so-called Copenhagen criteria concerning, *inter alia,* securing the rights of minorities. Liberals also argued for diversity, albeit connected with the general focus on rights. The preferred notion by liberals seemed to be 'pluralism' rather than diversity. Thus the primary interest is in the individual and the need to protect her from the majority, rather than the ethical status of the collective and its values.[21]

The second dimension in the value debate, concerning the nature of the Union's values, was more contentious. For example, there was reluctance to include diversity and social justice in the fundamental core of values in the first sentence of FD 2 for fear of legal ambiguity. However no one directly argued against the values of equality and diversity as such, even though differences in the conception remained. The conception of the values in the FD 1–16 was communitarian in kind, but non-religious. A substantial number of interventions pleaded for the inclusion of a reference to Europe's Judeo-Christian tradition or to God as a root and source of European values, while others were strongly against such references. The EPP faction in the Convention and others supported a solution taking the wording from the preamble of the Polish Constitution. The proposal was thus to insert the following text in the value article:

> The Union's values include the values of those who believe in God as a source of truth, justice, good and beauty, as well as those who do not share such a belief but respect these universal values arising from other sources.

Few, if any, based their argument on purely religious grounds – on the existence of God and the truth of religious teachings. One of those closest was Figel (Parl, SK, Christian Democratic Movement) who argued '[a] transcendent authority in regard to political structures can help us understand the limits of power, giving human dignity its highest meaning'.[22] Instead a communitarian approach prevailed, as exemplified by Fini, above. Four arguments supported this view. First, European values cannot be understood separately from Europe's religious tradition, and denying this is partly denying 'who we are and what we value'. Second, religion is a social (and institutional) force that has played, and still plays, a beneficial role in defending European values and creating social integration. According to Tajani (EP, IT, European Peoples' Party), lack of a constitutional recognition of the religious dimension disregards the lessons learned from the twentieth century totalitarianisms, which denied God, opening the way for the destruction of human dignity. In addition, the values of Christian humanism inspired the great statesmen who created the European Community in the post-war period.[23] Thereby Tajani emphasized the role of religion as a unifying power in Europe and as a force against violence and oppression. This also supported special recognition of churches and other organizations for the fundamental cohesive role they play in European societies, and for compensating shortcomings of public social institutions.[24] This recognition was later given in FD 37 (now Article 51) by the Praesidium by incorporating declaration no. 11 from the Amsterdam Treaty on the status of churches and non-confessional organizations. FD 37 added a crucial paragraph, that 'The Union shall maintain a regular dialogue with these churches and organisations, recognising their identity and their specific contribution' (CONV 2003, 650/03).

The third religion-oriented communitarian argument was that a lack of recognition would alienate those with religious affiliations, impeding their feeling of connection to Europe. This was also used in an ingenious pluralist argument. The fourth argument was meant to counter accusations of the creation of a 'confessional state'. The claim was that the principle of separation between state and church is a Christian principle: 'the laicism of the state is a typical Christian idea, born out of the distinction between what is due to God and what is due to Caesar'.[25] Officially, most religious communitarians saw themselves as involved in an inclusive project, seeking to clarify our common European identity. But there was also a clear exclusionary aim. Skaarup (Parl, DK, Danish Peoples Party), though a statist by inclination, bluntly stated that if there were to be a Constitution it should mention Christendom, because he did not 'think that we should include Turkey in the EU. Turkey is not a part of Europe, but an Islamic country.'[26]

Liberals and liberal communitarians alike were quick to counter this religious communitarian approach. One of the Convention's dominant liberals, Duff (EP, UK, ELDR), said:

> Concerning religion and Almighty God, he is responsible for bringing Christendom, Judaism and Islam graces, faith and duties, but he is not responsible for the flowering of liberal democracy and fundamental rights and therefore he should not appear in our Constitution. Amen.

Paciotti (EP, IT, PES), another liberal, reminded the plenary that the article defining the Union values should give guidance to the actions of public institutions and be the basis for sanctions against member states. References to God or the religious traditions would imply that the Union institutions would no longer be secular. Furthermore, she did not think that a full account of Europe could be given in terms of 'these traditions'. She added: 'if one ties the European identity to the past, Europe will look like a river of blood'.[27] Tajani's argument of the unifying force of religion was almost turned on its head. In addition the role of religion was questioned. According to Kaufmann (EP, DE, European United Left/Nordic Green Left), the reference to God would divide 'die Menschen in der Union' into two categories, the believers on the one hand and the non-believers on the other. She reminded the Convention that the European movement was founded by people who had suffered under and fought against German and Italian fascism in the Second World War, and who intended to overcome this type of division by securing a development for Europe based on freedom, security, and peace. This antifascist heritage of the founders of Europe should be safeguarded in the Constitution for the future.[28] Tajani's story about the anti-totalitarian role of the Church was denied, and his version of the foundation of Europe replaced with another. Likewise, the beneficial role of religious communities was questioned. De Rossa (Parl, IE, Labour Party), presenting himself as a 'retired

Irish Catholic' who knew 'a bit about God and the good and the bad he or she can do' objected to the inclusion of religious values in the Constitution since '[s]ome sects of religious believers' values are repugnant to equality, freedom and bodily integrity'.[29] The liberal argument is clear. The Union has to be neutral *vis-à-vis* religion, so as to not to endanger the principle of equal concern and respect for each individual. Together with the non-religious communitarians, liberals argue that inclusion of religious values or references to God or religion could endanger the principle of equal treatment and separate the non-religious from the possibility of identifying with the Union. Needless to say, the liberal and non-religious also criticized the inclusion of Declaration no. 11 from the Amsterdam Treaty with the new additional paragraph. As a solution to the question of religion they pointed to freedoms of thought, conscience, and religion in the Charter of Fundamental Rights incorporated into the new Constitution. Furthermore, churches should be treated as equals with all other civil society organizations.

The debate was characterized by a stand off between exponents of the two different types of view, each almost calling the other fascist, if only by implication. As Bellamy and Schönlau's contribution to this volume shows, it is naïve to think that these opponents were completely reluctant to make any kind of bargain and were perhaps overstating their positions in order to arrive somewhere in the middle.

There were two different pluralist attempts to form an agreement. Szajer (Parl, HU), himself a religious communitarian, tried, in contrast to some of other Christians, to show that the favoured wording from the Polish Constitution was actually providing for a high level of mutual recognition:

> [The text] is conscious that it does not speak about any specific religion. This is not a protest about Catholic, Muslim or Jewish faiths. It speaks about God – which could be the God of various beliefs. In opposition to those who criticise it in this Convention, it is a tolerant, non-discriminative and inclusive concept, giving equal respect to those who do not believe in God and those of different beliefs. [...] God may not be responsible for inventing or creating liberal democracy but, for many people under communist rule, religion has been one of the few remaining links to the common European heritage behind the Iron Curtain. These people now expect Europe to openly stand up for its principles.

He tried to justify the claim that religion is an important part of some peoples' lives which they cannot just abstract from, while at the same time acknowledging that others may not feel the same way. Haenel, as mentioned above, also took on a pluralist approach based on a more liberal than religious-communitarian point of departure. He accepted and

recognized the cultural, humanist, and religious influences on the fundamental identity of Europe without giving any special privilege to the one
specific belief or other.[30] He did however argue that this recognition
should be in the Preamble rather than in the article on values. Furthermore he approved of FD 37 (now Art. 51) because it acknowledged that
every state had its own solution to the question of the relationship
between church and state. Respect for diversity necessitates respect for
these historically achieved and fragile equlibria.[31]

Values: the end-result

The debate about the nature of the Union's values was transferred to the
Preamble, rather late in the Convention process. The first draft of a com-
munitarian-sounding Preamble had what turned out to be a very controversial rendering of the 'history of European values', giving leverage to the
Christian case for a reference to the Christian tradition:

> Drawing inspiration from the cultural, religious and humanist inheri-
> tance of Europe, which, nourished first by the civilisations of Greece
> and Rome, characterised by spiritual impulse always present in its
> heritage and later by the philosophical currents of the Enlighten-
> ment, has embedded within the life of society its perception of the
> central role of the human person and his inviolable and inalienable
> rights, and of respect for law

Christians thought it would be a falsification of history not to mention
Christianity alongside Greece, Rome and the Enlightenment (e.g. Cisneros Labourda (Parl, ES, Popular Party) 2003). One pluralist thought
that it would be of no sacrifice to '"agnostic" laicists' to cede place to
Christianity in the Preamble (Teufel (Parl, DE, CDU) 2003). Liberals were
more in favour of leaving history to the historians and not using a very
selective reading of history for political goals.[32] The 'solution' was to strike
direct references to Greece, Rome and the Enlightenment, but mention
the cultural, religious and humanist inheritance of Europe.

Overall, the debate about the nature of the Union's values seems to
have fallen to the advantage of the non-religious communitarians. While
the striking of the selective reading of history is in line with the liberal
approach, the citation from Pericles' funeral oration and the reference to
Europe as a 'continent that has brought forth civilisation' suggest that the
EU is founded on a community sharing a specific set of European values,
albeit of a liberal kind, and having a 'common destiny'. In this sense the
communitarian but non-religious approach that was found in the FD 1–16
seems to be maintained. This picture is not completely clear-cut. The
special role of churches is recognized in Article 51 of the draft Constitution, to the satisfaction of religious communitarians and pluralists alike.

Regarding the values in Article 2, equality was added to the important first sentence of the Article, while pluralism and non-discrimination were put in the second sentence. Diversity was not included in the Article on values, though included by way of Article 3(3), which states that 'the Union shall respect its rich cultural and linguistic diversity', and via the new motto of the Union, included in the Preamble: 'united in [its] diversity'. These elements show tensions within the conception of the Union's values as they are stated in the draft Constitution. Further, and importantly, the discussion following the final draft Constitution clearly indicates that the debate about whether Europe is united under God or not is not yet settled.

Conclusion

The Convention debate about the legitimacy bases of the European Union revolved around the constituents, the values, and the objectives of the Union. Regarding the constituents of the Union, the statist approach won out. Not only was the word 'federal' taken out of the Article 1(1), but it is stated that the states are the main constituents, and remain sovereign. The latter is confirmed by permitting unilateral withdrawal from the union, and by the ratification and revision procedures of the treaty, which stick to the unanimity rule. Concerning the objectives of the Union, the liberal and the communitarian approaches had a small victory in the moves from unanimity to QMV and co-decision and in the inclusion of new legislative competences. The value debate ended with the (tentative) success of the non-religious communitarian approach originally present in the FD 1–16, with some concessions to the liberal, the pluralist, and the religious-communitarian approaches. To a large extent the final draft Constitution is a compromise between the different approaches to the Union's legitimacy, all of which it tries to accommodate. This can be seen as positive as it allows the various parties to recognize their own version of the public philosophy of the EU in the draft Constitution, and could promote its immediate acceptance. However these public philosophies cannot easily coexist in public. The knowledge that others support the draft Constitution for ultimately different reasons may endanger willingness to comply with the rules of the Constitution because there is uncertainty as to what these rules actually are and how they should be interpreted.

The present analysis points in particular to two tensions inherent in the draft Constitution. First, it signals intergovernmental sources of legitimacy while the decision procedures on many issues have moved away from the intergovernmental decision mode. The increase in QMV in the Council points towards an emergent union of peoples or citizens who increasingly must share values and principles to willingly accept decisions made by majority rule. The stronger role of the European Parliament in the decision-making process points to a representation of the citizens and peoples of Europe who 'united in [their] diversity' act as an independent source of authority, distinct from the member states. Taking into account the forceful way states have been confirmed as the only real constituents, the Preamble's words of 'united more closely' to 'forge a common destiny' are rather contradictory. The citizens of Europe may be left confused as to whether they are to consider themselves as united or not. Therefore, is a common destiny really forged? Another tension concerns the question of the nature of the Union's values and the reference to Christianity. On the one hand, the symbolic Preamble and the article on values do not entail direct reference to Christianity besides the recognition of Europe's religious inheritance. On the other hand, the special role of churches is recognized under the title on the Union's democratic life. This may lead citizens to question not only whether they are united or not, but also whether this union is placed under God.

Of course, it could be argued that the Convention negotiations compromise the pluralists' prescriptions for 'good politics'. The present analysis has not addressed the process of the Convention directly, that is, on whether it should be characterized more as bargaining than as deliberation. However, in the latter stages the process lost its initial deliberative spirit and turned into a rather intense bargaining process. Under the pressures of time the Convention Praesidium sought to compromise between the different interests present, and this hindered a constitutional proposal based on a coherent vision of the Union. The controversy concerning the reference to Christianity, and the fact that the campaign for this continued after the Convention had finished its work, illustrates that a new mutually recognized set of beliefs and values has not developed out of the initial positions. At this point, it is unclear how the sources of Union legitimacy stand in relation to one another, and thus what kind of common ground the Constitution provides. While the Convention process as such can only be praised for the contribution it made to the effort of basing future European integration on an open democratic dialogue, the character of its end result points towards the need for continued debate about the constitution of Europe.

6 The open method of co-ordination in the European Convention

An opportunity lost?

Myrto Tsakatika

Introduction

Over the last few years the open method of co-ordination (OMC) has been the most intensely contested and the fastest spreading of the EU's 'new' modes of governance. The European Convention was faced with the question of whether it should be constitutionalized; and if so, how. Several members of the Convention wanted to see the open method of co-ordination explicitly mentioned in the draft Constitution as a distinct instrument of EU governance, independently of its mention in the context of the specific policy areas to which it is meant to apply. Such acknowledgement would have endowed it with independent status and legitimacy in the Union's governance. Yet this did not happen. The draft Constitution makes reference to the use of the method in the articles concerning economic policy (Art. III-71) and employment (Art. III-100) as well as to the possibility of using it in the articles concerning social policy (Art. III-107), trans-European networks (Art. III-145§3), research and technological development (Art. III-148§2), public health (Art. III-179§2), and industrial policy (Art. III-180§2). No specific article is dedicated to the open method of co-ordination as a policy instrument.

Following a brief description of open co-ordination and an account of what took place in the Convention's debate on it, the method's advantages and shortcomings in terms of efficiency and democracy, as well as the tensions they give rise to, are discussed, and some thoughts on how these tensions could be addressed are offered. It is argued that before deciding on whether and how to constitutionalize the OMC, deeper reflection on how the method could be improved and what its role really is in EU governance is called for.

The open method of co-ordination: a brief overview

In EU jargon, 'open co-ordination' describes all 'soft' policy co-ordination governance processes at work in the European Union, including not only the 'official' Lisbon open co-ordination processes operative in information society policy, enterprise policy, economic reforms, education policy, research policy, social inclusion and pension reform (European Council 2000), but also the Treaty-based and more actively pursued Broad Economic Policy Guidelines process and the European Employment Strategy (Hodson and Maher 2001; Vandenbroucke 2002; Radaelli 2003). Since Lisbon there have been proposals to extend open co-ordination to health care and care for the elderly (Vandenbroucke 2002: 15), common asylum and immigration (CEC 2001, COM 387 final; CEC 2001, COM 710 final) and aspects of defence policy (Wallace 2001), and elements of the method can be identified in the Lamfalussy Report's proposals concerning the regulation of an integrated securities market (Final Report 2001), the joint action plans concerning the preparation of accession countries' jobs markets for EU membership (Hodson and Maher 2001: 725–6), as well as in the concept of 'Environmental Policy Integration', meant to insure horizontal integration of environmental policy objectives in the different areas of Community policy (Scott and Trubek 2002: 5).

Without underplaying the differences between the various OMC processes, which are indeed considerable, for the purposes of this discussion one can put forward an 'ideal type' of the method (Radaelli 2003), that may be described as follows.

- The member states periodically (in some cases annually) set common policy guidelines, often translated into (more or less) specific objectives, the achievement of which is measured by (more or less) defined indicators or benchmarks, in a specific policy sector or area.
- Guidelines and benchmarks are incorporated into national action plans that member state governments are meant to formulate with the involvement of national parliaments, experts, and (where appropriate) subnational authorities, civil society and the social partners, in accordance with the particular institutional, social, legal, and political characteristics of each national reality.
- Member states' performance, as reflected in national action plans, is periodically subject to public joint evaluation and comparison against that of the best performers in the Union and in the world. This is conducted (to the degree that it is) mainly by the Commission.
- A high level Council-Commission committee (e.g. the Employment Committee for employment, the Social Protection Committee for social exclusion) plays an important co-ordinating role, while around this Committee widespread processes of consultation with the European level social partners, civil society, etc., are meant to develop.
- Public joint evaluation is meant to lead to member states exchanging best practices and learning from each other and provide them with incentives to strive toward the common goals. However, bad performers do not face sanctions: it is 'peer review' that is meant to provide incentives for member states to do better, not the application of penalties.

The emphasis in open co-ordination is on process, not on substance: it involves continuous evaluation and feedback rather than legislation or a series of hallmark decisions (Hodson and Maher 2001: 739). According to some commentators the long-term aim of the exercise is meant to be gradual, voluntary policy convergence, as opposed to harmonization (Jacobsson 2001: 8). For others, the aim is not policy convergence but to 'limit divergence, or even bring about a degree of convergence in some cases' (de la Porte and Pochet 2002: 15). Member states can profit from open co-ordination in improving their own policies, while co-ordinating with others (Radaelli 2003: 14; Vandenbroucke 2003: 9).

Open co-ordination has been described as a new mode of multi-level governance (Marks *et al.* 1996; Hooghe and Marks 2001) as it reflects a distinct type of 'interplay between different levels of governance' (Jacobsson 2001: 4) as well as a distinct set of horizontal interactions between governmental and non-governmental actors, operating at different levels (de la Porte *et al.* 2001; Jacobsson 2001; Eberlein and Kerwer 2002; Héritier 2002; Keiser and Prange 2002). The central actors in the process are the member states, which write the actual guidelines; the Commission, which plays a facilitating (rather than agenda-setting) role, by 'presenting proposals on the European guidelines, organizing the exchange of best practices, presenting proposals on potential indicators, and providing support to the processes of implementation and peer review' (Ardy and Begg 2001: 10; Hodson and Maher 2001: 729), as well as the high level Committees mentioned above, which co-ordinate the process among levels of governance and, in some cases, can act on their own initiative (Jacobsson 2001). A minor role is reserved for the European Parliament, similar to that assigned to the Committee of the Regions, ranging from the right of information to consultation. Guidelines are not amenable to judgements by the European Court of Justice (Ekengren and Jacobsson 2000: 8, 10). Finally, open co-ordination is meant, at least in principle, to actively involve European level social partners, civil society and NGOs, as well as national parliaments, subnational authorities, and experts at the national level, in the policy-making and implementation cycle.

Open co-ordination in the European Convention

In the first few sessions of the European Convention a number of participants raised the possibility of mentioning open co-ordination in the draft Constitutional Treaty (CONV 2002, 60/02: 8). In what followed, no fewer than four of the Convention's eleven Working Groups (WGV on Complementary Competencies, WGVI on Economic Governance, WGIX on Simplification of Legislative Procedures and Instruments, WGXI on Social Europe) debated the issue. Two questions were central: should open co-ordination be included in the Treaty? If so, how? As friends and critics of the OMC seized the opportunity to exchange their fire, both questions turned out to be highly controversial at Working Group level and in the plenary meetings.

In or out? After the end of Working Group level discussions, most participants seemed to be in favour of including open co-ordination in the Treaty. Putting open co-ordination on the constitutional map (CONV 2002, 375/1/02 Rev1; CONV 2002, 357/02; CONV 2002, 424/02; CONV 2003, 516/1/03 Rev1) by means of a general clause outlining its main features as a policy instrument and then leaving particular applications of the method to the provisions in each policy area ('double anchoring') (Vandenbroucke 2003: 8–12), so as to guarantee its operational flexibility, seemed a good idea. A solution of the kind was thought appropriate to endow the method with legitimacy and clarity of the kind only constitutional acknowledgement could bestow on it. Nonetheless, open co-ordination did not make it into the Constitution. This is because a heterogeneous but persistent minority remained strongly opposed to the constitutionalization of open co-ordination, finally managing to block it.

Some, attached to the Community method or to classic federalism, were against it because they were unhappy with the method as such. It was said to blur lines of responsibility between levels of governance, making the Union look as if it is doing things that in fact member states are responsible for and/or for actually representing an overall danger for Community competence, thereby being a hindrance to further integration (CONV 2002, WGXI/1: 64–7; CONV 2003, WGXI/42 Rev1: 124). Others, coming from an inter-governmentalist perspective, were happy with the method as it stood, but did not want it to be formalized as they were afraid that it would lose what they consider to be its greatest advantage, its flexibility (CONV 2002, WGXI/6: 17). Their real fear was that open co-ordination would be no more than a step in the direction of communitarization and that it augured ill for member states' ownership of the policy areas concerned. It seems that persistent opposition to communitarization of the OMC was (at least partly) about competence and power; not a matter of principle concerning the desirability of open co-ordination as a mode of governance.

As it is, or improved? The merits of open co-ordination according to most participants favouring its constitutionalization were its capacity to enable European level co-operation in policy areas where there would otherwise only be national action, as well as its advantages in terms of respecting and accommodating national diversity. Nonetheless, few participants would have claimed that the open method is a magic formula. In general terms, most people would subscribe to the idea of improving the efficiency of open co-ordination and rendering it more democratically legitimate.

However, in practice, it turned out that few Convention members were prepared to take radical steps in this direction: in constitutionalizing it, they would rather have kept open co-ordination roughly as it is at the moment, introducing only minor improvements.

A number of proposals for substantive changes concerning mainly the method's inefficiencies or its shortcomings in terms of democratic legitimacy were put forward by members who took the view that the constitutionalization of open co-ordination would have been a good opportunity to address its weaknesses. Concerning improvement of its efficiency, the radical proposal was to make the process more like fiscal policy co-ordination, that is, provide for more specific targets, attach sanctions to under-performance, and thus make the co-ordination process more binding, in order to ensure greater commitment on the part of member states (CONV 2002, WGVI/07: 54–5). The Commission, in a more moderate fashion, argued that more importance should be given to the implementation and monitoring of policy, where the Commission's role should be strengthened (CONV 2002, WGVI/08: 1), and to making the process more effective through measures like longer reporting cycles, greater co-ordination between the different co-ordination processes, and greater peer review (CONV 2002, WGVI/07: 63–4).

A number of proposals were put forward concerning the improvement of the method's democratic legitimacy. Some, coming mostly from the centre-left side of the European Parliament, expressed the view that democratizing open co-ordination (the Broad Economic Policy Guidelines process) would require 'communitarizing' it. This ought to be achieved by (a) giving the Commission formal rights of proposal on policy guidelines (CONV 2002, WG VI.3 rev: 3) in order to better take into account the common European interest (CONV 2002, WGVI/05: 2); (b) upgrading the EP's role by involving it in the preparation of the Broad Economic Policy Guidelines (CONV 2002, WGVI/9: 2); (c) by subjecting the guidelines to the EP's 'avis conforme', or by establishing a version of the co-decision procedure, in order to ensure some degree of democratic accountability (CONV 2002, WGVI/07: 44–5); and/or (d) by upgrading the involvement and consultation of the Social Partners with a special reference in the Treaty (CONV 2002, WGVI/14: 3). Against giving the European Parliament any substantial role in the open method of co-ordination were the Commission and UNICE, both of whom argued it would make no sense as the OMC is not a legislative process (CONV 2002, WGVI/9: 7–8, 20). Another proposal was to include the method in the Treaty, adding an obligation for as much transparency and participation as possible in the process (de Búrca and Zeitlin 2003). While proposals to attach sanctions to the process or to communitarize it did not fly with most people favouring its constitutionalizing, more moderate proposals like improving open co-ordination technically and adding a transparency and participation clause met with no opposition.

Efficient and legitimate?

Before the Convention, open co-ordination's vocal supporters took every opportunity to point out its numerous normative advantages. Open co-ordination was presented as a magic formula for addressing the EU's governance shortcomings. It was, first of all, said to be 'efficient', in offering an attractive mechanism for member states to take the first step in European level co-operation in policy sectors or areas where there would otherwise have been no co-operation because the Community Method would be unacceptable while inter-governmental co-operation would not suffice (Hughes 2001). These are mainly politically sensitive areas like economic and social policy, where member states have 'divergent problems, institutions and policy legacies' (Scharpf 2001: 8), and/or where there is no political consensus or an agreed ideological basis for reform among them (Ardy and Begg 2001: 22; de la Porte *et al.* 2001: 299); areas like education, where the obstacle to communitarization would not only be radical institutional, ideological or social diversity, but also national (or subnational) cultural diversity; and finally, second and third pillar policies where it might be felt that state sovereignty was at stake (Keiser and Prange 2002).

It was also claimed that open co-ordination could be expected to be 'efficient' in the sense of producing results. First, because it works as a confidence building mechanism: structure and regular repetition over time create 'trust and co-operative orientations' among participants (Ferrera *et al.* 2002: 1). In such a context, peer review mechanisms can put pressure on member states to do better, and thus succeed where legislation would have been likely to fail. Second, because it is flexible: it allows for different speeds in reforming policy while moving in the same direction (Mosher 2000: 7); it leaves member states the room to 'weigh their policy packages appropriately' (Ardy and Begg 2001: 11–12); it can be implemented without great – and potentially contested – legislative change (Ardy and Begg 2001: 11–2). It can, and does, take many forms, depending on the policy sector or area in question. Third, because open co-ordination facilitates mutual learning and policy experimentation, which makes it likelier for member states to find suitable solutions to common problems in situations where they are uncertain about which course to take (Sabel and Zeitlin 2003; Trubek and Mosher 2003; Zeitlin 2003).

Open co-ordination was not only argued to be desirable in terms of efficiency, but also in terms of 'legitimacy'. It was said to respect and accommodate the diversity of national (and sub-national) arrangements, which reflect 'legitimate differences of social philosophies and normative aspirations' (Scharpf 2002: 663). What the Union should do and is legitimately doing through open co-ordination is enabling member states to develop their own national solutions, appropriate to deal with their own particular problems, policy legacies and institutional realities (Scharpf 2001), rather than trying to impose a single one-size-fits-all best solution. Open co-ordination is also to be considered legitimate because (at least in principle) it provides for the participation of 'a multitude of economic, social and political actors at various levels (supranational, national, regional)' in the policy-making and implementation process (Goetschy 2000: 5), and also because it is meant to promote greater transparency (de la Porte *et al.* 2001: 293). Information becomes publicized, and so are the evaluation and comparison that take place on a regular basis, as this is essential to the practice of mutual learning and information exchange (Hodson and Maher 2001: 730).

Yet, open co-ordination attracted not only friends. There were also sceptics: suspicions were raised, particularly about the open method's efficiency in bringing about any notable results. The open method involves no formal sanctions against states departing from commonly agreed guidelines (Jacobsson 2001: 9; Goetschy 2001). As important as peer pressure and finger pointing may be, they may not be sufficient to enforce compliance and therefore achieve concrete results. Results essentially depend on the political will of member state governments and on the general social and economic context. The danger here is that when difficulties or adverse general conditions arise, 'the absence of hard law will mean that common aims are abandoned or watered down' (Begg and Berghman 2002: 13). Seen in this light, open co-ordination may amount to no more than an exercise in 'symbolic politics' (Mosher 2000: 8), or a 'talking-shop' (Hughes 2001). The open method may be used by member state governments as a cover for being 'seen to do something' (Ardy and Begg 2001) about unemployment and other politically sensitive issues, while in reality doing nothing more than repackaging their national programmes in the light of European pol-icies without making any substantial changes (de la Porte and Pochet 2002: 14–15).

But the critics have been most severe on the question of democratic legitimacy: it has been argued that the open method is extremely opaque. The institutional framework of open co-ordination is very complex, and there are many open co-ordination processes (Hodson and Maher 2001: 730) – not to mention that each process differs from all others in many respects, for example, how often guidelines are drawn up, how closely each is pursued, and how specific are the targets to be reached (see Hodson and Maher 2001, de la Porte and Pochet 2002; Ferrera *et al.* 2002). Undoubt-edly, transparency is limited to the core of elites that participate in the system (Jacobsson 2001: 9), as it is extremely difficult for the non-specialist, non-insider eye to follow the process (Hodson and Maher 2001: 730). Because it is not transparent, open co-ordination not only does little in the way of promoting participation, it ends up discouraging it.

Open co-ordination defies the logic of clear allocations of competences between levels of governance (Cohen and Sabel 2003: 351; de Búrca 2003: 15). It creates confusion about where ultimate responsibility lies (Ardy and Begg 2001: 10) for crucial issues, like reducing unemployment, reforming pension systems or dealing with immigration, which makes accountability for policy making and implementation impossible. Such confusion could damage rather than bolster legitimacy. If unpopular measures have to be taken, national governments might once again be prone to shift the blame to the EU, undermining its legitimacy. The EU would in other words become more of a scapegoat than it already is (Mosher 2000: 8; Ardy and Begg 2001: 12; de la Porte *et al.* 2001: 295, 300–1). Above all, the open method has been criticized for not being sufficiently informed by democratic scrutiny and public debate at both national and European levels (Jacobsson 2001: 9). The substantive political choices regarding the drawing of guidelines, the goals to be achieved, what can be considered 'one best way' outcomes against which benchmarking can take place (Terry and Towers 2000: 243–4), and even the choice of indicators to be benchmarked, which is argued to be a normative choice (Tronti 1999: 9, 12; Amitsis *et al.* 2003: 169), are not openly debated and questioned.

These were the assumptions, reasons given and (sometimes explicit) arguments that surfaced in the Convention debate in one form or another. The overall assessment of the method arrived at by most Convention members concerned with the desirability of open co-ordination can be summarized as follows: open co-ordination is an efficient mechanism in getting member states to co-operate in the first place, given its 'soft' and flexible nature, but there are serious questions about how efficient it may be in clocking up actual results. Furthermore, while open co-ordination seems to be a legitimate method of governance for the EU, as it respects and accommodates diversity, there are doubts about how democratic it is. It may not be as transparent and conducive to participation as is often thought; it may blur lines of responsibility between levels of EU governance and thus block accountability; it may, finally, lead to policy decisions whose formulation crucially lacks democratic scrutiny and public debate.

What could be done with the open method of co-ordination

Most Convention members quickly became well aware of the tensions at the heart of open co-ordination. One is that the more binding open co-ordination gets, the less flexible. As Ardy and Begg have put it: 'The more strictly any targets are monitored, the less the discretion available to a member state in shaping programmes' (Ardy and Begg 2001: 12). If member states are forced to conform to a particular standard at a mode, time and pace which is not of their own choosing, they are most likely to be pushed to do as best performers do, regardless of whether or not what best performers do suits their national institutional reality. On the other hand, the less binding open co-ordination is, the less it can produce results and solve problems: 'if there is no sanction (or, as was the case for the EMU convergence criteria, a reward) for failing to adopt suitable measures, let alone meeting targets, the attempt to co-ordinate could prove to be empty' (Ardy and Begg 2001: 12).

The second tension is between democratic legitimacy and respect for diversity. The more diversity open co-ordination accommodates, the more complex it becomes, and therefore the more participation and transparency become difficult to achieve. Furthermore, it would seem that diversity works against the possibility of democratic debate and public scrutiny in the context of open co-ordination. At the European level, debating and monitoring the implementation of one best alternative is out of the question, because there are said to be several legitimate alternatives, according to the needs and particular circumstances of each diverse unit. At the same time, at national level, where one such best alternative could be legitimately subject to democratic choice, it is easy for governments to avoid democratic debate and control through appeals to European priorities and European competence (Jacobsson and Schmid 2002: 7).

Probably, the choice that Convention members had to face was between the possibility provided by open co-ordination as it stands (or as it roughly stands) for member state co-operation in the first place, even if that meant few concrete results and little democracy (at least for the moment), or no co-operation at all. In these terms, participants made the first choice. That they did so is obvious from the fact that proposals to make the OMC more like fiscal policy co-ordination or to effectively communitarize it were quickly and without much discussion put aside, as their realization would probably have put member state governments off co-operation altogether. However, participants did not dedicate enough time – which was altogether lacking in the Convention – and energy – spending most of their energy fighting over competence – to consider a third option. They could have discussed the best possible version of open co-ordination, a version allowing for all normative concerns (bindingness, flexibility, democracy, diversity) to be addressed and reconciled and only afterwards thought about whether and how to constitutionalize it. What might such a formula look like?

One can provide only a very rough sketch here. Fritz Scharpf has come up with the proposal to combine open co-ordination with what he calls 'differentiated' framework directives, which has the potential to ensure both bindingness and flexibility. Discussing European social policy, he envisages a new type of directive to 'set differentiated standards for the stabilization and improvement of national social protection systems', taking account of 'differences in countries' ability to pay at different stages of economic development and of the existing institutions and policy legacies

of member states'. Such directives could be combined with open co-ordination: the Guidelines would provide the necessary direction for the realization of directives; nationally appropriate solutions would emerge
through the formulation of national action plans; benchmarking,
exchange of best practices and peer review would be used with all their
advantages; evaluation could continue regularly. Were such evaluation to
reveal problems, the framework legislation could be reconsidered and
modified. Were implementation problems to emerge, the Council could
authorize the Commission to use normal Community avenues to enforce
the law. In the social field, benchmarking and exchange of best practices
could be much more effective if they were used particularly among countries with similar welfare systems, according to Scharpf (Scharpf 2002:
662–5). Open co-ordination in this light would be a flexible instrument
for implementing framework legislation.

Yet this formula would still be subject to the tension between diversity
and democracy. It would still be too complex and lack transparency and
participation. It would also continue to mean little possibility for democratic debate and public scrutiny, as it would neither allow for substantive
discussion of alternatives, nor hinder member state governments' 'two
level' games. What is missing? For one thing, ensuring co-ordination and
coherence between the various processes of open co-ordination that have
been established in the social and economic policy fields in recent years
(Dehousse 2002: 16) would go a long way towards simplifying things.
Second, and most importantly, the open method of co-ordination, which
at the moment reflects a 'depoliticized', 'technical' approach (de la Porte
et al. 2001: 296; Raveaud 2003: 13–14), could be turned into an opportunity for political debate at both national and European levels, in a way that
would not be considered threatening for diversity, were a strengthening of
the parliamentary dimension at both national and European levels of governance to be seriously considered. Politicization would mean that policy
options would be sharper and therefore more accessible to citizens at
large, rather than only to experts and NGOs (Magnette 2001). Citizens
might still not be able to follow the procedure, but they would be clearer
about what is substantively at stake. Both participation and democratic
control would become more likely.

National action plans could be adopted after special – possibly parallel
– debates in national parliaments (Jacobsson and Schmid 2002: 13). Such
debates could be based on what de la Porte *et al.* call 'bottom up' benchmarking, which would involve each member state benchmarking other
member states by reference to its own policies. Since targets, indicators
and procedures would be chosen by national authorities, national
responsibility would be clear and public scrutiny concerning national
performance *vis-àvis* others' national performance would not be so easily
avoided (de la Porte *et al.* 2001: 299–302). But national governments
would need to justify not only their performance but also their substantive

policy choices in comparison to those of other countries, before national publics and opposing political forces.

While national level political debate would take a national perspective, European level political debate could take a European perspective. The EP would need to respond to proposals to change European (differentiated) framework legislation and in order do so would need to monitor and discuss the situation. For more regular monitoring purposes, the high level Council-Commission committees that are central to the co-ordination of the process at European level could include two members appointed by the EP's competent committee. Joint evaluation reports and proposed Guidelines could be discussed in a special (Spring, for social affairs) EP plenary session, where overall assessments of the situation in the EU could be made (Telò 2001: 17). Public exchange of best practices would be more profitable and mutual learning more likely, if public comparison was also made among and between what would be argued to be sets of ideologically akin policies. European political parties, party families and coalitions would be able to develop policy 'repertoires' and facilitate policy borrowing appropriately, as policies would need to be publicly justified in the context of a more comprehensive framework. Political confrontation and realignments could well be triggered by such a process, given that policies for sensitive areas like social policy and immigration would be discussed. Seen in this light, open co-ordination could be an instrument of democratic control as well as of political innovation.

Conclusion

In a last, ultimately unsuccessful attempt to reach agreement on an appropriate formulation to curb persistent objections to the constitutionalization of open co-ordination, the Final Report of the Working Group on Social Europe affirmed that the open method 'cannot be used to undermine existing Union or member state competence', it being 'an instrument which supplements legislative action by the Union, but which can under no circumstances replace it'. The approach chosen to make the case convincing involved an attempt to address the issue of competence: it was proposed that open co-ordination should be applied only where the Union does not have legislative competence; where Union competence in the area of sectoral co-ordination is not enshrined in the Treaty; and where the Union has competence only for defining minimum rules in order to go beyond these rules (CONV 2003, 516/1/03 Rev1).

This would in any case have been the wrong way to go in light of the above discussion. Distinguishing Treaty-based from non-Treaty-based open co-ordination processes would not do much for simplification. While one certainly could not expect the political dimension as described above to be 'constitutionalized', as the practice of open co-ordination increasingly shows, 'soft' and 'hard' regulation are and should be even more mutually supportive (de Búrca 2003; Trubek and Trubek 2003). Opposition to the constitutionalization of the OMC, coming from a discussion on power, rather than one on principle, blocked serious consideration of combining the OMC with EU legislation and of examining it seriously as an instrument for implementation.

The Convention debate on open co-ordination was an opportunity to re-think the method, whether that would have led to its constitutionalization or not. It cannot be said that the opportunity was completely lost as there was a lively debate on matters of principle raised by OMC. But on the one hand, the debate did not go far enough. Not enough effort was put into figuring out how open co-ordination could be turned into an instrument addressing all the normative concerns discussed above: how it could be flexible and produce results; accommodate diversity while promoting democracy in the EU. Discussing constitutionalization of the OMC would have been profitable only after good answers to these questions had been given. On the other hand, even if such answers had been provided, and even if these answers had pointed towards constitutionalization in one form or another, it is doubtful that advocates of open co-ordination could have succeeded in getting their views across. There were two parallel debates on open co-ordination rather than a single debate. One was concerned with the desirability of open co-ordination as a form of governance in the EU. The other was about the effect that open co-ordination actually has on the horizontal and vertical allocation of powers in the Union. It seems that the latter overshadowed and undermined the former.

7 Conceptions of freedom and the European Constitution[1]

Lynn Dobson

Introduction

Freedom is claimed to be one of the European Union's foundational principles. The Constitution lists liberty as a core value (Art. 2), and heads Title II of the Union's Charter of Fundamental Rights, now part of the Constitution, 'Freedoms'. Freedom – or liberty (used here interchangeably) – is, however, one of the most contested concepts in political philosophy (Gray 1991: 1). No consensus exists as to its meaning, its worth, its priority in relation to other strongly valued public goods, nor to its most hospitable political arrangements. Distinctly different conceptions of freedom are associated with different traditions of political thought, political movements, and modes of political organization. EU discourse deploys 'freedom' to legitimize disparate initiatives, but fails to situate it. Its meaning in EU politics is therefore opaque and its implications far from self-evident.

This chapter elucidates how the draft Constitution might affect political freedom. To begin with, three basic conceptions of liberty are outlined. The interplay of each with power engenders a characteristic conception of political order. These, in turn, are discernible in general accounts of the EU and in constitutional and institutional prescriptions offered for EU reform. In assessing the draft Constitution this chapter asks: how does it appeal to these underlying conceptions of freedom? Which conceptions of political order, if any, does it advance? What are its implications for liberty?

Whose freedom?

In approaching freedom in the EU we may wonder: freedom of what? This is also a methodological point. Clearly, a number of potential avenues are available: we could examine how EU activities bear directly on individuals' freedoms; we could investigate the EU's impacts on the freedoms of states; or we could take the EU itself as the unit whose freedom intrigues us. Different premises on the appropriate locus of moral standing will produce different conclusions about liberty. A full account of freedom in the EU therefore requires a theoretical model of the interrelationships of political freedoms at multiple co-existing (and only weakly hierarchical) levels of institutionalization. No such account is available. To proceed, some interim assumptions are adopted: first, polities are themselves justified by reference to individuals' values, and individuals are normatively prior to political entities such as member states or the EU. So we begin from normative individualism. Second, there may be grounds for holding that states make some independent contribution to individuals' freedom(s). If so, states' freedom must be of consequence to the individuals whom they serve, and that is sufficient reason to take states' fates within the EU as an object of normative concern. Third, when addressing questions of states' freedom the argument should be continuous with that for individual freedom: entirely new theories should not be introduced merely because the locus of freedom moves up a level of aggregation.

Freedom

Two conceptions of liberty?

In his celebrated 1958 essay 'Two Concepts of Liberty' (Berlin 1969) Isaiah Berlin claimed that two quite distinct concepts of liberty had been central in the history of political ideas. [2] The first of these, set out clearly for the first time by Hobbes ([1651] 1968: 261), is what has come to be called 'negative' freedom, or freedom as non-interference: the idea that freedom lies in lack of restraint or impediment. Freedom is therefore always 'freedom from' something or other that would otherwise interfere in such a way as to obstruct. As Berlin writes, 'liberty in this sense is simply the area within which a man can act unobstructed by others' (Berlin 1969: 122), and the more extensive that zone of non-interference, the greater a person's freedom.

The other, 'positive', concept of freedom refers to the source controlling action rather than to its space. On this understanding a person is said to be free to the degree that she determines her actions and pursuits herself rather than by being directed and moved by forces external to her. A free person is autonomous, not the instrument of another's will; a free person is a subject, not an object, conceiving and realizing her own decisions and projects. This freedom is freedom to live according to one's own values and to participate actively in the processes determining one's life. Negative freedom is thus the absence of constraint, while positive freedom is self-mastery, or autonomy.

Berlin went on to discuss these in the light of forms of rule. Where negative freedom is most prized there ought to be an area, the more extensive the better, independent of government control. This is staked out by individual rights. While such rights might (empirically) be better guaranteed by a democratic political system, there is no necessary conceptual link between democracy and negative freedom. Autocrats may be perfectly well able to refrain from interfering with their subjects' freedom. Positive freedom, by contrast, does necessitate self-government, because here what is important is not how far government encroaches but, instead, who governs. But, empirically, assertive self-government sometimes turns out to be illiberal.

Only two conceptions?

These linkages have been challenged. The identification of negative liberty with the minimal state, argues Skinner, is the result of a seventeenth century polemic (most self-consciously articulated by Hobbes) that successfully supplanted a previous tradition of classical republican thought connecting a negative idea of individual liberty to a polity that was positively free in two senses: it was self-governing internally, and self-determining in its relations with other states. A person was individually free only insofar as she lived in a free state; a state was free only insofar as it was governed neither by an internal faction nor by another state, and the only check on these undesirable eventualities was a citizenry prepared for active public service (Skinner 1984, 1986, 1998).

This classical thinking has been recast into a modern neo-republican theory of freedom (Pettit 1993, 1997, 2001). Pettit defends the view that freedom as non-domination is a distinctly different kind of negative liberty to that espoused by classical liberalism, incorporating, but surpassing, non-interference. Key here is the insight that an agent's individual behaviour and choice is conditioned not solely by what others actually do to him, but also by what others are in a position to do to him. Freedom is affected, *contra* Berlin, not only by another's exercising her power over us, but by her merely having the constant opportunity to do so, whether she exercises it or not. The slave of a kindly and caring master is nonetheless a slave. Clearly, the focus here is on the quality and structure of relationships, rather than the intentions or consequences of act-events as stressed by theorists in Hobbesian or Berlinian mould. But not every relationship where interference is a constant background possibility is an instantiation of domination. Whether interference is harmful to freedom turns on whether it is arbitrary: arbitrary interference is 'not forced to track the avowable interests of the interferee' (Pettit 2001: 139). Exposure to the power of such arbitrary interference is unfreedom (domination), and liberty (non-domination) is precisely freedom from such exposure.

Three conceptions of liberty

We now have three conceptions of liberty relevant to political organization. First, there is the conception of freedom as non-interference. Theorists in this tradition agree that intentional human acts, including intentional collective acts such as laws, may be restraints on freedom. Liberty as non-domination, the second conception, accepts the idea of liberty as non-interference in general but widens the idea of constraint on freedom in one way (to include structural relationships of power) while narrowing it in another (to exclude non-arbitrary interference, such as laws). Both of these signal the area and extent of freedom. In that sense they are passive, indicating the space in which action is potentially available. While the value of these sorts of freedom is high, it is limited, because they say nothing about what we can do, but merely something about what others may not do to us or be in a position to do to us. The third conception, liberty as autonomy or agency, picks out the active use of freedom in pursuit of ends. As Taylor notes, it is an exercise and not an opportunity concept (Taylor 1979).

Freedom (of all three types) is insufficient for the pursuit or the attainment of ends, and so its effective exercise depends on concurrent conditions: powers and capacities of one sort or another. And it is powers – those of others – that check positive freedom and intrude on both kinds of negative freedom. Any thesis about freedom necessarily ends up as also a thesis about power, so it is not surprising that all three conceptions refer to it. Liberty as non-interference and liberty as non-domination reject others' power to interfere with or dominate us; liberty as autonomy does so too, but adds to it approbation of our power over ourselves. This becomes even more apparent when considering what kinds of political arrangements each conception supports.

Freedom, power, and political order

In and of itself, none of these three is sufficiently determinative to furnish more than threads of a political theory. To get from any conception of freedom to politics we need to add to it an account of power, since it is in the interplay of power and freedom that political freedom of various kinds is to be found – or lost. The attitude to political organization and arrangements typical of each of the three approaches to freedom is conditioned not solely by its notion of freedom but also by its guiding conception and evaluation of power.

Power, again, is a contested concept in political philosophy. But, as Morriss writes, 'we can be interested either in the extent to which citizens have the power to satisfy their own ends, or in the extent to which one person is subject to the power of another'(Morriss 2002: 40). This is the analogue at the level of political society of Morriss's distinction between 'power to', (that is, power to effect some specified outcome) and 'power over' (power to affect another person or persons). The first usage relates to control over states of affairs in one's own life; the second refers to persons as objects of another's (or others') control. Usually, 'power to' do something or obtain some specified outcome is limited in its range of reference, but this is not so with 'power over' – in contrast, it implies the ability to get someone to do a wide range of things (Morriss 2002: 32–5). While analytically separable, in real life these two aspects of power are often intertwined. Our power to effect something may also involve (incidentally or purposely) having power over someone, and the converse is certainly the case, since power over someone entails the power to obtain outcomes by means of him or her. The three conceptions of liberty differ about which of these particular types of power they hold most salient, and differ too in their evaluation of power.

Liberty as non-interference

It might be thought that, since theorists of non-interference are most concerned with intentional acts constraining freedom, they would be most averse to another's (or others') 'power to' constrain. This may be so when considering freedom *simpliciter*, but once we examine how this concern enters into their account of political freedom we see that what they are most eager to prevent is 'power over'. Madison's recommendations in *Federalist Papers IX, X and LI* ([1788] 1987) as to the separation of political powers were not chiefly motivated by the desire to hinder a 'power to' bring about a specific outcome by some particular institution or group, but rather to prevent the formation of any power so concentrated as to be in a position to hold subordinate agents or bodies in its power over a range of outcomes. A generalized disposition to view 'power to' with suspicion, because of its capacity to interfere, leads these theorists to focus attention on the 'power over', allowing its holders the capacity to engage in an indefinite but large range of intentional acts encroaching on negative freedom. Since laws restrict freedom, on this account, and political institutions are ever-present threats to it, the champion of liberty as non-interference will consider only that form and extent of government justified that intrudes to the least degree consistent with preventing greater infringements. Political institutions restrict freedom, but are a necessary evil. Without them even worse outrages could be expected.

There are however ways of containing political organization so it serves negative freedom but is prevented from self-aggrandizement. The first is that 'in a society of free men the highest authority must in normal times have no power of positive commands whatever' (Hayek 1979: 130). The highest level of authority should promulgate only the most general regulations and rules. Institutions should be granted different types of powers and functions, they and their functionaries be chosen in different ways and for different and limited terms, and they should rest on independent and preferably competing social bases and sources of legitimacy. Inter-institutional mutual checks should be installed – ambition should, famously, be deployed to counteract ambition, and bodies should have effective defensive powers *vis-à-vis* each other. While decentralization and federalism are intrinsically desirable, they are the more welcome the more competitive they are. Decisions for positive actions taken at the higher levels of federal systems must have to cross high thresholds: unanimity, supermajority, concurrent majority, or double (or triple) majority systems. In particular, where redistributive measures are at issue libertarians of this kind distrust majoritarianism, since the many, if allowed to combine, may discover (and then organize to pursue) interests to the detriment of the few. Political authorities should have few or no powers to tax, and scant financial resources. Political power should be disabled and governing institutions disempowered as much as is compatible with preserving their capacity for checking infringements of an extensive area of individual freedom. Political institutions should inhibit, not facilitate, action. International institutions should be limited to prohibitions; supranational powers in particular should have no powers to do anything except restrain national governments (Hayek 1979: 108, 149).

In this tradition of thought, a constitution should not be written by those likely to enjoy the grant of powers under it. Second, it should not be adopted without consent. Third, it should contain no more than basic organizational and procedural rules. Finally, strong fetters should be placed on those able to amend or interpret it. Amendments should require unanimity or a demanding supermajority, whereas a minority should suffice for the withdrawal of consent (including repatriation of powers). The right of secession is inviolable.[3]

Liberty as non-domination

Law and the state receive a warmer reception from theorists of non-domination. Attention to 'power over' is constitutive of this theory and its evaluation of the polity is consequently ambivalent. An independent and self-governing political community does not restrict freedom. On the contrary: it underpins it, since it countenances only the kinds of interferences that enhance freedom overall (Maynor 2003: 171). Two sources of power threaten liberty: *dominium*, or private power, and *imperium*, or public power. The task of political institutions is to protect each citizen against abuses of private power. One important means is to ensure that public power is balanced across social forces such that no particular group is subject to any other (the 'mixed commonwealth'). But the cost of succeeding against *dominium* is that the state becomes both coercive and inescapable (Pettit 2001: 155), so raising the problem of *imperium*. While it is not possible or desirable to stop the polity exercising power, it is crucial to stop it from having arbitrary power. Hence, these theorists do not consider that freedom is necessarily at risk from others' 'power to'. Because 'power to' at the level of the polity is the only available check on what would otherwise be a clear field for relationships allowing the stronger to dominate the weaker, they see the polity – given adequate safeguards – as protective of liberty overall. This is why their prescription for the defence of negative liberties contrasts so sharply with that of the exponents of freedom as non-interference.

Pettit (1999, 2001) has explored in most detail the institutional technology to ward off these dangers. To be rendered non-arbitrary, political power must demonstrate that it tracks citizens' avowed interests, and that it tracks no other interests instead. The first can be secured by something analogous to a citizens' search and authorize function (Pettit 2001: 150), which prevents adoption of decisions not answering in any way to citizens' avowed interests, identifies possibilities that do, and authorizes those preferred by a majority. Standard electoral procedures (periodic elections, equal and universal franchise, electoral rules under popular control) under adequately competitive conditions should suffice for this (see also Shapiro 2003).

However, citizens may be vulnerable to elite manipulation, faction, or corruption. Majorities can ignore minority interests, can adopt only majorities' perceptions of common interests, and can pursue such interests in ways costly to minorities (Pettit 1999: 176). The remedy is 'editorial' control through contestatory democracy, establishing minorities' powers of challenge to force public review of contestable decisions in impartial settings. This requires procedural, consultative, and appellate resources. Procedural resources include constraints on the content of laws, and standard elements of liberal democracy (rule of law, separation of powers, deliberative democratic methods, bicameral approval, depoliticization of some kinds of decision-making, independent accountability, freedom of information). Consultative resources are especially important where decision-making is farmed out to agencies or taken by administrative bodies under delegated authority, and include devices such as advisory community bodies, hearings and enquiries, publication of proposals, access of groups to parliament, public opinion research. Appellate resources guard against governments being primarily responsive to something other than the public interest, and include mechanisms allowing challenges and review by courts and parliamentary committees, specialized tribunals' examinations of the substantive merits of decisions, and ombudsmen's investigations into maladministration (Pettit 2001: 167–72).

Positive liberty

The third conception of freedom has informed much democratic theory and state practice over the last century or so, and its suppositions still underlie most political positions, mainstream or marginal, in European states. We know it principally under the rubric of 'popular sovereignty', and its core tenets appear in their most uncompromising form in Rousseau's theory (1968 [1762]). Its adherents are a disparate group including, for example, varieties of both conservatives and socialists. While the deep structure linking freedom to political organization is (so I contend) much the same for all of them, the more specified that structure becomes the more extreme the differences in inflection between them. So on the face of it they seem very much opposed. What they share is a sense that individual freedom is tightly bound to collective autonomy embodied in a unified polity directed and determined from within itself. Freedom is advanced by the state's organs' 'power to' bring about certain positive outcomes, although which outcomes are most valued depends greatly on the ideological colouring of the particular position held.

If political institutions are to bring about desired substantive outcomes (whatever they are) they must have power over potential dissenters. Hence the advocacy of popular sovereignty and the strong statism or nationalism (or both) that accompanies it, and also the maxim that the freedom of all must sometimes override the freedom of individuals. Liberal egalitarians and social democrats insist that majority rule be accompanied by the constitutional entrenchment of minority rights. But they hold that the power of the majority over the minority is sometimes justifiable, being the only way the state can embark on desired policies – precisely because those policies will constrain the freedom of some. In contrast to neo-republicans, proponents of positive liberty are, then, affirmative of both aspects of power – 'over' and 'to' – on the grounds that they are either required for or contribute to positive freedom. The general disposition of this line of thought is to facilitate 'power over', perhaps within a specified set of side-constraints, in order to enable 'power to'.

Brian Barry's discussion of political arrangements most likely to secure impartially just outcomes and a politics of solidarity depicts a liberal egalitarian polity friendly to positive freedom (Barry 1991, 1995, 2001). Broadly, what he endorses is a representative system of government resting on election by majority but having to accommodate minorities' interests as the price of their cooperation. Before the point of voting is reached, outcomes must be produced in ways giving full chances for objectors to be heard, and must not be vulnerable to reasonable objection (i.e. not be substantively unjust). The criteria of a fair decision-making procedure are that all participants have adequate information and are able to express themselves effectively, that evaluations of participants' arguments are not influenced by their social standing, and, that consensus is aimed at and where it is not possible then everybody is treated equally by having an equal vote (Barry 1995: 110). Once proposals that participants can reasonably reject, as distinct from those they would just like to reject, have been dropped, a large number of cases where justice is not determinative will be left, and then the superior outcome is the one better according with fair decision procedures.

If some minorities are to be granted exemptions from public rules it should only be as a result of processes in which all citizens are able to take part on equal terms (Barry 2001: 305). 'Where the minority is merely the losing side, why should they have a veto, or be able to decide that the policy doesn't apply to them?' (Barry 2001: 300). However majoritarianism only works well where preferences are distributed in certain ways. An alternative principle, sometimes defensible, is that no minority should be expected to respect laws that disregard its vital interests (Barry 1991: 36–8). What about supermajorities? Where a prior inclination to accommodation is absent then supermajorities will stymie politics, the tyranny of minorities will be allowed, and conflict will be exacerbated. Requiring extraordinary majorities favours the status quo, since its beneficiaries will have veto power over more equitable arrangements (Barry 1995: 107). Institutionalized deliberative bodies such as public commissions and cross-party parliamentary committees, together with facilitative institutional conditions, should be strongly encouraged. Barry takes these conditions to include electoral systems that are not plurality voting in one-member constituencies, multiparty systems where no party has a majority, and weakly cohesive political parties (Barry 1995: 105–6).

To summarize so far, liberty as non-interference is hostile to both 'power over' and 'power to', and sees freedom as residing in the greatest possible diminution of both that is consistent with basic societal order, protection of the institution of property, and procedural rules. Liberty as non-domination is averse to 'power over' but not to 'power to', since political institutions must have powers to prevent private domination. Positive freedom argues for 'power over' in order to assure 'powers to', else current beneficiaries of the status quo will block justifiable change, thus privileging the autonomy of some over that of all.

Political order and European Union

Non-interference

From the 'non-interference' point of view, states' relations with EU-level institutions are like individuals' relations with state-level institutions. EU institutions should have no 'power over' states, lest they are granted dispositional 'powers to'. All such powers are restraints on states' freedoms. Specific measures and laws may sometimes be needed to prevent worse infringements, but these should be no more than are required to maintain relations of mutual non-interference. Once basic protections against interference are assured the only positive policies the common institutions should undertake are those protecting these gains. Individual freedoms are secured within and by states, and since they are negative involve merely restraint by supranational institutions. Therefore there is no need for any direct relationship between individuals and EU political institutions.

Frank Vibert (2001) sees the EU's constitutional problem as how to strike the optimal relationship between two systems of choice: market and political. In Hayekian vein, Vibert believes the EU should be restricted to regulatory rules of general application, while rules suited to particular cases should remain lodged with nation states or lower levels of political authority. This distinction stacks up with two others. First, for Vibert there are rights that are preconditions for systems of (rule-governed) choice, and then there are rights that function as ways of expressing priorities within such systems of choice. Next, there is a politics that is rights-based – it carves out fundamental rights as side constraints (Nozick 1975) and sets institutions to jealously watch them – and a politics that is vote-based, deciding priorities within the limits set by those constraints. The three are coherently related, and in each case, only the former of each pair is justifiable EU business.

In practice, Vibert argues, the danger of tyranny comes not from the inert and silent majority but from intense minorities. So EU institutions should mediate between minorities (not assist them in finding common purpose). The European Commission cannot be a quasi- or para-executive; it is a multi-tasking regulatory agency. The Parliament should see itself as a scrutiny and review body analogous to the second chamber of a bicameral parliament rather than a continent-wide version of a national assembly. Its political parties should not receive funding. Since the EU breaches freedom if it moves beyond regulatory activity confined to preserving market choice and a system of general political procedural rules, it follows that it needs no budget. And since decisions about social priorities ought to be made nationally, the EU should eschew a Charter of Rights imposing a centrally determined set of values.

Non-domination

On the non-domination account of freedom, states should form an EU-polity but in ways precluding the domination of any faction. This suggests that freedom-preserving balances should be struck between large states and small, and that different parts of the EU machinery should be under the control of different social and political interests. Laws and policies should track avowable common interests and only those, so institutions should have procedures that authorize and also procedures that edit: majoritarianism plus minorities' opportunities to challenge. Further, the EU should not as an entity enter into or sustain relationships that are structurally dominating, that is, where an external power might interfere at will. This might have resonance for transatlantic relations.

From this perspective, there is no reason why the individual should not have a direct relationship with the EU-level institutions: were the state to insist on mediating that nexus, it would have become a dominating presence – able to interfere at will. Bellamy and Castiglione have articulated and defended a neo-republican account of political order for the EU (e.g. Bellamy and Castiglione 2002). Indeed, the EU is held up as a real-life exemplar of a 'mixed sovereignty' system (Bellamy forthcoming): its multiple levels coalesce in different ways, its varying institutions co-exist alongside member states' diverse orders, norms and criteria, and it is liable to member-state and EU-level processes of scrutiny and ratification. Further, it incorporates diverse channels of representation balancing multiple *demoi* as well as other types of interest. From a non-domination perspective its main shortcomings are its weak governance and poor accountability, and these should be remedied by means of enhanced dialogic processes between its various stakeholders (Bellamy forthcoming: 187–8). Similarly, and informed by Tully's theorizations of an agonistic and diverse constitutionalism (Tully 1995, 1999, 2000), Shaw has emphasized the desirability of procedures encouraging dialogue and review in the EU's constitutional process (e.g. Shaw 1999, 2003a).

Autonomy

The problem for a theorist of positive freedom is how to conceptualize multiple self-directed agents at different levels of aggregation. This view of liberty is linked most immediately with the idea of a self-sourcing 'power to' (i.e. autonomy), and this in itself does not get us beyond individual mastery towards any kind of collective mastery. However, in conditions of proximity and interdependence, where none can escape the effects and influence of others, self-determination can only be achieved where others' impacts can be made to be (or understood as) consistent with one's own self-determinations. Autonomous agents' compatibility with each other comes through their having common ground, so that each can identify with collective purposes as expressive of their own individual autonomy. Since such organization then allows greater power to group members in pursuit of their aims, political power over individuals is legitimated (also) as an extension of their individual autonomy. Hence we move from individual mastery to (national or other) popular sovereignty.

If this applies to individual–state relations, it should also apply to state–EU relations. One (currently influential) version of this including some liberal side constraints would see the EU as a moderately perfectionist federation. The underlying intuition here is as follows: the individual member states have similar desired aims or values they are hampered in pursuing on their own for reasons pertaining to intrinsic features of the problem or for reasons of scale or scope. If they combine and organize in certain ways ('pooling sovereignty') they will each be able or better able to pursue and accomplish their objectives. This will allow each state more capability than it would otherwise have, and since the states' objectives and values are similar, each is not directed by another's objectives and values when they do concert in this way. So collective EU decisions can be seen as an expression and enhancement of each member state's positive liberty. However, if they have values in common, it seems difficult to argue that states' populations must be very different from each other. And this raises questions about a European identity and common EU-wide values. In this outlook, then, there is no need for disquiet about the EU's power over states and populations in order that it may have powers to bring about desirable substantive outcomes, just so long as there are EU-wide majorities, and minorities' interests are protected by side constraints.

Van Parijs explicitly ties the promise held out by a self-assertive EU to his left-libertarian theory mandating a citizens' income as the condition of 'real freedom for all' (Van Parijs 1997a), noting that the EU could be a significant way of attenuating competitive pressures and providing the opportunity for 'massive and permanent interpersonal transfers' across nation-state boundaries (Van Parijs 1997a: 229). In particular, he champions greatly increasing the powers of the EU on distributive matters (Van Parijs 1997b: 291). But to do so would require a more powerful Union (Van Parijs 1997b: 292) and 'democratic scale-lifting': transnational solidaristic patriotism amongst persons and transnational democracy including a powerful parliament working under majority rule (Van Parijs 1997a: 229–30). It is crucial to reconstitute the EU as a single constituency whose people is no longer 'represented' intergovernmentally. The European Parliament should be made up of subsets of (member-state) populations, but structured along ideological or social, not national or ethnic, lines. EU-wide lists with proportional representation and multiple voting should be introduced so political discourse 'will gradually be reshaped so as to construct "our" interest on a Europe-wide scale' (Van Parijs 1997b: 295). The European Council's and Council of Ministers' decision rules should move from unanimity to 'not too qualified' majority, their discussions ought to be held in public, and where appropriate regional representation should be allowed. A President of the Council should be directly elected in a pan-EU election – again, to cater to general (EU) not partial (national) interests (Van Parijs 1997b: 296–7). *Contra* Pettit, contestation is not enough for freedom: the EU needs more centralization (Van Parijs 1999: 197). Democratic accountability should be considered owed to the people of Europe as a whole, not to multiple *demoi* (Van Parijs 1997b: 299).

With some sense now of what each conception's approach to individual freedom, to political freedom and forms of rule, and to freedom and the EU comprises, we can now summarize their nature and implications for the constitution of the EU. First, to each of the three conceptions of freedom belongs a distinctive account of what ought to be the principles of systemic order. Second, each has a characteristic preference relating to action. Third, specific sorts of aggregation (on a majoritarian–minoritarian continuum) flow from each conception. Finally, they differ on which particular substantive goods the polity exists to safeguard or promote.

A non-interfering order

For freedom as non-interference, the important principle is that the political order should be a self-regulating system of veto points where action can be blocked or slowed down. Access should be permitted to a plurality of actors with competing interests, and incentives should be organized so that actors are motivated to frustrate each other. Indeed, a system replete with veto points will itself help to institutionalize mutual distrust (Weale 2001: 75–7). The system's whole thrust should be to inhibit alterations to the status quo. This position is anti-majoritarian, in the main – the few substantive measures that the political system does need to be responsible for are usually best left to smaller groups of well qualified people insulated to some degree from popular pressures. As for individual and social goods, these are essentially to be had in the private sphere by free activity amongst free people. The political system has no business interfering in social life beyond the minimum required to uphold basic societal and economic order.

A positively free order

Positive liberty's approach is to a large extent the mirror image of that of freedom as non-constraint. Its organizational principles are hierarchy and coordination. That is because its force of action is facilitative; the point is to move from the status quo to a more desired state of affairs, and the institutional energy needed to overcome the forces of institutional inertia must be as effectively harnessed as possible if it is to succeed in enabling political action. Federations should be structured to be cooperative rather than competitive. Majoritarianism is favoured, both instrumentally as a greater mobilizational resource, and also non-instrumentally because it embodies collective autonomy. The vision of substantive goods held by positive libertarians ties them to the notion of the common good or the public interest. A unified government and common popular identity are often seen as goods in their own right, and for social democrats and liberal egalitarians are vital preconditions for the provision of economic and social goods implied by the ideas of social justice. At EU level, the European social model is frequently associated with positive liberty.[4]

A non-dominating order

For non-domination, the important systemic principles are those of mix and balance. Separation and pluralization of institutional powers is favoured, but it should be cooperative as well as competitive, and be combined with a balance across social forces so that all major perspectives and interests are represented through the organs of the system. Action may be either inhibitory or facilitative, as is required to maintain balance, but most importantly it should be revisable. Both majorities and minorities should shape and revise political outcomes. Since political stability of the neo-republican order is the most important social good its account of substantive goods leans heavily on the idea of active citizenship, sometimes conceived as a good in its own right as well as a crucial precondition of the political freedom without which no other freedoms are available.

Freedom and power in the draft Constitutional Treaty

Systemic organizational principles

In some ways the draft Constitution does import more veto points and actors with veto power into the EU's workings. Most obviously, ten new member states are set to join the EU. The introduction of a President of the European Council and a Foreign Minister affiliated to both the Commission and the Council of Ministers, alongside the existing President of the Commission, means plenty of potential for confusion and infighting between three EU figureheads (Hughes 2003: 5). National parliaments have, for the first time, a role in the EU architecture, as watchdogs of subsidiarity, and have been awarded powers of the yellow and pink cards: the 'early warning system' allowing them to indicate an EU proposal's noncompliance with the subsidiarity protocol, and their ability to require the Commission to review a proposal where one third of national parliaments (one quarter on proposals relating to 'Freedom, Security and Justice') claim non-compliance. The principle of conferral (Art. 9), seen as of 'paramount significance' (House of Lords 2003b: 17), states explicitly for the first time that member states are the source of all legitimate measures under the treaties (and now the Constitution). Taken together with the principles of subsidiarity and proportionality, it acts to limit both the extent and the exercise of EU action.

Where qualified majority is the decision rule in the Council of Ministers it remains, until 2009, a supermajority; indeed the threshold for a winning coalition has risen slightly from 71 per cent to just over 72 per cent, though on the other hand it is now a double majority (232 out of 321 votes plus at least 60 per cent of population) rather than the cumbersome triple majority scheme introduced by the Nice Treaty. Further, unanimity has been retained in some eight policy areas, including trade and cultural industries and asylum and immigration.[5]

On the other hand, a number of changes strengthen the principle of hierarchy: the attribution of legal personality to the Union (Art. 6), the open avowal of the primacy of EU law over national law in Article 10 (long *de facto* but never before asserted in a treaty), the streamlining of the Commission, the introduction of the European Council President, the division and ordering of competences into exclusive, shared, and supporting, and by no means least the apparent consolidation of the large member states in the proposed institutional architecture (Baldwin and Widgren 2003;

House of Lords 2003a: 7; Temple Lang 2003). Further, there is a repeated emphasis on coordination. The EU is characterized as a single institutional framework aiming at consistency, effectiveness and continuity of political action (Art. 18.1). For the first time a principle of loyalty, reminiscent of the federal concepts of Bundestreue (German) and comity (American), is invoked. The draft Constitution contains a mutual solidarity clause in case of natural disaster or terrorism (Art. 42), bases the Common Foreign and Security Policy on the 'development of mutual political solidarity' in Article 39, and includes a mutual defence pact in case of armed aggression (Art. 40.7). Throughout it talks of identifying and defining common or convergent interests and coordinating policies, and of mutual confidence and mutual recognition.

Neo-republicans can take heart that power in the draft Constitution remains dispersed over many institutions and many kinds of actors, and indeed, with enlargement and the incorporation of national parliaments and other new institutions, rather more of them. The Convention process itself demonstrated more mixing and balancing, over a wider range of participants, than seen in IGCs. It can, however, hardly be said that it strengthened all institutions and actors, much less that it strengthened them equally. Baldwin and Widgren's analysis of decision-making rules operative from 2009 concludes that the institutional balance will be disrupted in two ways: first, the Commission will greatly gain in power and the Council will lose (briefly, because more possible winning coalitions in the Council increases Commission ability to play them off against each other), and second, once power indices are brought into play, it is evident that 'about 40 per cent of the voting power is concentrated in the hands of the four largest nations: Germany, Britain, Italy and France' (Baldwin and Widgren 2003: 8). Any three large states will be able to form a blocking minority (House of Lords 2003b: 32). Temple Lang warns the six largest states will dominate CFSP (Temple Lang 2003: 2). Parliament will gain in influence, but the Committee of the Regions and the Economic and Social Committee remain little more than advisory bodies.

Other treaty components do seem to mix and balance in the required manner. The arrangements for enhanced cooperation, for example, try carefully to prevent factionalism. Most of all, the detail of the division of competences shows that shared competence is now the norm – precisely the kind of non-hierarchical and politically inclusive attribution of functions favoured by theorists of non-domination. Whether it will be able to function adequately in the absence of clear jurisdiction to settle boundary disputes remains moot.

Action, and principles of aggregation

The draft treaty adds few inhibitions, quite possibly as a result of its violation of the neo-liberal precept that its authors should not enjoy powers granted by a Constitution. There is now for the first time a codified right of state secession, but as its want would hardly prevent a member state's leaving, Article 59's contribution is simply to sketch out the applicable procedure. In calling the bluff of reluctant parties it may be just the opposite of inhibiting: as the House of Lords drily comments, it would 'not wish to see this provision used to force Treaty change on members' (House of Lords 2003b: 24).

In general the decision rules are becoming less anti-majoritarian, but supermajoritarianism will prevail until 2009. The Constitutional draft's real 'chilling' factors, however, are its requirements for entry into force and for amendment. The draft has an intergovernmental gauntlet to run before being decided by unanimity and then ratified by each contracting state, with many states bound by their own constitutions to put the matter to popular referendum. Repeal of previous treaties is contingent on entry into force of the Constitution, so if any one state or population prefers the *status quo*, the Constitution's prospects are not good. Amendments are also to be decided by unanimity after an IGC (which may be prepared by a Convention) and ratification in each state according to national constitutional requirements.

Overall the draft Constitution is overwhelmingly facilitative. It expands the areas in which the EU is involved (Dougan 2003: 4; House of Commons 2003a: 99). It reduces the need for unanimity and makes the 'ordinary legislative procedure' (that is, qualified majority voting in the Council plus co-decision with the Parliament) the default procedure. Thirty-six areas shift to QMV plus co-decision – a doubling, more or less (Peers 2003a; House of Lords 2003b: 20, 33). More sensationally, from 1 November 2009 – when the EU may have more than 25 members – votes will no longer be weighted, so that the ordinary legislative procedure will be simple majority in the Council (representing at least 60 per cent of population) and co-decision in the Parliament (Art. 24). Parliament's default voting rule will be majority of votes cast rather than absolute majority. Funding for Parliament's parties may help them to craft distinctive platforms and to mobilize EU citizens, but the Parliament's expanded budgetary powers, the many additional areas falling under co-decision, and the reduction of the need for absolute majorities will probably make more of a difference in the longer run. After these changes, it will be 'dramatically easier to pass EU legislation' (Baldwin and Widgren 2003: 1). The proposed *passerelle* clause (allowing shifts from unanimity to majority voting without treaty revision) joins the arrangements for constructive abstention and enhanced cooperation as devices to circumvent obstructive states and facilitate action where a substantial body of member states wishes it.

Depillarization has large structural implications beyond bringing into the purview of the Commission and Parliament policy areas previously immune from scrutiny. General principles and clauses of general application now apply across all three pillars, meaning, for example, that the supremacy and direct effect doctrines of EU law now apply to CFSP, and that 'flexibility' (Art. 17, the clause allowing the EU to act in areas not provided for in the treaty) now applies across all policy areas and not – as previously – just the internal market, though its requirement for unanimity diminishes its practicability (Dougan 2003: 2–4; House of Lords 2003b: 19, 42; Peers 2003b: 1). In the area of criminal justice, constitutional provisions would entail a 'very large' transfer of power to Union institutions from member states (House of Lords 2003b: 44). The Court's jurisdiction is now expanded by incorporation of the three pillars and by removal of some former restrictions, and member states have no choice about accepting the jurisdiction of the ECJ or specifying the level of court permitted to refer to it for preliminary rulings (House of Comons 2003a: 102–3). The provisions of Article 35, delegating powers to act, will significantly enhance the powers of the Commission (Dougan 2003: 10). The EU's history so far suggests these empowerments of the Court and the Commission will facilitate rather than impair EU action.

For proponents of contestation and revisability the picture is less clear-cut. It could be argued that the very endeavour to impose a constitutional finality fails to respect freedom (Shaw 2003a) and perhaps imperils the adaptive and dynamic nature of the EU (Weatherill 2002). One problem here is that since one purpose of a Constitution is precisely to insulate some aspects of political organization and method from easy or hasty revision it is a device inherently and intentionally inimical to free contestation. Even so, some are more rigid than others, and the current draft's amendment procedures are plainly intended to reduce the possibilities for revision (by anything short of a replacement treaty) to vanishing point. It is sometimes said the incorporation of the Charter of Fundamental Rights into the Constitution will have an ossifying effect on freedoms, and the draft Constitution's provisions for the 'Justice and Home Affairs' dossier in particular permit worrying gaps in scrutiny, review, and accountability (Peers 2003c: final paragraph, pages unnumbered).

Elsewhere, the scope for contestation and inclusion of majorities and minorities does seem to have been opened up. A number of commentators noted the shift to more inclusive and deliberative modes of work in the Convention itself (e.g. Closa 2003; Hoffmann and Vergés-Bausili 2003; Magnette 2003; Shaw 2003a). The European Council's assumption of actions previously taken by the Heads of State and Government implies they are now liable to judicial review, and its express adoption as an EU institution makes it liable to the access to documents, rules and jurisdiction of the Ombudsman (Peers 2003a: 2nd page), though on the other hand the right of access to documents has not been extended to all persons in the Union (House of Lords 2003b: 40). Article III-235 allows Parliament to set up committees of enquiry, and Article III-270 now allows any natural or legal person standing before the Court. The Charter adds the right to effective remedy and a fair trial, including legal aid where necessary (Art. II-47).

Interestingly, Title VI, Part I: 'The Democratic Life of the Union', adds some flesh to the somewhat emaciated provisions on citizenship in Title II. Its way of doing so is in tune with a neo-republican emphasis on multiplicity of sites and forms: political parties are described as contributing to the formation and expression of citizens' will, there is mention of the EU's intention to foster a public sphere (Art. 46.1), of the importance of civil society, representative associations, social partners, churches, religious associations and communities, and philosophical and non-confessional organizations; the Title expresses commitments to both participatory and representative democracy, to broad consultation, to public exchanges of views, to open, transparent, and regular dialogues; to public meetings of decision-makers, open access to documents, and appeal to the Ombudsman; and not least, there is the late and surprising addition of citizen's rights of initiative (Art. 46.4), though how far it 'will allow the individual citizen, as opposed to lobbyists, groups and organizations, to have an impact on the Commission remains to be seen' (House of Lords 2003b: 39; see Smismans, this volume). The current draft does not include the procedure for strengthening citizenship and the requirement to monitor its development provided for by Article 22 TEC.

Substantive goods

Insofar as citizenship is a primary substantive good for non-domination theorists, as well as a useful prop to contestation, the Constitution moves – a little – in a direction congenial to them. The 'Social Europe' project did not fare so well, despite eliciting widespread support among *conventionnels*. Indeed, it was they who forced it onto the Convention's agenda, late in the day and apparently against Giscard's wishes. Its working group became the largest, attracting over sixty participants. Despite that, the draft Constitution does not alter the predominance of internal market liberalization over social policy matters (Brown 2003). It does specify principles to be integral to all EU policy areas: gender equality; non-discrimination on grounds of sex, racial or ethnic origin, religion or belief, disability, age or sexual orientation; environmental sustainability; and consumer protection (Arts III 2–5). Some of the Charter's articles could be interpreted to imply rights to social provision, such as housing. In the main though, framework legislation to assure systems of property ownership, price stability, and open markets, as preferred by classical liberals, continues to be the bedrock of the EU's constitution.

Conclusion

What does the work of the Convention suggest about freedom in the EU? In terms of the three conceptions of freedom we began with, the draft treaty – taken in the round – moved the EU a greater distance toward an ideal of positive liberty than it moved it towards rival ideals. On the substance of policy the classical liberal's view of freedom is still ahead overall, though the distance is slowly diminishing. On the form of political rule, the draft Constitution shifts the EU decisively toward a conception of freedom combining a more hierarchical organization of power with popular sovereignty. This is moderated by the still wide dispersal of power, and conditioned by a diversity of consultative, contestatory, and constitutional, restraints. Two points are offered for further reflection. First, there is no reason to think that all of an individual's freedoms are best secured through the nation state, nor that any particular freedoms are in all circumstances best secured by the nation state, nor that the individual/state nexus exhausts the possibilities for enhancing individuals' freedoms. So we need a theoretical and conceptual model recognizing the state's effects on individual liberty, but able to specify how other levels of political organization bear on it, too. Second, in concentrating power amongst the largest three or four members and dispersing it over the smaller the proposed constitutional arrangements strengthen the autonomy of the EU, but do so by boosting disproportionately the capabilities of the largest states. So we also need to understand the potentials for domination between large and small political units, and think further about how to ward it off without surrendering hard-won capacities to formulate and pursue worthwhile common goals.

8 The constitutional labelling of 'The democratic life of the EU'

Representative and participatory democracy[1]

Stijn Smismans

Introduction

According to the European Convention the future European Constitution needs a clear statement on the democratic nature of the EU. Regarding 'The democratic life of the Union' the draft Constitution states that the EU is based on both the principle of representative democracy and of participatory democracy. Such specificity is new: the current Article 6 EU Treaty only mentions 'democracy' as one of several 'principles on which the Union is founded', 'common to the Member States', the others being liberty, the rule of law, and respect for human rights and fundamental freedoms. The Rome Treaty, with its functionalist logic, did not mention the principle of democracy. The concept entered the constitutional debate primarily as a political signal to candidate member states and subsequently as an ongoing condition of European Union membership (Verhoeven 1998b: 219) rather than as a requirement for the Union polity *in se*. 'Democracy' was first referred to in the Preamble to the 1986 Single European Act in light of the enlargement to Spain, Portugal, and Greece. The Preamble of the Maastricht Treaty, agreed in light of potential enlargement to central and eastern Europe, stresses the member states' 'attachment to the principles of liberty, democracy and respect for human rights and fundamental freedoms and the rule of law' (European Council 1991; and Simon 1995: 86). In addition, Article F, paragraph 1 TEU provided that 'the Union shall respect the national identities of its Member States, whose systems of government are founded on the principles of democracy'. The Amsterdam Treaty introduced a sanction mechanism that may be applied when a member state seriously and persistently violates the fundamental values of the Union – such as the principle of democracy.[2] The Nice Treaty also allows the making of recommendations if there is a clear risk of such a serious breach.

The current Treaty does not define democracy;[3] nor does it suggest how the principle of democracy should be interpreted as a 'principle on which the Union is founded'. As a foundational principle for the European polity *per se*, 'democracy' need not be reduced to the common denominator of the democratic traditions of the member states but could take account of the particular features of the EU. Nevertheless, the normative (political and academic) debate on 'EU democracy' has long taken as paradigmatic our thinking on democracy at the national level, namely representative democracy (section 2). More recently, 'participatory democracy' has become salient within the European polity, emerging in the 'governance debate' and shaped by its dominant actors. To a great extent the normative arguments for participatory democracy are not congruent with those for representative democracy (section 3). In the Convention debate representative and participatory democracy finally seemed to meet. However, this was coincidental, and the relation between those two forms of democracy remains unclear (section 4).

The 'democratic deficit' debate and the predominance of representative democracy as normative framework

The EC could long be considered a 'special purpose association' (Ipsen 1972: 176), to which a limited amount of well-defined functions were delegated. The 'democratic nature' of the European construction was thus not a matter of serious concern and could be assumed to be 'absorbed' by the democratic credentials of the delegating member states. The initial European Communities were then said to be based on a 'permissive consensus' (Lindberg and Scheingold 1970: 41). Little popular interest in an elite-driven and technocratic project coincided with a diffuse support for the idea of European integration (De Búrca 1996: 350). From a normative-legal point of view the legitimacy of the EC/EU has primarily been thought of in terms of 'the rule of law' rather than in terms of democratic participation. The European Community/Union is based on a set of fixed and identifiable rules and principles, and judicial remedies are available to ensure respect for these rules and principles. The European Court of Justice (ECJ) has played a major role both in establishing the rules – describing the Treaties as the 'constitutional charter'[4] of the Community – and in guaranteeing their application.

The institutional expression of the rule of law was formulated in the principle of 'institutional balance'. Formulated already in 1958 in the *Meroni* case,[5] the concept of institutional balance was clearly defined in *Chernobyl*. '[T]he treaties set up a system for the distribution of powers among the different European Community institutions, assigning to each institution its own role. Observance of institutional balance means that each of the institutions must exercise its powers with due regard for the powers of the other institutions'.[6] The Community's legitimacy is then based on the readiness of the European citizen to 'conform with ... rules that are formally correct and that have been imposed by accepted procedure' (Roth and Wittich 1968: 37). This traditional legal reading of EU legitimacy identifies legitimacy in terms of 'legal validity' with legitimacy in terms of 'the generalised trust of the governed'.[7] However, rules cannot justify themselves simply by being rules, without reference to considerations beyond themselves (Obradovic 1996: 197).

In light of increased transfer of decision-making power to the European level, combined with the process of constitutionalization pushed for by the ECJ, the merely functionalist and legalistic approach appears unsatisfying for addressing the legitimacy of the European construction. Therefore, both the political and the legal discourse have gradually made reference to the normative framework that has also dominated our thinking about legitimacy and democracy at the nation-state level, namely the idea of representative democracy, and in particular the idea of parliamentary democracy (Dehousse 1998: 598).

Thus the initial concern about the 'democratic deficit' of the EC focused on the need for popular involvement via the European Parliament. It should be directly elected, and subsequent changes increased its powers – budgetary and legislative powers, and control over the Commission. Such direct parliamentary representation of European citizens at the European level has always been combined with indirect territorial representation of citizens via governmental representatives in the Council of Ministers, and (more recently) the European Council, assumed accountable to their national parliaments. One can argue that the EU is coming ever closer to a bicameral parliamentary democracy (Nentwich and Falkner 1997), and close to the institutional system of a number of federal countries, in which the legislative power is shared by two branches, representing the population of the Union and its member states respectively (Dehousse 1998: 606), especially with increased use of the co-decision procedure and strengthening of the Parliament's position within it.

Representative democracy is also the normative framework with which the European Court of Justice has sought to go beyond the purely legalistic rule of law interpretation of the legitimacy question. The idea of democratic participation entered the case law of the ECJ in 1980. According to *Roquette Frères* 'the consultation provided for in the ... Treaty is the means which allows the Parliament to play a ... part in the legislative process of the Community. It represents an essential factor in the institutional balance intended by the Treaty [and] although limited, [ ] reflects at Community level the fundamental democratic principle that the people should take part in the exercise of power through the intermediary of a representative assembly'.[8] Although the Court links the democratic principle with the concept of institutional balance, and thus acknowledges the roles that the Council and Commission play, only the European Parliament is explicitly recognized as ensuring the democratic principle at the European level.[9]

The intensified democratic deficit debate of the 1990s has also placed other elements on the political agenda. Since the end of the 1980s, normative discourses on the legitimacy of the European construction have stressed the need to respect regional and local autonomy and to involve these actors in European policy-making. The Maastricht Treaty therefore established the Committee of the Regions (COR), and allowed member states to be represented in the Council by a regional representative. Again, representative democracy and accountability via territorially elected representatives emerged as a central normative framework. Similar concerns about representative democracy in a multi-level context emerged also concerning the role of national parliaments in European decision-making. While the European institutional set-up ensures a central position for the member states via the (European) Council, at national level European integration has strengthened the executive to the detriment of the parliament (Moravcsik 1994). Thus emerged the idea of giving national parliaments a direct stake in the European institutional set-up, though in practice the solution has mainly been sought in member states' internal regulations increasing parliamentary control over their ministers in the Council (Westlake 1995; Smismans 1998). The debate on subsidiarity is also coloured by the framework of representative democracy. That concept emerged in the European debate on the one hand from the pressure from certain regions – in particular the German Länder – to use it as a way to protect the regional autonomy recognized at their national level, and on the other hand from certain member states – in particular the UK – that saw in subsidiarity a tool to protect themselves against creeping Community intervention (Van Kersbergen and Verbeek 1994: 225). In both cases, subsidiarity is linked to a conceptualization of democracy in terms of electoral representation at the (lowest possible) territorial level. This contrasts with the original more horizontal and participatory conception of the subsidiarity principle. According to Catholic social doctrine, to which the origin of the concept has commonly been attributed, state intervention is only desirable in so far as smaller social units, like the family, cannot do the job. Such (horizontal) subsidiarity is a more participatory and pluralist concept (Ward 1996: 203), ensuring decentralized organization of responsibilities and protecting the sovereign sphere of smaller social groups.

Finally, the political debate on European citizenship has conceived of it as a formal, legal rights-bearing status rather than as a participatory political status (de Búrca 1996: 358). Related political rights are mainly linked to territorially based parliamentary representation[10] such as the right to vote and stand as a candidate at municipal elections (in the member state in which the citizen resides) and at European Parliamentary elections (even if the citizen resides in a member state other than his or her own), supplemented by the right to petition the EP (see below). Only the right to apply to an Ombudsman broadens the idea of democratic participation beyond the parliamentary assembly.

The issue of transparency, noted in the democratic deficit debate since the beginning of the 1990s, allowed most room for re-interpretation of the normative framework (Dehousse 1998). Transparency plays a vital role in any democracy, by informing the public so that the citizen can know which decisions are taken, why, and on the basis of which arguments. Consequently it enables scrutiny and accountability of decision-making (*ex post*). Within the framework of representative democracy transparency ensures parliamentary control over the executive, and enables citizens to go to the ballot box well informed. Within a more participatory model of democracy transparency also ensures that citizens can reinforce accountability through access to courts or to an ombudsman. In a participatory democracy transparency also enables participation by organized interests in the policy process *ex ante*.

At the European level, no fundamental debate has taken place on how transparency may contribute to a reduction of the democratic deficit, and the debate has not been very focused (Curtin 1996: 97). It is often connected with bringing the EU closer to the citizen and building confidence in its institutions. Some elements of the debate fit the framework of representative democracy, such as the request for openness of Council deliberations given its legislative function, and efforts to make the relations between individual Members of Parliament and external interests transparent by registering contacts between MEPs and lobbyists (Schaber 1998). Some elements come closer to the idea of participatory democracy. In particular, the Commission has always linked transparency to participation in the decision-making process *ex ante*. Not by accident, its first communications on transparency and on relations with special interest groups were adopted simultaneously, in 1992 (Lodge 1994: 350). It is mainly from this focus on interest group participation – related to an increased need for a legitimating discourse – that the concept of 'participatory democracy' emerges at the European level.

The governance debate and the emergence of the idea of 'participatory democracy'

The first traces of the concept of participatory democracy in EU official documents can be found in efforts to strengthen the involvement of NGOs in European policy-making. In its Discussion Paper 'The Commission and non-governmental organisations: building a stronger partnership' (CEC 2000, COM 11 final), the European Commission argued that although 'the decision making process in the EU is first and foremost legitimized by the elected representatives of the European people, NGOs can make a contribution fostering a more participatory democracy'. In its Opinion on this Discussion Paper, the European Economic and Social Committee (EESC) stated that 'participatory democracy requires that parties who are affected by legal provisions should be involved in the opinion-forming process at the earliest possible stage and should be given the opportunity to bring their wishes to bear in this process and put forward their proposals'. It added that 'this principle, in particular, chimes with the participatory model of civil society, under which a form of civil dialogue is already being practised via a public discourse' (EESC 2000, indent 3.1.4). In fact, the idea of participatory democracy should be located in the discourse on civil society and civil dialogue developed by both the European Commission and the EESC since the end of the 1990s (Smismans 2003). In 1996 the concept of 'civil dialogue' was coined by the Commission's Directorate General responsible for social policy to stress the need to encourage interaction with social NGOs, in addition to the already existing 'social dialogue' with the social partners. Initially thought of as a tool to build a supportive network favourable to European social intervention (Kendall and Anheier 1999: 294), the discourse on civil society involvement has subsequently broadened to include other policy sectors. It has also become part of the Commission's promises on administrative reform, not least as a reply to the legitimacy crisis which injured the Santer Commission. In the Commission's White Paper on European Governance (CEC 2001, COM 428 final), the key document around which the administrative reform of the Commission was structured, participation through civil society organizations held an important place to ensure 'good governance'. The concept of 'civil society organizations' no longer merely refers to (social) NGOs but is interpreted ever more broadly. The Commission does not resist the temptation to use the discourse on civil society involvement and participation to legitimate the variety of (existing) structures of interaction with all sorts of actors, including private lobbyists.

The connection between 'participatory democracy' and the involvement of civil society organizations in European policy is also made by the European Economic and Social Committee. Even before these concepts entered the Commission discourse, the EESC started to play with them in an attempt to redefine its proper role. Created by the Treaty of Rome, the EESC is a body with advisory powers across a wide range of areas dealt with at the European level, composed of representatives from national employers' organizations, trade unions and 'various interests' (such as liberal professions, small and medium enterprises, consumers and social economy organizations). The Committee felt itself further marginalized due to the gradual increase of alternative consultative fora, the creation of the Committee of the Regions and the development of the social dialogue outside the EESC (Smismans 1999). In reply to this marginalization the EESC tried to revive its role as a 'forum of organised civil society', claiming a particular representative role in EU democracy (Smismans 2000). In its Opinion of 1999 on 'The role and contribution of civil society organisations in the building of Europe' (EESC 1999) the EESC argued that 'strengthening non-parliamentary democratic structures is a way of giving substance and meaning to the concept of a Citizens' Europe'. It defined its own role as guaranteeing 'the implementation of the participatory model of civil society; [enabling] civil society to participate in the decision-making process; and [helping] reduce a certain "democratic deficit" and so [underpinning] the legitimacy of democratic decision-making processes'. Referring to the difficult definition of the 'demos' concept within the EU, the Committee argued that 'the democratic process at European level – even more so than at the national level – must provide a range of participatory structures in which all citizens, with their different identities and in accordance with their different identity criteria, can be represented, and which reflect the heterogeneous nature of the European identity'. The EESC concluded that, enshrined in the Treaty, with a consultative role and composed of representatives of intermediary organizations, it could act as a representation of the people's way of identifying with civil society organizations, and complement the legitimacy offered by the EP as the representative of citizens' national (territorial) identity. The Committee – in its contribution to the White Paper – did not claim a monopoly of this role, and argued that 'the "European democratic model" will contain many [. . .] elements of participatory democracy'; but it also stressed that 'a basic precondition and legitimising basis for participation is adequate representativeness of those speaking for organised civil society' (EESC 2001).

The institutional debate on 'participatory democracy' is thus framed in a particular way, with several characteristic features. First, one should point to the ambiguous use of the term 'participatory democracy'. Political theory has mostly linked the concept of 'participatory democracy' to ideas of 'direct democracy', although the two are not synonymous. 'Direct democracy' has long been part of the dichotomy between representative and direct democracy, referring to both the referendum model and the classical city-state democracy of Ancient Greece. 'Participatory democracy' emerged as a concept to revive the idea of direct participation in the complex society of the second half of the 20th century (Korsten 1979: 81–119; Pateman 1970; Barber 1984). Direct and participatory democracy both refer to a democratic system in which individuals participate personally in the deliberations which concern them, in which there is no intermediary between those who make the decisions and those affected by them. Yet, the concept of 'participatory democracy' extends the idea of direct participation from the political world to other sectors of social life, such as the workplace, education, and local public administration. The original 'direct democracy' debate focused especially on the referendum issue. In contrast, 'participatory democracy' gives particular attention to 'self-realisation' and to deliberation in face-to-face relations, so stressing mostly a 'small-group' model of democracy (Sartori 1987: 112). The issue of direct citizen involvement in European policy-making has recently started to be addressed in the academic debate (Nentwich 1996; and in particular regarding e-democracy, Weiler 1997 and 1999; Curtin 1997 and

Verhoeven 1998a). It has acquired only very marginal attention in the political and institutional debate.[11] What the governance debate mainly focuses on is not direct citizen participation, but an alternative form of representation, i.e. not territorial representation but functional representation, or representation via associations and interest groups. The White Paper still leaves some room for interpretation since it (also) intends to 'communicate more actively with the general public', making more intensive use of communication technologies; which could, in principle, also involve individual citizens.[12] Yet, the White Paper's discourse on 'openness' and 'communication' is mainly concerned to make the institutions understandable and improve confidence, whereas proposals to encourage and structure participation focus on groups and not on individuals. Using the concept of 'participatory democracy' creates the illusion that such functional representation automatically implies direct citizen participation from the base upwards.

Not only the political debate, but also European integration literature performs 'epistemological sliding' on participatory democracy, meant as civil society involvement (De Schutter 2002) or social partners' participation (Betten 1998) rather than direct citizen participation. In its broadest interpretation 'participatory democracy' is used for 'the direct involvement in decision-making of those that are most affected by it' (Lenaerts 1993: 23; Verhoeven 1998a: 379).[13] The point is not that everybody needs to co-decide on everything, but that all should be able to be involved in the decision-making by which they are most affected. In theory, such a conception could imply the decentralization of decision-making to ensure direct citizen participation, but it has mainly been used by legal scholars to structure participation in 'central' European decision-making, potentially via e-democracy (Curtin 1997) but especially via the involvement of civil society organizations.

The reason for this 'epistemological sliding' may lie in the evolution of political theory. Some participatory models, such as Barber's (1984), have paid attention to the *deliberative interaction* of citizens in small fora such as neighbourhood assemblies and 'television town meetings', which may lead to a conflation of 'participatory' and 'deliberative democracy'. Such a tendency may be strengthened by work on citizens' juries and deliberative opinion polling (Stewart *et al.* 1994; Smith and Wales 2002) which resonates with the insights of deliberative democrats. However, it does not follow that all deliberative fora (such as those established at European level) ensure direct citizen participation.

Moreover in the debate on deliberative democracy (Bohman and Rehg 1997; Elster 1998; Eriksen and Fossum 2000) that has influenced democratic theory over the last decade, the attention to the communicative and discursive character of the deliberative model has often overshadowed the question of who is actually supposed to participate.[14] Even in the version inspired by radical or direct democracy, namely 'directly-deliberative polyarchy' (Cohen and Sabel 1997), the concept of participation has never been clearly defined. In an 'EU version' of the deliberative democratic model, namely 'deliberative supranationalism' (Joerges and Neyer 1997; Everson 1999; Joerges 1999), the focus is on the deliberative and science-based nature of decision-making procedures rather than on the participation of groups or – even less – individuals.[15]

Second, the Commission's concern with 'participation' (as well as transparency) has been introduced largely from a functional efficiency-driven perspective – as a tool to reply to the Commission's information needs and to ensure compliance (Smismans 2003; Follesdal 2003). In the White Paper, participation is identified as one of the five principles underpinning 'good governance' (together with openness, accountability, effectiveness and coherence), but it is defined in the following way: 'The quality, relevance and *effectiveness* of EU policies depend on ensuring wide participation throughout the policy chain – from conception to implementation. Improved participation is likely to create more *confidence* in the end result and in the institutions which deliver policies. Participation crucially depends on central governments following an inclusive approach when *developing and implementing* EU policies' (stress added).

Put differently, the focus is on effectiveness and confidence building, rather than on democratic procedure and the recognition of participation rights – a tendency already noted with regard to the issue of transparency in the 1990s (Craig 1997: 120). The Commission's governance debate seems at best an efficiency-driven exercise, and at worst an attempt to provide a legitimating discourse for its own institutional position and functioning, without including profound reforms (Curtin 2001; Magnette 2001; Scharpf 2001). Vague rhetoric on participation fits with such a legitimating discourse, but the Commission refrains from developing explicit considerations on what 'participatory democracy' might mean in the EU.

The EESC more explicitly claims a role for participatory democracy complementary to representative democracy. Moreover, it proposes a more horizontal and participatory interpretation of subsidiarity which 'not only concerns the distribution of powers between the various territorial levels, but is also the expression of a participatory conception of relations between public authorities and society and of the freedoms and responsibilities of citizens. When deciding who is to be involved in the preparation of decisions, account should thus be taken not only of territorial (vertical) subsidiarity but also functional (horizontal) subsidiarity, which is a major factor in good governance' (EESC 2002, para. 3.5). The phrasing of this horizontal subsidiarity principle illustrates the Committee's predominant approach to the idea of participatory democracy. The EESC recognizes its proper role as just one element of participatory democracy, yet its redefinition of democracy in the EU does not imply (decentralized) participatory rights – for individual citizens or via organizations – other than representation through the Committee.

Third, the emergence of the issue of 'participatory democracy' in the European constitutional debate is linked to the institutional interests of the Commission and the EESC. Other institutions have been much more reluctant about the discourse of participatory democracy – interpreted as civil society involvement. Thus the European Parliament argued in its comment on the White Paper that 'democratic legitimacy presupposes that the political will underpinning decisions is arrived at through parliamentary deliberation' (EP 2001, para. 10b) and that 'the involvement of both the European and national parliaments constitutes the basis for a European system with democratic legitimacy' (para. 8). 'Organised civil society [...] whilst important, is inevitably sectoral and cannot be regarded as having its own democratic legitimacy' (para. 11a; and EP 2000, para. 30). The Parliament stresses that 'elements of participatory democracy in the political system of the Union must be introduced *cautiously* with a constant eye to the recognised principles and structural elements of representative democracy and the rule of law' (para. K, stress added). The Committee of the Regions, rather than talking about 'participatory democracy' (or involvement of civil society) prefers a normative discourse on subsidiarity, 'proximity', 'closeness to the people' and 'grassroots democracy' (COR 2001a and b) and argues that 'the democratic legitimacy of representatives elected by direct universal suffrage must not be confused with the greater involvement of NGOs and other arrangements for the representation of individual interests within society' (COR 2002, Cdr 103/2001 final, para. 3.2).

Obviously, political actors with an electoral mandate claim the importance of representative democracy, whereas non-elected political actors like the Commission and the EESC may search for alternative or complementary sources of legitimacy in civil society involvement. This tension between elected and non-elected political actors may explain the 'schizophrenic nature' of the European normative and constitutional debate, where arguments on representative and participatory democracy have not met. The 'democratic deficit' debate has developed in the context of the subsequent intergovernmental conferences (IGCs). No surprise then that the debate has been framed in terms of representative democracy, given that representatives from governments elected on a territorial basis are the main actors of the IGCs. The 'governance debate', on the contrary, was initiated by the Commission to increase confidence and efficiency by starting the reform of governance without awaiting new Treaty revisions. The debate developed outside the context of the IGCs, with its centre of gravity in the exchange of ideas among Community officials and academics. Yet, the governance debate also aspired to set down markers for institutional reform that in the longer run would have influence – perhaps in the next IGC.

Most of the governance issues did not figure among the priorities for future institutional reform, as set out at the Nice and Laeken Summits,[16] to be discussed first in the Convention and subsequently in the IGC. Moreover, since most Convention members had a national or European electoral mandate, the predominance of 'representative democracy' as the normative framework for institutional reform should not surprise. In fact, the Convention tended to confirm the schizophrenic nature of the European constitutional debate: the fora for Treaty revisions (Convention and IGC) focused on the vertical, territorial-representative dimension, whereas the governance debate focused on the horizontal dimension – as if this dimension were not a constitutional issue. Nevertheless, some traces of the governance debate emerged in the Convention.

The Convention debate; the accidental meeting of representative and participatory democracy

The draft Constitution adopted by the Convention on 13 June and 10 July 2003 stated in Article 2 that 'the Union is founded on the values of respect for human dignity, liberty, democracy, equality, the rule of law and respect for human rights. These values are common to the Member States in a society of pluralism, tolerance, justice, solidarity and non-discrimination', and thus echoed the current provisions of Article 6 EU Treaty. However, contrary to the current Treaties, the draft Constitution included a separate title on 'the democratic life of the Union' qualifying democracy in the EU as 'representative' and 'participatory'. To understand these qualifications it is useful to see how the title on 'the democratic life of the Union' was shaped throughout the drafting process of the Convention.

The first preliminary draft of the Constitution proposed by the Praesidium to the Convention on 28 October 2002 (CONV 2002, 369/02) suggested an article (Article 34) that would 'set out the principle of participatory democracy' stating that 'the Institutions are to ensure a high level of openness, permitting *citizens' organisations* of all kinds to play a full part in the Union's affairs' (stress added). This led in the draft of 2 April 2003 (CONV 2003, 650/03) to the following formulation:

'Article 34: The principle of participatory democracy
1   Every citizen shall have the right to participate in the democratic life of the Union.
2   The Union institutions shall, by appropriate means, give citizens and representative associations the opportunity to make known and publicly exchange their opinions on all areas of Union action.
3   The Union institutions shall maintain an open, transparent and regular dialogue with representative associations and civil society.

This Article has several striking features: first, it is placed under the title 'The democratic life of the Union', among articles concerning the principle of democratic equality, the European Ombudsman, political parties, transparency, protection of personal data, and the status of churches and non-confessional organizations. Surprisingly, no mention was made of a 'principle of representative democracy'. This is even more surprising in the light of our argument regarding the composition of the Convention and the schizophrenic nature of the constitutional debate. The assumption seemed to be that 'representative democracy' did not need an explicit mention since it would result automatically from constitutional provisions on the European Parliament or the voting rights recognized under the title of citizenship. Nevertheless a considerable number of proposed amendments asked for references to representative democracy, either in Article 34 or as a separate article under the title on 'the democratic life of the Union'.

Second, according to the preliminary draft of October 2002, Article 34 had to provide a 'framework for dialogue with citizens' organisations', and thus confirmed the Commission's and EESC's tendency to see 'participatory democracy' mainly in terms of functional representation. Yet, the proposed formulation seemed to follow the 'original' participatory democracy dimension addressing the individual citizen, where it stated that 'every citizen shall have the right to participate' and shall have (like associations) the opportunity to make known and publicly exchange his/her opinions on all areas of Union action. However, these general statements were not accompanied by direct-participatory procedures. Therefore, three proposed amendments (out of 50 concerning Article 34) asked for the introduction as 'participatory democracy' (also) of such democratic tools as a European referendum and the right of petition and legislative initiative (under various forms). Four proposed amendments suggested that the Article on participatory democracy should require a more pro-active approach by the Union to promote and encourage the participation of its citizens.

Third, the terminology used to indicate the intermediary organizations is confusing. The concept of 'representative associations' was used twice, in the third paragraph even apparently in opposition with 'civil society'. At first glance, 'civil society' might be thought to be 'everything but the state', aimed in particular to indicate the private sphere and the individual citizen, in opposition to 'representative associations'. Yet, according to the explanatory note, 'associations are mentioned in addition to civil society since there are associations which do not come under the civil society heading (employers' and employees' trade unions, associations representing the interests of the regional and local authorities etc)'. Many amendments criticized the terminology, for instance asking for deletion of the qualification of 'representativity' for associations, and for explicit inclusion of the social partners into the concept of civil society and/or participatory democracy.

Some of the amendments were introduced in the final version of the draft Constitution presented by the Convention on 18 July to the European Council of Rome. The title on 'the democratic life of the Union' included, among others, the following:

Article I-45: the principle of representative democracy
1   The working of the Union shall be founded on the principle of representative democracy.
2   Citizens are directly represented at Union level in the European Parliament. Member States are represented in the European Council and in the Council by their governments, themselves accountable to national Parliaments, elected by their citizens.
3   Every citizen shall have the right to participate in the democratic life of the Union. Decisions shall be taken as openly as possible and as closely as possible to the citizen.
4   Political parties at European level contribute to forming European political awareness and to expressing the will of Union citizens.

Article I-46: the principle of participatory democracy
1   The Union Institutions shall, by appropriate means, give citizens and representative associations the opportunity to make known and publicly exchange their views on all areas of Union action.
2   The Union Institutions shall maintain an open, transparent and regular dialogue with representative associations and civil society.
3   The Commission shall carry out broad consultations with parties concerned in order to ensure that the Union's actions are coherent and transparent.
4   No less than one million citizens coming from a significant number of Member States may invite the Commission to submit any appropriate proposal on matters where citizens consider that a legal act of the Union is required for the purpose of implementing the Constitution. A European law shall determine the provisions for the specific procedures and conditions required for such a citizens' initiative.

This final version differs from the previous ones in several interesting aspects. First, and most obvious, the title on the democratic life has been 'enriched' by the introduction of the principle of representative democracy, in a different article than that of participatory democracy. It clearly says that 'the working of the Union shall be founded on the principle of representative democracy', but no comparable statement is made regarding participatory democracy. Combined with the priority given to the article on representative democracy, this seems to suggest that participatory democracy is only a complementary – second-order? – form of democracy. The precise interrelation between the two principles of democracy remains unclear.

Second, Article I-45 provides, for the first time, a clear constitutional statement that the democratic representative nature of the EU is based on both the role of the EP and the Council. While this is in line with the 'traditional' reading of the European institutional framework in terms of a bicameral federal system, this has never been clearly stated in the Treaty. Yet, one can still question whether this is an accurate description of the 'representative democratic nature' of the European multi-level institutional set-up. Shouldn't, for instance, the 'representative democratic' role of the Committee of the Regions also have been mentioned? Or the institutional role of the national parliaments beyond their control function with respect to their government representative in the Council, such as their in role in Treaty ratifications or as guardians of subsidiarity as proposed in the Convention? In a comparable way one would have expected the article on participatory democracy to refer to the European Economic and Social Committee, which on the basis of the Treaty is supposed to play a (central) role in the civil society dialogue the article aims at.

Although not an accurate description of democracy in the European multi-level polity, the explicit recognition provided by Article I-45 of the multiple or at least dual representative democratic basis of the Union (EP and Council accountable to national parliaments) may induce the Court to revise its standard understanding of EU democracy discussed above, linking a rule of law interpretation of the institutional balance to the mere democratic input of the EP. At least the Court will have to recognize – given the clear Constitutional statement – that within the institutional balance not only the EP but also the Council plays a representative democratic role. It may even be argued that a normative democratic reading of the institutional balance should take account of the representative nature of *all* institutions being part of that balance (in various combinations according to the rules of the Treaty). 'Since each of the institutions (...) represents a different constituency, the notion of institutional balance can be presented as a way of ensuring the adequate participation and representation of different constituencies within the European Community process' (de Búrca 1999: 59; Craig 1999; Lenaerts and Verhoeven 2002). Such an interpretation of 'institutional balance as interest representation' (Smismans 2002) raises the question whether non-elected bodies like the Commission, or the EESC, could be considered to have a representative role within the institutional balance. Yet it may provide us with a more accurate account of and (therefore) normative guide for our conceptualization of EU democracy.

Third, the formulation that 'every citizen shall have the right to participate in the democratic life of the Union' has moved from the principle of participatory democracy to that of representative democracy. This confirms the dominant tendency to confine the direct involvement of the citizen to voting in elections, leaving 'participatory democracy' mainly for civil society organizations. Similarly, the phrase that 'decisions shall be taken as openly as possible and as closely as possible to the citizen' is placed under the heading of representative democracy. It should therefore be seen as a request to respect subsidiarity in territorial terms, ensuring accountability through parliamentary assemblies at the lowest possible level, rather than as a request for decentralized direct citizen participation – in which case it should have been placed under the heading of participatory democracy.

Fourth, while the right of every citizen to participate has been moved to representative democracy, the principle of participatory democracy is further defined in line with the dominant interpretation it had acquired in EU official discourse, namely linked to the Commission's efficiency-driven consultation practices. In order to ensure that the 'Union's actions are coherent and transparent', the new third paragraph requires the Commission to carry out 'broad consultations with parties concerned'. The concept of 'parties concerned' leaves further place for interpretation, adding to the confusion created by the wording of 'representative association and civil society'. Yet the requirement is not to consult '*the* parties concerned'. Requiring simply 'broad consultation of parties concerned', the proposed Constitution article confirms the reluctance to create any participatory rights and a willingness to leave the consultation process to the discretion of the Commission.

Fifth, the fourth paragraph of Article I-46 introduces a surprising exception to the tendency to conceptualize participatory democracy as consultation with civil society organizations. A new instrument allows 'direct citizen participation' through a 'citizens' initiative'. Citizens, no fewer than one million, may invite the Commission to take a legislative initiative on a particular issue. This provision is surprising. It deviates from the dominant tendency to define participation in terms of representation through associations. And it appeared in the draft Constitution at the very last moment, for it was not mentioned in the draft of 26 May (CONV 2003, 724/03). On 3 June, Professor Meyer, a German delegate in the Convention, circulated among the Convention members his proposal for a 'citizens' initiative', finding large support – 60 signatures – for it. This amendment was subsequently formally proposed to the Convention Bureau. In light of the large support across various parts of the political spectrum, it decided to include the (slightly modified)[17] amendment into the draft presented to the plenary of 11–13 June. Some amendments of this kind had been presented earlier on during the Convention, but had been discarded from the debate because presented by single Convention members without broader support. These amendments – one by Alain Lamassoure, another by Caspar Einem and Maria Berger (CONV 2003, 670/03) – went considerably further than the proposal of Meyer's that ended up in the draft Constitution. Lamassoure's amendment provided that a citizen's initiative could also be with respect to the abolition of a law whereas Einem and Berger linked the citizen's initiative to a referendum.

Without such a 'sanction mechanism', the opportunity to invite the Commission to submit *any* appropriate proposal appears to pay no more than lip service to 'participatory democracy'. It remains entirely at the discretion of the Commission to decide whether it will or will not take a legislative initiative if invited, and to define its content. It is doubtful whether the European law required by Article I-46 para. 4 will be able to give the citizens' initiative a minimum of compulsory flavour.

Moreover, one may question whether this new 'citizens' initiative' will add much to the existing right to petition the European Parliament (Art. 21 and 194 EU Treaty). Any citizen of the Union, and any natural and legal person residing or having their registered office in a member state, has the right to address, individually or in association with other citizens or persons, a petition to the European Parliament. The petition must deal with an issue coming within the Community's fields of activity and must also directly affect those who present the petition. These requirements are more demanding than the citizens' initiative. On the other hand, the petition may have the same effect as the citizens' initiative since on the basis of it the Parliament can ask the Commission to take action,[18] and there is no minimum requirement for signatures. Moreover, the petition right as a way to introduce political ideas and topics into the legislative policy-making process has been strengthened by the EP's ignoring the Treaty requirement that one should be 'directly affected' in order to present a petition (Baviera 2001). Interestingly, the draft Constitution does not include this right of petition either in the article of participatory democracy nor in that on representative democracy.

Sixth, it is notable that several 'intermediary actors' are situated outside the Article on participatory democracy. The role of political parties is explicitly recognized (as already by the Nice Treaty), and clearly placed in the context of representative democracy. The social partners are placed in a separate article (Art. I-47), suggesting that (autonomous) social dialogue as part of the Union's democratic life escapes both logics of representative and participatory democracy. Finally, according to Article I-51 the Union shall 'maintain an open, transparent and regular dialogue' with churches and non-confessional organizations. The formula is identical to the 'civil society dialogue' under the principle of participatory democracy. Was it deemed necessary to state this explicitly for churches and non-confessional organizations since these are not always considered part of civil society? Or the separate Article may imply that such a dialogue should be particularly looked for more than it is with other parts of civil society, as Tore V. Olsen explores in his contribution to this volume.

Conclusion

If one starts from the hypothesis that the future IGC will approve (all) proposals made by the Convention, the future European Constitution will label EU democracy as both representative and participatory. Today the Treaty only mentions democracy *tout court* as one of the principles on which the Union is founded. Moreover, the concept has entered into the Treaty primarily as a political signal to (candidate) member states rather than as a principle for the European polity as such. The 'democratic deficit debate' has directed attention to the (un)democratic nature of the European polity *in se*. Since this debate mainly developed in the context of successive IGCs where the dominant actors have an (indirect) electoral mandate, it has been informed mainly by the idea of representative democracy. More recently, and independently, the 'governance debate' has been initiated by Community institutional actors lacking electoral mandates. Addressing constitutional issues under the label of 'governance', this debate has introduced the concept of participatory democracy. This has been defined mainly as the interaction between the Community institutions, in particular the Commission and the EESC, and civil society organizations. Although the Convention did not entirely overcome the split nature of this constitutional debate, some governance issues nevertheless entered its deliberations. Thus the democratic principle on which the Union is founded is henceforward qualified as representative and participatory. Yet, representative democracy is not well defined in its multilevel context, and participatory democracy has a strong efficiency-driven flavour. Moreover, the (desirable) relationship between representative and participatory democracy remains unclear. However, in particular regarding the latter point, political theory also has still some way to go.

9 Transparency and legitimacy

Daniel Naurin

Should meetings of the Council of Ministers, at least in its legislative capacity, be held in public? That was one of the many questions put to the Convention by the Laeken Declaration. It soon turned out, however, that the European Council already knew the answer. At its subsequent meeting in Seville, in June 2002, the European Council decided that debates in the Council on the most important legislative acts under the co-decision procedure should be public. The Convention goes even further. Article 49(2) of the draft Constitution reads 'The European Parliament shall meet in public, as shall the Council of Ministers when examining and adopting a legislative proposal'. The article applies to all legislative acts, not only the most important (as interpreted by the presidency), and not only co-decision acts. The main argument in favour of such a reform is that it would increase the democratic legitimacy of the EU.

The value of transparency for 'input-oriented legitimacy' (i.e. the democratic quality of the decision-making procedures), to use a well-known terminology, seems to be indisputable. This is so regardless of which model of democracy one prefers. For those favouring representative democracy, transparency increases the chances for citizens to gain access to the information they need in order to make enlightened choices in the voting-booth. If one prefers deliberative democracy, transparency is valued to enable deliberation in the public sphere. If participatory democracy is the championed model, transparency is valued for participatation in decision-making (Curtin 1996; Weiler 1999; Hoskyns 2000; Harlow 2002. See Smismans in this volume on tensions between these models).

However, and more interestingly for the EU, where institutional structures for input-oriented legitimacy are largely absent (Scharpf 1999), transparency is also often promoted as an important instrument for providing output-oriented legitimacy, i.e. high quality decisions in accordance with the public interest (Curtin 1997: 23; Lord 1998: 88). It is often argued, especially by theorists advocating different versions of deliberative democracy (Elster 1986, 1998; Gutmann and Thompson 1996), that transparency promotes decisions more in line with the public interest. Factional self-interest and agency shirking (i.e. deviation from assigned public interest mandates) is assumed to thrive in secrecy. As Woodrow Wilson put it, 'publicity is one of the purifying elements of politics' (quoted in Gutmann and Thompson 1996: 95). Majone too argues that transparency (in combination with clear objectives and judicial review) may be a strong check on independent agencies' agency shirking (Majone 1996). Thus, given the common assumption that the EU will not develop input-legitimate political structures such as European parties, first order European elections, a European public sphere, and a European identity thick enough to allow majority rule on salient issues, for the foreseeable future, transparency may be a very welcome help on the output side for a European Union in need of legitimacy.

While not disputing that transparency has 'purifying' effects on policy outputs, in this chapter I will argue that transparency as a tool for output-oriented legitimacy is very much dependent on the institutions and structures on the input side. Therefore there are clear limits to the extent to which transparency may be used as a substitute for reforms on the input-side when seeking democratic legitimacy. Furthermore, there are also reasons to suspect that while transparency may strengthen output-oriented legitimacy by 'preventing wrongdoings' (Scharpf 2003), another part of the output-side – effective problem-solving – may be weakened. This chapter is not, as I will clearly emphasize, an attempt to argue against opening up the meetings of the Council of Ministers or any other EU institution. The Convention is right, in my view, to continue to push forward the transparency agenda. Rather it is an argument for more nuanced claims, based on empirical research, aimed at specifying under what circumstances transparency reforms may strengthen or weaken the decision-making processes of the EU.

Transparency as a promoter of the public interest

'Public discussion tends to promote the common good', according to deliberative theory (Elster 1986: 113). Opening up closed decision-making arenas has the effect that political actors have to face two challenging social norms. These norms, the theory goes, put pressure on the actors to argue instead of bargaining and to refrain from using self-regarding and immoral arguments. According to the first – the-force-of-the-better-argument norm – political positions must be backed up by rational arguments rather than by threats and log-rolling. The second – unselfishness norm – assumes that politics is 'public in nature': 'we' are using politics to solve 'common' problems. Therefore, in order to 'avoid the opprobrium associated with the overt appeal to private interest in public debates' (Elster 1998: 102), political positions are publicly justified with other-regarding or ideal-regarding arguments. 'There are certain arguments that simply cannot be stated publicly. In a political debate it is pragmatically impossible to argue that a given solution should be chosen just because it is good for oneself. By the very act of engaging in a public debate – arguing rather than bargaining – one has ruled out the possibility of invoking such reasons' (Elster 1986: 112f). The force-of-the-better-argument norm and the unselfishness norm thus have the power to 'launder' political discussions on the surface, according to this theory. Laundered arguments are used because political actors do not want to lose face in the short term and reputation in the long term.[1]

But how do we go from rhetoric to policy? The question was whether transparency can improve output-oriented legitimacy, by bringing policy decisions closer to the common good. Since political actors must be careful not to be publicly discovered as hypocrites, the argument continues, policy positions (and eventually decisions) are laundered as well, as a result of laundered justifications. Elster recognizes two components of this hypocrisy constraint. First, since justifications are supposed to support positions, there must be some reasonable connection between the two. If it is too obvious that other-regarding or ideal-regarding justifications are just cover-ups for self-interested positions, the actor in question will not only be discovered breaking the unselfishness norm but will also be revealed as a hypocrite. Therefore, if justifications must change, positions may have to change as well. The effect of publicity will then not just be to replace the argument 'Policy option B should be chosen, because it is good for us' with 'B should be chosen, because it is good for the environment'. Instead we will hear 'A should be chosen, because it is good for the environment', A being a position at least a bit more in line with the common interest (the environment in this case) than was B.

Second, actors may become entrapped by a consistency requirement. 'Once a speaker has adopted an impartial argument, because it corresponds to his interest or prejudice, he will be seen as opportunistic if he deviates from it when it ceases to serve his needs' (Elster 1998: 104). Hence there is pressure on the actors to hold to positions and justifications that have been once expressed in public throughout the whole decision-making process. Actors will be punished if they first support A publicly, 'because it is good for the environment', and then in the end vote for B, provided that the political process is transparent all the way through to the actual decision-making so that the hypocrisy can be discovered. Therefore, rhetoric is not just rhetoric.[2]

Apart from checking for self-interests including institutional self-interests (i.e. agency shirking) transparency may also affect other aspects of the moral quality of decisions, as well as more simple forms of 'good governance'. The most straightforward form of laundering is simply strengthening the incentives for actors to keep to basic standards of good governance: trying to be as cost-effective as possible, securing high technical quality and efficacy in policy and, of course, refraining from any kind of corruption. More 'advanced' effects involve ideological and moral laundering. Immoral behaviour, as defined by politically accepted social norms, is suppressed when transparency puts decision-makers in front of a public audience they perceive they will have to please. Via the decision-makers' anticipation of its reactions, the public forces its moral convictions upon them so that unacceptable arguments and positions are censored.

It is important to note that for this moral laundering to be a positive process from a normative point of view, two assumptions have to be made. First, we have to assume that the social pressure levied on political actors by the public does not violate liberal norms of autonomous decision-making. This is more relevant, however, in considering the political choices of individual citizens, rather than government officials, and explains why the act of voting in elections should not be in public (Goodin 1995). Second, we also have to assume that the dominant social norms of the public, activated by transparency, fit with our own moral ideals. If we disagree with the views of the moral majority we may still advocate transparency for democratic input-legitimate reasons, but we are not going to like the effects on the output side.

In the following I will leave aside questions about the effects of transparency on prejudice and moral ideals in policy-making and focus only on interests. According to the theory, as shown above, transparency has the power to make political actors argue and act in favour of the public interest rather than partisan interests. It does so by increasing the costs of violating the unselfishness norm and the force-of-the-better-argument norm. The first step is laundered arguments. From there the hypocrisy and consistency constraints transfer the laundering effect to policy positions and eventually to policy decisions, steering them towards common interests and avoiding factional biases. This is, in Elster's words, 'the civilising force of hypocrisy' (Elster 1995: 251).[3]

Input procedures condition the output effect

If policy-makers can be pushed to take decisions more in line with the European public interest, as the transparency argument goes, it is tempting to conclude that this could be a way for the EU to compensate for the lack of democratic procedures resulting from the 'triple deficits' on the input side: 'the lack of a pre-existing sense of collective identity, the lack of Europe-wide policy discourses, and the lack of a Europe-wide institutional infrastructure that could assure the political accountability of office holders to a European constituency' (Scharpf 1999: 187). The logic of the argument of the civilizing effect, as described above, is clear. The real question, however, is not whether transparency can promote output-oriented legitimacy in theory, but rather under what conditions it might actually do so. Unfortunately, as I will argue, those conditions are the very same factors we found lacking in the EU and wanted to compensate for.

Condition 1. A Europe-interested public

Deliberative theorists argue that transparency promotes the public interest in policy making by censoring self-regarding arguments. For this to be true, however, they have to make some important assumptions about who the public comprises which are seldom made explicit. First, they must assume a public that (at least after the deliberation) has a clear view of what the public interest is and prefers that over any other outcome. Second, they have to assume that the public audience does not consider the public interest to be in part constituted by private interests. If it did, self-regarding arguments would be part of the expected type of justification. What follows from these assumptions is the unselfishness norm, which means that if you do not show your commitment to what can be credibly presented as in the public interest, and not to your private good, you will incur some type of social cost.

But for an unselfishness norm to develop there must exist some degree of common identity in the first place. Without any notion at all of a 'we' being 'together' in this process of collective decision-making there would be no reason to consider a 'higher' public interest than the sum of private interests. If everyone is convinced that the only purpose of political engagement is to get as much as possible out of it for oneself, there is no need to pretend to care about collective values. Therefore there will be no public-regardingness from the decision-makers as an effect of transparency if the public audience is itself not public-regarding. The stronger the collective identity, the stronger will be the notion of a public interest beyond the sum of private interests, and consequently the stronger the unselfishness norm. And the stronger the unselfishness norm, the stronger the effect of transparency when it comes to censoring self-regarding behaviour.

The implication for transparency's potential to provide output-oriented legitimacy for the European Union is clear – again we are up against the first deficit on the input side, to follow Scharpf: the lack of a collective identity. A heterogeneous society in terms of identity, history, culture, language and political and economic institutions will develop a relatively weak unselfishness norm. The European interest will not be as strong a normative reference point in public discussions in Europe, as the national interest is in more homogeneous nation states.[4]

Condition 2. A European public discourse

A European public audience is thus the first condition for transparency to promote output-oriented legitimacy by forcing officials to focus on European public interests. The second condition is a European-wide public discourse, which unfortunately is also the second part of the triple input-deficit. Strictly speaking transparency in itself does not have any effect at all on political behaviour. In order to affect arguments, positions and decisions, transparency must be accompanied by (at least the risk of) publicity. Making information about political actions legally available to a larger public does not have any effect on behaviour if decision-makers have no reason to think that the information will be disseminated.

The key to making information public in large modern societies is the mass media. Very few citizens will go to Brussels to watch the open debates in the Council live (although this is actually possible now, according to the new working order of the Council (2002/682/EC)) or apply for documents themselves. If it is not in the media most people will never hear about it. Therefore the effect of transparency on political actions will be stronger the more media attention policy-makers anticipate. The fact that 'European mass media are largely absent, the most important media structures – the newspapers and television channels – are still firmly placed within the national borders of the member states' (Karlsson 2001: 71) has two important consequences in this respect. First, media attention will most likely be focused mostly on national events. For national media EU politics tend to be less interesting to report than national politics, and that moderates the effects of transparency in the EU compared to those at national level. Second, media framing will tend to be national. Information made available by transparency rules, such as open Council debates, will be reported and interpreted from a national perspective. Such national domestication of EU information is an obstacle to the formation of a European public able to press decision-makers to act more in accordance with a European public interest.

Condition 3. (Real) accountability

Transparency and accountability are two closely linked concepts. From an input-oriented perspective transparency is a necessary condition for accountability. Without access to information about what decision-makers actually do, accountability is impossible and any sanctions put on decision-makers will be arbitrary. Increasing transparency in the EU therefore promotes accountability.

From an output-oriented perspective, on the other hand, accountability is a condition for transparency to have an effect on political behaviour. The effects of transparency, as we have seen, come from decision-makers' fears of incurring costs by failing to fulfil public expectations. The first two conditions – a European public audience and a European public discussion – define those expectations. But even if those two conditions were to be fulfilled there would be no reason to assume any change of behaviour on the part of the decision-makers if there were no costs involved with breaking public expectations. A decision-maker would have little reason to avoid self-regarding behaviour, including national interest-regarding behaviour, in public, if he or she was not likely to be punished for it. Again we are back to the 'triple deficit' which we started from; there has to be in place an institutional infrastructure assuring accountability of office holders – including real sanctions for bad behaviour – in order for transparency to have an effect on output-oriented legitimacy.

The accountability problems of the EU are well known and need no detailed review here (Lord 1998; Harlow 2002). For the Council of Ministers, where (indirect) electoral accountability applies, one problem is the lack of Europe-wide elections able to focus sanctions on deviations from European rather than national interests. A second problem is the lack of European issues in national election campaigns. If the governments' record in Brussels is not on the electoral agenda, because national parties prefer to compete on national issues (Hix 1999), transparency in the Council will have a small effect on behaviour.

Generally, the further away from public sanctions, the less the chance, *ceteris paribus*, that transparency will steer political actions towards the public interest. The European Central Bank is an interesting case. Lacking any type of formal sanctioning mechanism, the only type of cost that the executive board and the governing council have to think about when taking decisions affecting the European economy is public embarrassment if it should be discovered that they have not been doing a good job, or that they have been more sensitive to the needs of certain European regions than others. While losing face should not be underestimated as a form of punishment, and credibility is crucial for a newly created central bank, the effect of transparency in such cases is very uncertain. The extent to which publishing minutes and voting records of the bank will promote output-oriented legitimacy – government for the people – will depend to what extent (1) public critique facilitated by transparency actually represents the public interest (and not just some factional groups such as financial actors or large state governments) and (2) how much central bankers value the avoidance of such public critique (i.e. how much it hurts).

The risk of weakened problem-solving capacity

Even if the EU could produce a strong unselfishness norm and effective public accountability the primary effect of transparency might not diminish focus on national or sectoral interests. If we take negotiation theory into account we soon realize that transparency may be a problem for output-oriented legitimacy as well as a solution (Naurin 2003). A thin collective identity, and a consequently weak unselfishness norm, aggravates these problems.

Negotiation theorists make a distinction between integrative and distributive bargaining[5] (Walton and McKersie 1965; Elgström and Jönsson 2000). Distributive bargaining is characterized by mistrust. Actors perceive the situation as zero-sum and seek agreement by pressuring their opponents to make the biggest concessions possible. Integrative bargaining, on the other hand, is a co-operative game in which the parties work together in order to find non-zero sum solutions which everyone can be satisfied with (everyone invited to the negotiations, that is). Transparency does not change the basic nature of the distributive bargaining game. Even though actors need to be aware of the unselfishness norm, to the extent that there exists one, and the force-of-the-better-argument norm, which makes threats and log-rolling more difficult (Elster 1998), the main strategy will still be 'rhetorical action' (Schimmelfennig 2001), i.e. using manipulated information in order to advance one's position.

Integrative bargaining, on the other hand, will be more fundamentally disturbed by transparency. The integrative bargaining process is dependent upon actors trusting each other and being willing to share non-manipulated private information. Participants need to understand each other's real preferences and motives in order to find mutually advantageous solutions (Fisher *et al.* 1999). For discussions to be 'free and frank' the participants must feel safe about giving away that information. They need to know that it will not 'somehow be used against them' (Walton and McKersie 1965: 159). Transparency will put pressure on actors to hide self-interested motives, as an effect of the unselfishness norm, as well as making them generally more careful in revealing private information.

An additional reason why publicity makes integrative bargaining more difficult is that hesitancy is often seen as a sign of weakness in politics. Political actors are expected to appear principled and assured of themselves. Integrative bargaining is dependent upon the parties agreeing that they do not already know all the answers. The process of searching, 'thinking out loud', putting different options on the table and throwing them out again if they are found to be no good, is blocked if the parties are not allowed to be unsure or to change their minds. By introducing transparency into the negotiation processes of the Council of Ministers we run the risk, therefore, of losing problem-solving capacity should ministers become afraid to speak their minds.

There is also a risk that the ministers simply stop talking to each other and instead start to address the public audience. Public relations rhetoric may substitute for problem solving: big words with little substance. When communication between the parties stops, decision-making stops. This, in turn, may lead to a real stop in the sense that no decision is taken and problem-solving capacity is lost. An alternative scenario is that decision-making leaks out of the public meetings into informal arenas (Wallace and Hayes-Renshaw 1997). Increased formal transparency may thereby lead to less actual transparency, if actors choose to negotiate in corridors instead of at the formal meetings. A misguided transparency reform could in fact have the unwanted effect of shrinking the number of participants having access to the core decision-making arena as some, probably the less powerful, participants, are lost between the public meeting and the corridor. While containing the hope of higher quality outputs, in the form of policy decisions closer to the public interest, transparency thus also involves risks for the output-oriented legitimacy of the EU by weakening its problem-solving capacity.

A civilizing or politicizing force?

Transparency also involves an additional risk that runs completely contrary to the hypothesis of deliberative theory. The civilizing force of transparency may in fact turn out to be the opposite when we take the dynamics of representation into account. Transparency may under some circumstances increase, rather than censor, the degree of self-regardingness in the decision-making process. The risk for increased politicization of group-interests when decision-making is made public comes from the fact that 'the public' is a much more complex set of audiences than deliberative theorists tend to assume. Political representatives of parties and groups do not only have to answer before an abstract general public that demands justifications in line with the common good. They are facing different audiences who want to hear different types of arguments.

First, as emphasized in classical pluralist theory, politics involves conflicts of interests between social groups. 'If a fight starts, watch the crowd', Schattschneider wrote, meaning that parties involved in political conflict must try to make allies in the audience in order to win the battle (Schattschneider 1960: 3). Potential allies may be won over by specific emphases on how they in particular are affected by a particular policy option. 'Policy B should be chosen, because it is good for you' is by all means an other-regarding justification, but it has nothing to do with the common good.

Second, and more problematic for the output-oriented legitimacy potential of transparency, is the fact that representatives have home constituencies watching them. Often this domestic audience is hoping and expecting to hear something very different from the abstract 'general public'. They may not want to hear their representative covering up their interests in public interest rhetoric. Rather they may want to be assured that he or she is on their side, fighting for their interests. When taking into account that representatives are involved in 'nested games' (Tsebelis 1990), both external and internal, the idea of hearing someone in a public debate saying 'Policy B should be chosen because it is good for us' suddenly does not seem that odd. It may not persuade anyone who is not a member of this particular representative's constituency, but that would not be its purpose anyway. Its purpose would be to rally support in that part of the audience able to determine whether this representative will be re-elected or not. When it comes to the Council of Ministers that part of the audience is not European but national – and arguably not improperly but legitimately so.

Both in negotiation theory and in corporatist theory (Streeck and Schmitter 1985; Williamson 1989) there is a worry that transparency increases the pressure from members and home constituencies, potentially disrupting the representatives' search for common solutions. If this kind of group-pressure puts a stop to compromise and instead leads to flirting with members and constituents and more focus on 'our interests', the civilizing force of hypocrisy may turn into a politicizing force. From a normative point of view we have to remember that this is a problem only if we agree with the basic assumption of deliberative theory that politics should be about common rather than special interests. From a pluralist perspective, where the notion of a collective public interest as a uniquely defined outcome and something more than the sum of individual interests is rather suspect in the first place, open conflicts of interest are healthy and should be welcomed rather than avoided. If transparency makes compromise among elites above the heads of grassroots, as in the corporatist and consociational models, more difficult, from a pluralist point of view that would be a strong output-oriented argument in favour of opening up the Council of Ministers.

Specifying the conditions for an output effect

From an empirical point of view the main conclusion of taking negotiation theory, representation, and nested games into account is that it is no longer so clear what the effects of transparency on political behaviour would be. They would vary, both in strength and content, on the particular issue at hand, the political actor being exposed and the characteristics of the public audience. Considering the centrality of transparency in the future of Europe debate this is a strong argument for more empirical research. Specifying the circumstances under which transparency might have a civilizing or a politicizing effect, and under what circumstances it could lead to fewer 'wrongdoings' and/or less problem-solving capacity, would substantially improve the discussion on institutional design. Formulating and testing hypotheses on the effects of transparency is therefore an important research task.[6] In this section I will merely indicate some obvious hypotheses that may already be formulated. When it comes to the characteristics of 'the public' I have already discussed above the special conditions pertaining to the European Union. The less collective identity the weaker we should expect the selfishness-censoring effect of transparency to be. This may be studied by comparing European and national public discussions, bearing in mind the problems with finding a comparable European public discussion. To what extent is the common good used as a reference point in open Council debates, compared to debates in national parliaments, for example?

In terms of actor characteristics we should expect a difference between the supranational and the intergovernmental institutions of the EU.

Ministers are representatives of national constituencies while Commission officials must leave all their national allegiances at home and forget about anything but the European interest when they take up their jobs in Brussels. While the Commission certainly is still to a large degree infused with national interests, illustrated for example by the dispute between small and large states over the question of whether every member state should have a commissioner or not, commissioners are much less affected by pressures from national constituencies than are ministers. The hypothesis would therefore be that transparency has a smaller and more easily predictable effect on the Commission than on the Council. In the Council there will be, on the one hand, much more self-regardingness for transparency to do something about, and hence a stronger potential output-oriented legitimacy effect. On the other hand there is a greater risk/chance for politicization due to national pressures. Whether the effect will be civilizing or politicizing (again, beware of the normative bias of deliberative theory in that terminology) depends to a large extent on whether there is a European identity strong enough to produce a powerful unselfishness norm.

Although agency shirking has historically been proven to be substantial (Tallberg 2003), for the Commission the European public interest will feature more strongly than it does in the Council due to the Commission's special mandate. Hence there will be fewer special national interests for transparency to moderate. Apart from agency shirking, transparency will have a job to do in the Commission when it comes to sectoral interests, such as industries, agriculture and fisheries. Although the effect of transparency on the Commission will probably be less radical than in the Council, the direction of the effect will probably be civilizing rather than politicizing. Rather than playing down the European interest when acting in public, which is something ministers with an eye to home audiences may do, commission officials will want to appear as nothing but devoted Europeans.

The effect of transparency will also depend on the type of issue at hand. A common distinction is that between efficiency- and redistributive issues, often used in the discussion on how to legitimize delegations of power to independent non-majoritarian institutions (Majone 1996). Transparency may promote output-oriented legitimacy in both types of issues, but in different ways. Pure efficiency-issues assume a positive-sum game and in principle consensus on the public interest, which makes the question of group-pressure and politicization irrelevant. The role of transparency in that case would be to secure good governance (efficiency, technical quality, lack of corruption) and prevent agency shirking. The selfishness-censoring effect is more relevant for redistributive issues.

Generally, therefore, the hypothesis should be that transparency has the greatest potential for positive effects on output-oriented legitimacy in the Council of Ministers, when it is taking decisions on issues involving strong conflict of interests on redistributive issues and issues concerning the allocation of values and risks. This is also the case, however, where transparency entails the greatest risks from an output-oriented perspective, in terms of politicization and lack of problem-solving capacity. It is in intergovernmental negotiations on contested issues that transparency can do most good – and bad – in output terms. Opening up the Commission should therefore be less controversial, which also seems to be verified by the fact that the Commission has had less trouble implementing rules for access to documents than the Council (Deckmyn 2002).

Conclusion

The power of transparency to launder political arguments, positions and decisions, and hence improve output-oriented legitimacy, is derived from 'the power of the public'. Who this public is, how it is informed and what it can do to sanction policy-makers, ultimately decides what the effect of transparency on policy will be. The output-oriented legitimacy potential of transparency is therefore contingent on the institutions and structures on the input side. Without government by the people transparency in itself will not be able to deliver government for the people. Given the usual assumption that a collective identity, a public sphere, and proper accountability mechanisms are lacking, transparency will not by itself improve the output-oriented legitimacy of the EU. Instead the effect may be politicization and weakened problem-solving capacity. The research challenge is to specify how transparency should be institutionalized to do the best job possible. Having said that, and as emphasized in the introduction, transparency still has an important role to play on the input side. For those who have not yet joined Scharpf and Majone in giving up any thought of democratizing the supranational decision-making procedures of the EU, this may be a sufficient argument for pressing the transparency case.

10 An institutional dialogue on common principles

Reflections on the significance of the EU Charter of Fundamental Rights

Claudia Attucci

Beyond the dualism of international and domestic law

The relationship between the normative claims of individual rights and membership in a polity has long been an uneasy one for political theory. The EU Charter of Fundamental Rights (hereafter, the Charter) sheds light on this relationship. It increases the legitimacy of the EU by raising the universalistic claims of individual rights in a polity where different political cultures are coming together. The Charter's significance rests not in granting ultimate authority to a higher Court, but in enabling an institutional dialogue among different actors on the basis of common principles. Since the decision of the European Council to draft a Charter of Fundamental Rights in 1999, its purpose has always been ambiguous. The aim of the Charter oscillates between increasing the protection of human rights and the almost opposite one of safeguarding national traditions and practices allegedly threatened by EU integration. Arising from a tension between the principle of the equal treatment of human beings, and that of respect for diversity between member states, the normative thrust of the Charter appears to be ambivalently inspired by both normative universalism and particularism.

The reflections that follow assume as a working hypothesis that the *sui generis* character of the EU as a supranational polity, together with a conception of fundamental rights that departs from natural-law theories of human rights, supersedes the dualisms of international and national law, as well as that of universalism and particularism. While these are often implicitly assumed in political theory, a study on the EU cannot take them for granted. Many of the problems that normative theories encounter in studying the EU, including the ambiguities that scholars read in the Charter, derive from the attempt to encapsulate the EU within these dichotomies.

The normative approach implicit in the Charter is a 'contextual universalism'.[1] This entails that the value and function of the Charter lie not so much in what one expects from a traditional bill of rights, but rather in enabling an institutional dialogue whereby different choices ought to be justified against a background of common principles vis-à-vis other actors. These are choices regarding which fundamental values ground the rights of persons. Thus, the Charter does not foster European integration by promoting homogeneity, but rather by underscoring the legitimacy, and the limits, of different normative stands between the member states and between them and the EU.

The following section considers several hypotheses regarding the function of the Charter within the dichotomy of international and domestic law, concluding that these categories are not sufficient. Another source of the rights of the Charter is explored: the common constitutional traditions of the member states. Rawls's 'overlapping consensus' proves a useful, but deficient, instrument to understand the role of general principles. Elaborating on Rawls's idea of constitutional essentials, I argue that these principles are not universal principles from which particular policies and rights should be deduced, but rather abstract principles based on concrete practices and beliefs. As these are abstract, however, the definition of concrete rights must draw on decisions about what constitutes a fundamental interest of the person. Their lack of definitive validity, due to the plurality of possible legitimate choices, needs to be recognized. I thus conclude that these choices must be justified by the abstract principles recognized as common within the EU, based on a common concern for persons as human beings.

Why an EU Charter of Fundamental Rights?

The Charter should serve to increase the legitimacy of the EU institutions. This is explicit in the mandate of the Cologne European Council: 'Protection of fundamental rights is a founding principle of the Union and an indispensable prerequisite for her legitimacy' (European Council, 1999). Since the late 1990s politicians and other informed observers have seen a need to make these rights more explicit, following decades of jurisprudence on fundamental rights by the European Court of Justice (hereafter ECJ) drawing on the constitutional traditions of the member states and on international human rights law (notably, the European Convention on Human Rights). The mandate speaks of a need to make the 'overriding importance [of fundamental rights] visible to the citizens', yet why this need was felt is less obvious. In addition to human rights protection, the public debates and drafting debates referred to the need to establish a core of common principles as a yardstick in view of enlargement, the strengthening of a sense of common values as the basis for a more ethical EU and a strengthening of its identity, and, finally, the possibly opposing aim of curbing an overly active ECJ and protecting member states' sovereignty.

Subsidiarity of rights?

The ambiguity of ultimate aims is reflected in the text of the Charter. It purports to protect the rights of all persons, but often formulates them in principles, leaving the formulation of norms to member states' discretion 'according to national legislations and practices'. Protection of rights may still vary considerably among member states, raising doubts regarding the Charter's safeguarding of the universal rights of persons.[2] A central question is whether the Charter primarily checks EU integration, ECJ activism and supremacy to safeguard member states' constitutional traditions, or whether on the contrary it contributes to constituting the EU as a legitimate autonomous actor with its own values and identity. The Working Group on the Charter in the Convention on the Future of Europe (hereafter, WGII) addressed this. WGII reinforced the principle that the Charter does not extend EU competences (Art. 51, in particular), and justified leaving the definition of rights to national practices and legislation as an application of the principle of subsidiarity (CONV 2002, 354/02).

The principle of subsidiarity responds to the twofold task of enforcing common principles (equal rights) and respecting diversity of member state traditions. However, if rights are subject to subsidiarity, this may conflict with their normative thrust. In response, subsidiarity for rights can be seen as regulating the relationship between the definition and the implementation of the same rights: defined at Union level, their interpretation and application are still left to member states. But is this 'division of labour' between the Union and the member states only a matter of interpretation if it affects individuals' extent and enjoyment of rights? Traditionally, interpretation of rights in the domestic sphere presupposes that legislative bodies, courts and constitutional courts belong to the same 'constitutional tradition', yet in the EU interpretations may vary according to different constitutional traditions. It is perhaps misleading to regard references to the national legislations and practices as issues of interpretation. The normative approach of contextual universalism suggests instead that general principles be regarded as constructed from particular cultures, rather than to regard particular norms as derived from general rights, as applications and interpretations.

This will be explained with reference to the idea of 'common constitutional traditions'. This combines two aims: setting a common normative ground for the EU, and respecting pluralism. We must first consider why other traditional interpretations of rights – as negative constraints on political power – do not fully explain the significance of the Charter.

The Charter and the constraining function of human rights

While the Charter certainly serves a negative, or defensive, function of constraining political power, this does not exhaust its function, which cannot be completely identified with that served by bills of rights within international and domestic law. In constitutional law, bills of rights provide an internal constraint, whereas in international law they impose an external constraint on states' sovereignty regarding treatment of their own citizens. Note that the Charter speaks of 'fundamental' and not of 'human rights'. Despite their frequent conflation, the two terms are analytically distinct. 'Fundamental' qualifies a right that prevails over others in a political and legal system, while 'human' indicates its extension to all human beings – the first term is functional, the second extensional (Palombella 2002, Ch. 1). One's view on the extension of rights is certainly related to one's views on the function they should have as positive rights – their being 'fundamental' may depend on their being universal human rights. Yet this normative stand need not be assumed *prima facie* in the following.

The Charter could exercise a constraining function in at least three ways: by enabling the ECJ to constrain member states, analogous to the external constraint of human rights in international law; by allowing the ECJ to constrain EU institutions, analogous to the internal constitutional constraint of bills of rights in domestic law; or, finally, by giving member states means of protection against supranational EU institutions. The last role has no precedent in the dualistic order of international and domestic law.

According to the first hypothesis, the Charter would exercise a 'constraining' function by placing external checks on the member states, similar to international (regional or universal) Charters of human rights. Despite its popularity in public opinion and the media, there are good reasons to deny that the Charter can be reduced to this function alone. It is important that the EU shows a strong commitment to international human rights, but this Charter may not be the best instrument to do so. First, a new human rights Charter for the EU is redundant. Weiler points out that it is not bills of rights that are lacking in domestic and international arenas, but rather human rights policies, monitoring committees, and accession to the ECHR (Weiler 2000). Furthermore the Charter would be rather ineffective as things stand: the European Court of Justice lacks political capacity to act as a check and enforce rights against member states in fields beyond EU competence, while the Charter is mandated and adopted on the (maybe misplaced) condition that it ought not increase the Union's competences.[3] Finally, from a substantive viewpoint, as a human rights Charter it is both deficient and too ambitious: it lacks definition on the most important human rights (Parmar 2001), while containing rights that are far from being universally recognized as human rights.[4] Moreover, the formulations sometimes avoid taking any position where there are conflicts between different constitutional traditions.

In sum, if the Charter had solely the function of placing an external check on member states, it would be redundant, deficient in its substance, and lacking in the most important capacity of human rights Charters – namely, to challenge abuses of power by sovereign states against their own citizens. Other bodies may be more suited for undertaking such a task, e.g. the European Court of Human Rights with the European Convention on Human Rights. The ideal role of the Charter in granting more visibility to these human rights may carry further significance in shaping the normative foundation of the EU.

The second hypothesis is more appropriate: that the main purpose of the Charter is to constitute a self-imposed constraint on the Union's institutions, reflecting at supranational level the self-binding function of constitutional bills of rights in domestic law (see Holmes 1995). Arguably, this is indeed the main legal function of the Charter, in its horizontal clause explicitly saying that it is addressed to EU institutions and to its member states only when implementing EU law (Art. 51). However, the analogy with domestic constitutions is asymmetric: if the Charter is an act of self-constraint, who binds itself? The European people, the peoples of Europe forming a new collective, or the member states (and their peoples) aiming to defend themselves against the EU? The hypothesis that it may be all these at the same time underscores the originality of the EU, raising the question of what idea of common principles is implicit in the Charter. Moreover, the principles for areas outside the competence of the EU (education, marriage, etc.) require special attention to avoid inconsistencies within the self-binding view. Reference to fields outside EU competence may be justified, as was done by WGII, by the fact that polities of the EU may have some sort of spill-over effect also on other issues (as a 'side wind', Goldsmith 2001: 1207). But the emphasis placed on those rights seems to go beyond this concern.

This leads us to the third hypothesis, that the member states place a defensive constraint on EU institutions. Here we envisage states as protecting their own systems of rights, not so much (or not primarily) on the basis of a universal human nature that requires the same human rights for all humans, but on the common constitutional traditions of the member states. The Cologne mandate suggests that the Charter may be binding on the grounds of fundamental rights whose definition is not dictated only by universal human nature. It speaks of 'fundamental', rather than 'human', rights and explicitly states that the rights in the Charter should also be those 'derived from the constitutional traditions common to the Member States, as general principles of Community law' (European Council, June 1999). In speaking of 'common', across the plurality of traditions, this phrase highlights a classic paradox of unity in diversity.

Before turning in the next section to its 'constructive' function we must consider whether the common constitutional traditions may also be invoked with a 'negative' function. Common constitutional traditions might be thought to provide a source of rights viewed as constraints by coordinated member states against the supremacy of EU institutions and against the supremacy of the Union's interests over national interests. This constraining function might be of two kinds. First, as an idea of the universalism of rights, as an aspiration or approximation towards universal principles through inclusive consensus.[5] Without a pre-given conception of human nature, this interpretation might see the reference to common constitutional traditions as a sort of approximation towards universal human rights – hence, the Charter would serve a function similar to other international bills of human rights. More interestingly, the constraint of common constitutional traditions may be understood as a defence by member states to protect their achieved principles against EU institutions. While sub-units impose the constraints on higher institutions, the member states exercise an 'external' constraint as separate actors, rather than as components of a collective that binds itself. This leads us to explore whether the idea of shared principles can instead be constitutive of a sense of commonality in the EU built around the rights of persons.

Towards a European sense of 'common'?

Since the Charter cannot be seen as only serving a negative function, we now turn to the hypothesis that the common constitutional traditions identify a core of European values, forming common principles constitutive of a body politic that is not merely the sum of its parts. A charter of rights may have a positive function – that of setting the shared values through which common goals can be pursued in a political community.[6]

The common constitutional traditions as a lowest common denominator

One recurrent interpretation considers the common principles deriving from the common constitutional traditions as a *lowest common denominator* – a minimum threshold of rights-protection outlawing legislation or practices that trespass it. Such a minimum standard would be compatible with other, thicker, standards in the member states (Besselink 1998; Weiler 1999: 107ff). While this is an important view, the pluralism and incommensurability of values that constitute a legal system make the notion of a common minimum denominator of rights problematic (Raz 1986, Ch. 13). This has indeed posed concrete problems for the ECJ when faced with cases that would receive different interpretations according to different traditions of the member states. As Weiler pointed out, the ECJ has given up interpreting rights on the grounds of the common constitutional traditions of the member states, which served only as a source of inspiration. Instead the ECJ made its own choices 'in the light of Community law'. The difficulties are due to the fact that the constitutional traditions and practices of the member states differ greatly in how they rank values, even when they share them. In making its choice in view of the objectives of the Union, the ECJ has thus contributed to establishing, using Weiler's terms, the 'fundamental boundaries' that define the nature of the Community (Weiler 1999: 102).

In what follows I argue that the Convention that drafted the Charter responded to the ECJ's difficulties by recognizing that establishing common principles does not always lead to the definition of a European set of rights, instead leaving their definitions to the member states. It is important to bear in mind that 'fundamental boundaries' do not privilege collective interests against individual interests. Rather, Weiler implies that fundamental boundaries are not opposed to fundamental rights: the definition of fundamental rights that political institutions are to protect draws on an idea of the person, and an idea of what is of value in a particular community. In this sense, they are two sides of the same coin.

An overlapping consensus on political values?

When conceptualizing the idea of common constitutional traditions, Rawls's 'overlapping consensus' seems a particularly apposite model. Both the idea of the common constitutional traditions and the idea of an overlapping consensus attach normative value to those principles that meet consensus, without presupposing normative homogeneity. Rawls's 'overlapping consensus' identifies the role of some set of values on which all different 'comprehensive doctrines' need to converge. The many philosophical beliefs and conceptions of the good that people hold as individuals or groups in a pluralistic political society may draw on such a shared overlapping consensus to secure long-term compliance with the public principles of that society (Rawls 1993, 2001).

Moved by the 'political virtue' of reciprocity, people who live in the same society and who believe in different comprehensive doctrines compare their principles in order to find out what can be shared with others so as to form the basis for stable cooperation. After a process of generalization where they become aware of the general principles in which they believe, they can engage in the construction of political values forming the basis of an overlapping consensus by a process of abstraction from their comprehensive doctrines. The values so identified by overlapping consensus are recognized as political, or public, and form the fundamental constitutional principles – for determining the 'constitutional essentials' of a well-ordered society. Political values in overlapping consensus are thus collective constructions that aim at universalism understood here as a principle of inclusion. These values thus find their roots in particular contexts where people believe in different comprehensive doctrines.[7] Applied to the common constitutional traditions of the member states in the EU,[8] overlapping consensus would identify core *political* values on which a European identity can be based, without covering the whole spectrum of values (and thus, of rights) of the member states.

A common political identity transcending and capable of including the plurality of more substantive cultures within particular societies is also envisaged by the idea of a 'constitutional patriotism'. In developing this idea, Habermas has proposed that a sense of common belonging based on constitutional principles, rather than on substantive doctrines, is particularly applicable in the context of the European Union, for it is capable of providing a common identity for Europeans without threatening the cultural diversity that characterizes the continent (Habermas 1996b, 1999; Eriksen and Fossum 2000; Friese and Wagner 2002). Without denying its importance, however, I shall argue that a constitutional patriotism for Europe along these lines often takes the over-simplistic route of a separation between a public and a cultural identity. Principles that transcend particular substantive beliefs are often insufficient for any particular public issue to be decided.

From the general to the particular, or from the particulars to the abstract

Based on the principle of reciprocity, Rawls's normative view suggests that we recognize public values as those that fall within an overlapping consensus. This approach of *Political Liberalism* can be called a contructivist 'contextual universalism', because general (or more appropriately, abstract) principles are justified on the basis of a normative aspiration towards universality understood as inclusiveness. It is constructivist because normative principles are not given *a priori*, but are justified by being preferred in procedures that are deemed to be 'fair'. Thus, its universality is based on the praxis of inclusion, which finds its origin in particular contexts – it is, for this reason, 'contextual' – and these contexts are in great part determined by political institutions.

Because such political – or public – values are by definition agreed upon by all members of the society in which they apply, disagreement in politics is not, for Rawls, a disagreement on these political values. He recognizes that disagreement may remain (Rawls 1993: 240). This is due, he argues, to the 'burdens of judgement' – that is, to our incapacity to fully evaluate all the elements that are at stake in a political decision, and therefore about which value to give priority. According to Rawls, public values always ought to override beliefs deriving from particular comprehensive doctrines. Thus, public reasoning ought to be 'political' all the way down, from the general to the particular, and concrete cases should be defensible on the basis of a complete set of general principles (Bellamy and Schönlau, this volume, and Waldron 1999).

However, even on this 'constructivist' reading one can reject the idea that no disagreement on values stemming from comprehensive doctrines should enter the constitutional politics that sets the basic structure of a society. Indeed, nothing guarantees that general political principles provide an answer for all political issues based on a complete theory.

Rawls seems to overlook that when acting in accordance with the civic virtue of reciprocity, people may choose different 'ways [in which political values] can be characterised' (Rawls 1993: 240) for reasons that may rest on those same comprehensive doctrines. Think of the very abstract notion of human dignity as stated in Article 1 of the Charter. While there is almost universal overlapping consensus on this provision, the fact that people support it from different comprehensive doctrines may cause disagreement in how 'constitutional essentials' should be transformed into rights. The meaning of the right to life, for example, is heavily affected by comprehensive doctrines when it comes to cases such as abortion. Likewise, the meaning of the general principle of 'body integrity' is differently interpreted by those who disagree on whether infibulation decreases the dignity of women, likewise by those who disagree about whether organ transplant is a violation of human dignity. Finally, it seems that the prohibition of human cloning and restrictions on eugenic practices (Art. 3) rests on philosophical (albeit not necessarily religious) beliefs about the nature of human beings. My contention is that the borders between public and non-public cannot be so sharply defined as to exclude public concrete decisions having to draw on beliefs of comprehensive doctrines. Consider, for example, the role of reasoning in universities – which Rawls considers non-public – in determining fundamental choices to be taken in public (Rawls 2001: 93–4).

Having pointed to the problems of the most recurrent interpretation, I put forward another conception of rights and their function that rests on the impossibility of their being grounded on purely political and uncontroversial values. Once one admits the inescapability of controversial substantive choices about values in the public realm, it becomes all the more important that a dialogue between different publics be fostered. This is necessary to prevent entrenched majorities' neglect of the fundamental interests of minorities, and to avoid the identification of group decisions with a personified 'collective will'. I conclude that abstract principles are useful for such a dialogue, provided that they are not intended as a complete theory from which particular cases are derived.

Towards a more substantive conception of rights?

The very structure of the Charter suggests a move towards a substantive view of rights. It is composed of six chapters (plus the 'horizontal clauses') referring respectively to the values of dignity, liberty, equality, solidarity, citizenship and justice. The drafters grouped rights on the basis of the values that they aim to promote, instead of dividing them into different kinds (civic, political and social rights). This choice reflects the principle of 'indivisibility': there is no hierarchy or distinction in the nature of rights. What characterizes a particular right is not its structure – for instance that negative rights have priority over more positive – but the value it aims to achieve. The claim of indivisibility and the introduction of social rights on the same ground as other rights challenges the idea that rights be only the conditions to secure freedom and autonomy. If one recognizes value pluralism, this conception of rights implies that choices are taken about values – choices that can never be safe from contestation.

An interest-based conception of rights

What makes rights fundamental? According to an interest-based approach to rights, it is the fact, or the belief, that the interest they promote is sufficiently important for the rights-holders to hold some other person(s) to be under a duty (Raz 1986: 166; Fabre 2000: 14). To identify an interest as *sufficiently* important coincides with assessing in particular contexts that this is to be publicly promoted against others (Waldron 1989) – and this may well depend on societal arrangements and not solely on the 'nature' of human beings.[9] Rights are collective decisions about rules as to how society's institutions are to evaluate and weight persons' interests. Those decisions are taken on the basis of beliefs about which interests of individuals are so important as to hold others to some duties, and under what circumstances. Thus, while rights are based on a concern for individual interests, they are not in conflict with collective goals. Representing views about what a person enjoys in a society, they are part of a collective good that establishes how people are to be treated in the community in which they reside (see Raz 1994).

Dealing with disagreement

It is on the basis of a conception of individual rights as interests that Waldron grounds his rights-based argument against entrenched bills of rights (Waldron 1993). He recognizes that disagreement about the fundamental interests of persons leads to disagreement about fundamental rights, and rejects the idea that they should be constitutionalized and place inviolable limits on democracy. The latter, he argues, responds to a principle of authority required by the grounds of the same respect for people that is also at the foundation of the idea of rights. Since citizens who are responsibly committed to the principle of reciprocity still disagree sincerely about what people's fundamental interests are, respect for their responsibility and judgement demands that we recognize disagreement with regard to the substance of rights.

However, rights are supposed to counter the risk that majoritarian representative democracy will always be partial and may neglect fundamental interests of minorities. For this reason, one cannot neglect the normative significance of principles constructed on the basis of reciprocity, which transcends personal interests in guiding public choices, and allows the legitimacy of different choices between values to be justified.

For this reason, I conclude, the search for an overlapping consensus on principles reached by abstraction plays an important function, provided that these are not understood as complete rules, but rather as open-ended principles.

The relevance of regulative abstract principles

The distinction between principles and rights is identified as crucial in the Charter by both scholars and political actors (Goldsmith 2001; Heringa and Verhey 2001). It reveals a complex relationship between abstract common principles and actually enforceable rights, which does not always result in a shift of ultimate legal authority from national courts to the ECJ. I do not take the distinction between principles and rights to refer to the nature and the substance of different categories of provisions, as is often claimed when it is argued that social provisions should be considered as principles, as opposed to rights (Goldsmith 2001). Rather, this is a matter of degree of abstraction that applies to all rights. The normative point to be made is by whom and on what grounds the principles are to be transformed into rights.[10]

As mentioned above, the Charter contains some vague principles that are not sufficiently supported by enforceable norms, in that they refer to 'national legislations and practices'. This has been often criticized by commentators, who for this reason see the Charter as a mere rhetorical exercise that risks ratifying the *status quo*, and subjugating the ECJ to national practices rather than increasing rights-protection. There are, indeed, reasons to be disappointed, if one expected the Charter to put an end to many of the controversial issues that are rightly a matter of concern for civil or social rights advocates. With reference to national legislation and practices, disagreement is not eliminated.

This is lamented by almost everyone: by those who wanted liberal rights to be imposed on particular cultures, by those who expected the Charter to build a strong constitutional patriotism, and also by those who fear that these provisions represent an attempt to simply mask (and thus, manipulate) disagreement under an alleged consensus on vague principles. In contrast, in light of the conception of rights outlined briefly above, general principles may still play an important critical function and foster change.[11] I do not suggest that principles should be a substitute for rights. It seems impossible to achieve a conception of rights that is actually universal, just and inclusive, and does not partly depend on contingent worldviews and goals chosen in a political community. Hence, it is misleading to attach to them the function of 'constitutional essentials'. With this I mean that they are not sufficient for determining and freezing the 'basic structure' of the political community, understood as constituted by a set of overarching principles that can always override comprehensive doctrines and thus allow decisions independent thereof. General principles, instead,

are to be considered as open normative frameworks that trigger reciprocal justifications, even if they do not call for a univocal interpretation by
one court.[12] This is possible as long as they are seen as abstract, incomplete and regulative. Abstract, rather than general, in that they are constructed from existing contexts, cultures, beliefs and traditions, through a
process of inclusion by abstraction – rather than being based on an *a
priori* idealized notion of human nature (O'Neill 1988). Incomplete,
because practical substantive decisions not wholly derivative of abstract
principles are inevitable.[13] Regulative, in that they demand that national
legislations and national courts justify their own practices as compatible
with them.[14]

Once principles are understood in this way, particular substantive
choices need to be framed within them, for this forces courts, legislative
bodies, and the public to bring to the fore the beliefs of entrenched
majorities and provide justifications for them. Some choices may thus
appear unfair impositions on others, when judged under the principle of
mutual recognition of other people's interests and claims. For this reason
abstract principles, even if not enforceable at EU level, exercise a powerful
critical function against entrenched majorities from within, triggering
changes that may in the long run be more effective than if they were
regarded as norms imposed by alien bodies. Viewed in this sense, the function of the principles in the Charter is not the same as that of international human rights – of imposing respect for recognized universal
rights and challenging the sovereignty of states in respect of how they
treat their citizens. This requires that the principles be clearly defined and
enforceable, and consensus exist on their content.

While more legal clarity and more enforceable rights may well be
needed regarding some of the provisions in the Charter,[15] I see it as fruit-
ful to view the principles in the Charter as aiming to broaden the scope
for exploring the possibility of consensus, establishing acceptable limits of
divergence in the definition of rights, and finding acceptable compromises where these are deemed necessary (Bellamy 1999; Bellamy and
Schönlau, this volume). Even when not enforceable as rights, principles of
this kind may have a greater impact than they would have if left in the
political void (or what pretends to be so) of international law. These principles are supported in the EU by an institutional framework in which the
actors recognize each other as having embarked on common projects,
sharing political goals. The fact that choices about values need to be justified vis-à-vis others who have mode different ones forces explicitness about
assumptions that may conflict with other accepted principles. This raises
internal debates within societies that can bring about profound transfor-
mations.

Conclusion

These reflections on the Charter arose from perplexities regarding the normative function of the Charter in the field of rights protection. Having shown that the Charter does not have solely the same function as international human rights law or constitutional bills of rights, I explored how common constitutional traditions of the member states may help identify common principles by abstracting from different political cultures. As abstract, these principles purport to transcend the particular cultures, thus allowing trans-cultural justification. I then raised doubts whether political values can be isolated from 'omni-comprehensive' values when they have to provide guidance for political decisions in concrete cases. Therefore, they prove insufficient to define rights whose interpretation can be fully remitted to Courts.

I then turned to look at the nature of fundamental rights. I identified a view of rights that does not try to escape from substantive choices about values, and yet does not aim to impose one set of values as the only justifiable grounds for rights. This may be an empirically bounded interest-based conception of rights that recognizes value-pluralism. Once the necessity of substantive choices is recognized, I concluded that abstract common principles remain important. They regulate and allow an institutional and intercultural comparison between those choices. They engage both historically developed collective actors (including peoples represented by state institutions, where the term 'people' does not have a collectivistic meaning) and individual persons. Principles of this kind have a critical function in challenging entrenched majorities. While they may not have the function often attributed to constitutional rights, representing the 'set of values' on which a European identity may be built, they do provide the framework for confronting and justifying the politics of rights in the EU and in the member states.

The EU Charter of Fundamental Rights offers a chance to reconsider the formulation of fundamental principles and rights as means of legitimating political institutions. This escapes the familiar, traditional dualism of general universal rights as in international human rights law, and particular culturally-based rights. The structure of the EU polity offers a new possibility in this sense, precisely because not all the provisions included in the Charter fall within EU competence.[16] In disentangling them from the level of decision-making it is possible to open up the debate to different publics. The Charter thus challenges path-dependent decisions in the member states about values, without superimposing other (equally path-dependent) choices.

11 Motivating judges

Democracy, judicial discretion,
and the European Court of
Human Rights

Roberto Gargarella

The purpose of this study is to call attention to the scope of powers usually granted to judges, and the limited controls usually established over them. More specifically, I want to examine different attempts made at limiting the action of judges, or 'motivating' them to decide in specific ways, and the difficulties confronted by each of these solutions. These problems are not being properly addressed during this constitutional period. On the contrary, the tendency is to strengthen the powers of the judiciary, neglecting the profound normative questions raised by this institutional choice – an institutional choice that directly touches upon the democratic character of the Constitution.

I want to begin by emphasizing a few obvious points. First, tribunals like the European Court of Human Rights or the European Court of Justice deal with enormously important issues. Let me mention just a few among hundreds of good examples. In *Borelli* (3 December 1992) the ECJ began to specify the relationship between community law and national law. With the 'TCECA' decision (29 November 1956), and the 'AETR' decision, the ECJ began to develop a theory about the implicit powers of the different branches of government. In *Dundgeon v. United Kingdom* (22 October 1981, n. 45, 4 E.H.R.R. 149), it examined the demand of a homosexual who was persecuted by Northern Ireland laws that made certain homosexual acts between consenting adult males criminal offences. In *Tyrer v. United Kingdom* (25 April 1978, n. 26, 2 E.H.R.R.1) it reflected upon the meaning of the notion of corporal punishment.

The second point is also obvious, but probably more important. The fact is that, in all these cases, different people proposed to adopt not only different, but often diametrically opposed solutions. What it is important to notice is that these substantial disagreements were not limited to the 'political sphere.' In contrast, they were also present within the 'judicial sphere,' as is evinced in the dissenting opinions present in the judicial sentences. For example, in the *Dundgeon* case, the majority of the Court found that Irish laws violated the rights of homosexuals, while dissenting opinions denied that view, emphasizing that 'Christian and Moslem religions are all united in the condemnation of homosexual relations and sodomy.' In the *Tyrer* case, the majority affirmed that the birching of Mr Tyrer represented a degrading punishment, while magistrates like Judge Fitzmaurice maintained that the punishment that Mr Tyrer had received was insignificant compared to what students received in his time, in his place.

Now, each of us, as citizens of democratic communities, may have reasons for being concerned about this situation. It seems that the members of the Court disagree as much as we do, but the fact is that their role in these discussions is clearly more important than ours (Waldron 1999). What they say comes to be our 'law,' while we have almost no possibility of challenging their judgments. Probably as a consequence of this fact, there have been numerous attempts at establishing limits to their decisions in one way or another. In the next part I will refer to different initiatives adopted in order to 'move' judges to decide in certain ways; describe the limits of each of these initiatives; and explore the possibility of overcoming these limits.

Diverse interpretative theories

Obviously, the first thing that every community does in order to obtain certain specific legal outcomes is to write down legal norms. Thus, for example, the European Convention on Human Rights and its associated protocols have been drafted in order to define or publicly affirm certain basic goals, and to favour their realization. However, one initial problem regarding these decisions is that legal language, like all other languages, is full of ambiguities and vagueness. The 'open texture' of the language (Hart 1961; Carrió 1968) forces us to engage in difficult struggles in order to ascertain or make precise the actual meaning of what we have written down. Granted, there are many well-developed strategies in order to overcome at least some of these problems. For example, there are hundreds of *dictums* that belong to ancient Roman Law, which are directly aimed at solving these problems. They tell us how to decide when we have more than one norm for the same crime (*non bis in idem*); how to decide when a newly-enacted norm appears to contradict one already in place (*lex posterior*); how to decide when a more general rule seems to contradict a more specific one (*lex specialis*), etc. These techniques are actually very helpful when we need to solve some of these problems, even though we should never lose sight of the fact that they are just normative solutions that also need to be publicly discussed and agreed on, which does not normally happen.

Now, documents such as the European Convention on Human Rights, like most constitutional documents, raise more troublesome interpretative problems. In effect, these constitutional texts are even more difficult to interpret than other legal texts, because they are normally created at an early stage of a community's development and they usually have the aspiration of staying in place during ages, generation after generation. This aspiration creates some difficulties, which some authors called an inter-temporal problem (Ackerman 1984). The main difficulty is that our original, constitutional initiatives may come into conflict with some of our present aspirations (i.e. we may have committed ourselves to protect property or liberty in ways we currently find unacceptable). In addition, our understanding of the meaning of particular concepts (*freedom* of speech; *cruel* punishment; *fair* trial) may dramatically differ from the one that the creators of that document had in mind when they included them in the Constitution. Situations like these create an 'interpretative gap,' which needs to be filled mainly by the decisions of the judiciary. This situation creates a serious risk, namely, that of having the rule of law replaced by the will of judges.

Legal theorists and other academics have developed new complex interpretative theories in order to tackle these issues. They have mainly been trying to show judges what is the right way of interpreting the Constitution. In other words, they try to show them how to 'close the interpretative gap,' how to avoid adopting arbitrary decisions. Some authors, for example, suggest that constitutional documents should be read as 'living texts' and propose to approach these texts with a 'dynamic' conception in mind (Eskridge 1987). Others believe that the Constitution should be read according to its purposes and final objectives, and propose what has been called a 'teleological' interpretation of law. Yet others defend an 'originalist' approach, and look for the precise meaning of Constitutional words in the intentions of its authors or in the ideas that were dominant at the time of the approval of the Constitution (Bork 1990; Scalia 1997). In addition, there are those who defend a 'moral' reading of the Constitution, and try to connect its meaning with the best reading of the moral principles that underlie its content, a reading which properly 'fits' with our legal history (Dworkin 1986, 1996).

If the European Court of Justice or the European Court of Human Rights were to adopt one of these alternative readings, it should present and defend this decision publicly. Undoubtedly, the choice would be difficult, and so would the argumentation in its favour. However, it should be clear that we, as participants of this legal community, would be, in a way, better off, given that we need to know what our norms 'really' mean. Of course, as may be expected, the choice of a particular interpretative theory will have significant consequences: the Constitution will look very different depending on what particular interpretative theory is chosen. For example, if judges were to interpret a term, say decency, according to its 'original understanding,' then the outcome will be very different from the one we would obtain if they decided to read that term through a 'dynamic' interpretative theory. Similarly, the best 'moral reading' of the term might be contrary to the meaning we could infer if we were to define its meaning by exploring the 'context' in which the term was inserted, and so on. That is why we need to have more certainties regarding how judges are going to interpret our norms.

The problem is, however, that Courts do not choose one single interpretative theory and then stick to it in all subsequent decisions. In contrast, the tribunal tends to adopt many different interpretative theories at the same time, and make use of them more or less at will, depending on the case at hand.[1] Thus, what usually happens is that the Court decides one case taking into account one particular interpretative theory, and the following by using the same or a different method. Let me illustrate my argument.[2]

In the famous *Golder* case, for example, the ECHR made a defence of a certain type of originalism, mainly deciding the case by reference to the 'textual' meaning of the terms at stake. The Court employed the same interpretative strategy on many other occasions, such as in the *Engel* case (8 June 1976, n. 22, 1 E.H.R.R. 647); or in the *Lithgow* case (8 July 1986, n. 102, 8 E.H.R.R. 329). On this latter occasion, the Court established that 'the words of a treaty should be understood to have their ordinary meaning … and to interpret the phrase in question as extending the general principles of international law beyond their normal sphere of applicability is less consistent with the ordinary meaning of the terms used' (Merrills 1993: 70). By contrast, in cases such as the *Tyrer* case the Court made use of a 'dynamic' interpretative theory, and stated that 'the Convention is a living instrument which, as the Commission rightly stressed, must be interpreted in the light of present-day conditions.' In yet other cases, the Court defended a teleological interpretative theory, and looked for the final purposes of the articles at stake. Thus, for example, in the *Wemhoff* case (27 June 1986, n. 7, 1 E.H.R.R. 55), the Court maintained that its mission was to 'seek the interpretation that is most appropriate in order to realize the aim and achieve the object of the treaty, not that which would restrict to the greatest possible degree the obligations undertaken by the Parties' (Merrills 1993). In sum, the Court has not been maintaining a consistent interpretative approach, which has an obvious impact on its final decision. In the end, this is what explains, for example, the European Court of Justice's radical change of opinion from *Stork* (4 February 1959) to *Stauder* (12 November 1969); *Internationale Handelsgesellschaft* (17 November 1970); *Nold Hauer* (13 December 1979).[3]

Defining the democratic role of judges

The lack of a shared interpretative theory creates two serious public risks, among others. First, it makes it difficult for us as individual citizens to know what 'the law of the land' is. Second, and most important, the absence of an interpretative agreement makes it more difficult for us as a group to carry out our democratic will. The will of judges may come to prevail over our democratic will, as expressed in the norms we collectively create. Given these problems, many authors began to elaborate theories capable of reducing both these serious risks. What these authors tried to do was to define principles capable of guiding the judges in their daily activities. They sometimes recommended specific principles of interpretation, but they framed these recommendations into more general theories about what judges should do. To give just a few examples of these theories, I will briefly summarize three of them. First, I will mention John Ely's view, which gained a lot of respect from legal scholars and from political scientists as well, and then I will refer to Owen Fiss's and Cass Sunstein's views on the issue.

According to Ely (1980), judges should concentrate their efforts on safeguarding the political process, conceptualizing the process to have failed where:

> 1) the ins are choking off the channels of political change to ensure that they will stay in and the outs will stay out, or 2) though no one is actually denied a voice or a vote, representatives beholden to an effective majority are systematically disadvantaging some minority out of simple hostility or a prejudiced refusal to recognise commonalties of interest, and thereby denying that minority the protection afforded other groups by a representative system.
>
> (Ely 1980: 103)

In spite of some internal problems, Ely's theory is very good at confronting the two risks that we associated with more traditional views about the judiciary. According to this view, citizens keep their final authority on all the important questions of private and public morality. In other words, according to Ely, judges' only mission is to ensure that the community and each of its members are allowed to live as they want. To do so, judges would have to safeguard the preconditions of democracy and, within that general mission, make a special effort to ensure that 'discrete and insular minorities' are not 'systematically disadvantage[d].'

Authors like Owen Fiss have insisted on this last point, emphasizing the importance of ensuring judicial protection to disadvantaged minorities. In Fiss's view, judges should see themselves as the 'voice of the powerless minority.' By assuming this task, he presumes, judges would be simultaneously able to overcome all criticisms regarding their non-democratic background. Thus, in 'Groups and the Equal Protection,' Fiss affirmed that:

> [w]hen the product of a political process is a law that hurts [disadvantaged minorities], the usual countermajoritarian objection to judicial invalidation – the objection that denies those 'nine men' the right to substitute their view for that of 'the people' – has little force. For the judiciary could be viewed as amplifying the voice of powerless

minority; the judiciary is attempting to rectify the injustice of the political process as a method of adjusting competing claims.

(Fiss 1976: 153)

Authors like Cass Sunstein, in contrast, have concentrated their analysis on the contributions that judges may make to democracy. In this respect, Sunstein developed an innovative theory regarding the judicial role, which recommends a highly self-restrictive role on the part of the Court. According to him, the Court should allow itself to 'leave things undecided;' avoid abstract generalizations; reason by analogy and not through broad general principles; and to move carefully, step by step, taking 'one case at a time' (Sunstein 1999). In his opinion, a Court that decided through 'incompletely theorised agreements,' would decisively favour democracy, by leaving ample room for public debate.

Now, theories like the ones we have mentioned seem to properly address the concerns we have been discussing. If judges behaved as these theorists recommend, it would be much more difficult for any critic to challenge what judges do. Typically, the common criticism that points to the non-democratic character of judges would tend to evaporate because, allegedly, judges would be working for the reinforcement of democracy. The question is, however, why should we expect judges to act in such a way? In other words, what reasons do we have for thinking that judges would be *motivated* to adopt and enforce one of such views? What reasons would we have for thinking that our favourite theory would come to be the dominant theory among the community of judges? The functioning of our democracy cannot be dependent on the good luck of having a judge who acts in a way we believe is better for democracy.

Formal and informal constraints over judges

In the section above, we examined some interesting theories regarding the role that judges could reasonably play in a democracy. As we pointed out, however, the 'success' of these theories depended on the judges' willingness to abide by one of them. I am now going to explore some formal and informal remedies that, supposedly, may give incentives to judges, in order to adopt 'routes' like the one described (ensure the preconditions of democracy; protect minorities).

One formal constraint over judges would be the democratic right to impeach them. This limitation, however, is not really an interesting one. As we know, the right of impeachment is not only difficult to carry out but also normally reserved to very extreme situations that do not interest us at this stage, namely, situations where the judges commit crimes or openly violate the norms they have to enforce. Another, quasi-formal constraint would be the one imposed by previous judicial decisions. This limitation, which is particularly important in common law systems, is as imperfect as the one established by written laws. In effect, the importance of these limits will depend heavily on the strictness of the interpretative theory in place, and the decision of judges to properly abide by those previous decisions and the interpretative theories that they chose to use.

Another more interesting answer would say that judges are 'naturally' inclined to, say, defend minority rights, given that they are neither elected nor re-elected by the people directly, and consequently do not need to win the people's confidence during their tenure. In this sense, and as a consequence of their 'independence' from majority will, they will be inclined to behave in a way that seems theoretically plausible. Moreover, the defenders of this position may add, judges tend to use the best arguments available in order to gain reputation, and/or win their discussions with their peers. Now, it seems clear that this common view implies an obvious misunderstanding of the situation at stake. In effect, the mere fact that judges do not depend on majoritarian will says nothing about their possible inclination towards protecting minority rights. The judiciary may be independent from the majoritarian will and still be insensitive towards minority interests. We may reasonably associate 'majoritarianism' with a certain hostility towards minorities, but we cannot associate judicial independence from the majority will with a proclivity towards defending minority rights. A 'counter-majoritarian' institution may or may not be hostile both towards majority and minority interests. But in the case of judges, we lack the motivational connection that we found in the case of majority institutions ('dependence on the majority' – 'inclination to defend the majority').

Finally, some others may think that judges will be particularly inclined to protect minority interests as a consequence of their peculiar institutional position. These theorists also assume that we neither have nor need to have virtuous or socially committed judges in order to obtain appropriate judicial decisions. Instead, they refer to the institutional conditions under which the courts do their job and that, supposedly, 'move' them to act, reason, and decide in specific ways. For example, Alexander Bickel observes that judges 'have, or should have, the leisure, the training, and the insulation to follow the ways of the scholar in pursuing the ends of government' – which in his opinion, is crucial to sorting out 'the enduring values of society' (Bickel 1978). Owen Fiss seems to defend a similar view. According to him (Fiss 1999: 98–9, emphasis added), there are

> certain procedural norms that have no counterpart in politics ... not just ... the independence of the judiciary from the will of the electorate, so uncharitable these days, but also ... the requirements that judges *must respond to grievances that they might otherwise prefer to ignore, hear from all aggrieved parties,* assume individual responsibility for their decisions, and justify their decisions in terms of publicly accepted norms. Judges engage in a special dialogue with the public. Through

this dialogue they achieve a certain distance from their personal pro- clivities and come face to face with what Mark Tushnet might call uni- versal reason.

Now, the institutional obligation of judges to hear 'all aggrieved parties,' or to 'engage in a special dialogue with the public' (Bickel 1978; Fiss 1999) does not tell us much regarding the way judges tend to act, or the way in which they are actually constrained. For example, for those judges who are personally hostile or unsympathetic towards the rights of certain minorities, the obligation to hear the aggrieved party will surely mean very little. They will probably not see what they do not want to see. Although an adequate institutional system should not accept this outcome as normal, it is hard to see how Fiss would avoid it. In a similar fashion, Fiss's idea of a 'special dialogue' between judges and the public seems also questionable. Clearly, the idea of a dialogue sounds interesting because it appeals to an egalitarian situation where two parties are more or less equally situated and have equal chances of succeeding in the defence of their own arguments. But this idea has no clear resemblance to the legal world where we see different 'players' situated in asymmetrical positions. Judges, in particular, have the (discretionary?) power to accept or reject all the arguments of one of the parts, if they were to decide to do so. They have the chance to simply 'put an end' to the alleged conversation when- ever they want, thus 'imposing' their own view upon us.

Things do not improve substantially by appealing to judges' insulation, to their training, or to the time they have for taking decisions. It is true that the members of the political branches act under different conditions, and that this fact surely has an impact on the content of their respective decisions. However, it is not easy to know whether the aforementioned conditions (time, isolation, experience) would have a 'positive' impact, for example, with regard to the defence of minority rights. This would undoubtedly be the case if we defended 'epistemic elitism,' that is, a posi- tion according to which an isolated, individual reflection, increases the chances to decide impartially. But, as democrats, we should *at least* be equally open to an alternative view that links impartiality with a process of collective reflection.

A lost battle? Judicial motivation and personal commitments

The above analysis helps us recognize how differently we treat judges and politicians and how different are the incentives we provide each of them with. Typically, and through the adoption of electoral mechanisms, we establish very strong incentives for 'forcing' our politicians to act in a certain way. We can select our favourite representatives and reward or punish them according to their behaviour in office. These mechanisms are certainly very imperfect, but nevertheless allow us, as citizens, to somehow 'orient' or control the decisions of our representatives. However, what is true for politicians is not true for judges. There are neither popular elections that allow us to select, reward or punish a judge, nor good institutional means for 'pushing' them to decide in one way or another. This situation re-opens all the risks we have examined above. In effect, given this lack of controls over them, judges may be inclined to play their institutional role out of very unattractive theories about the judicial role, or use very implausible interpretative theories, putting democracy, and with it all the most important legal norms created by the people, at risk.

Of course, there are some good things to say in favour of such a situation. First of all, one may say that judges should never be dependent upon the collective will. Rather, they should be impartial, and placed 'above all interests.' Similarly, one may say that the whole point of having a judicial branch is to prevent our democracy from becoming a 'simple' democracy, that is, one where the majority rules unrestrainedly. If this were the situation, minority rights would be put under the most serious risk: who would then take care of such rights? What would happen if majorities suddenly became moved by passions or oppressive interests? It is just because we want to counteract these possibilities that we create a judiciary like the one described, namely, a judiciary that is 'isolated' from the people, which is not tempted to respond to their more immediate, unreasoned and sudden demands.

Now, all these claims sound very well, but the truth is that they demonstrate less than what they aim to demonstrate. In effect, as we have already suggested, by having a judiciary that does not depend on majority will we do not increase the chances of ensuring respect for minority rights or the preconditions of democracy. Judges do not become 'impartial' as a consequence of not being elected by majorities. They do not tend to rule from a position 'well above all interests' just because we 'disconnect' them from majoritarian pressures. In this way we do nothing to avoid other pernicious influences that may still affect their decisions. For example, one may think that a majority of male judges would be 'naturally' inclined to rule in favour of male interests or, to put it differently, would have problems in properly understanding and balancing women's interests, demands or needs. These judges may be 'independent' from the majority but still be clearly 'partial' in favour of one group within society. Even worse, the fact that judges are so severely separated from the majority may directly affect the impartial character of the judiciary. In this sense, for example, the black majority in South Africa would have good reasons to be afraid of the lack of impartiality of their judges if the main tribunals of their country were totally or almost totally composed of white judges. This would be so even if they knew that their judges were honest and well-educated persons. Of course, nothing prevents a white judge from properly understanding the rights of black people, in the same way that nothing ensures that a female judge will properly understand and defend women's rights. However, the absence of black or female voices within the Court may raise significant doubts regarding the impartiality we were trying to ensure. As Anne Phillips suggested, 'in querying the notion that *only* the members of particular disadvantaged groups can understand or represent their interests [one] might usefully turn this question round and ask whether such understanding or representation is possible without the presence of *any* members of the disadvantaged groups?' (Phillips 1995: 89, n. 12; Kymlicka 1995: 146–7). In sum, it is difficult not to think that judges, in their decisions, will tend to reflect who they are (i.e. white, middle/upper class men) and will have more difficulty in putting themselves in the place of others (i.e. members of a disadvantaged minority).

Given that difficulty, the common claim which says that 'the only thing we need from judges is their competence' is inadequate or incomplete. Nothing guarantees us that non-elected, isolated, and well-educated judges will act in a reasonably impartial way. In this sense, an article such as Article 39 (3) of the European Convention of Human Rights seems to be too limited, when it says that candidates for election shall be 'of high moral character and must either possess the qualifications required for appointment to high judicial office or be jurisconsults of recognised competence.' Granted, the conditions included in this article may be conditions necessary to achieve impartial outcomes. However, these conditions also seem very inadequate for obtaining what we want from judges: we want them to be motivated to decide in certain ways, i.e. to give special protection to powerless minorities.

Now, could someone still insist, against our claims, that the judiciary should be examined in a totally different way? Would it be reasonable to say, for example, that the very idea of 'motivating' judges, i.e. by giving them incentives to become the 'voice' of disadvantaged groups, already represents a violation of impartiality? I do not think so, particularly when we are studying European Courts, such as the European Court of Justice. As we know, Article I-28–2 of the draft Constitution states that 'The Court of Justice shall consist of one judge from each Member State.' It seems apparent that we do not see these provisions as unfair but, by contrast, as an expression of our commitment to the equal respect of each of the affected parties. It seems apparent, then, that the choice of having one judge from each country seems clearly in tension with the proclaimed ideas that judges should be 'above' all interests, that the judiciary should not be treated as a 'representative' body, that impartiality has nothing to do with personal inclinations. Clearly, it seems that we emphasize a certain view about impartiality in our public discourse, while applying a different view when we have to organize our institutional system. The fact seems to be that, if we care about impartiality we must care about the personal characteristics of the judges, not only about, say, their legal knowledge or academic qualifications. We care, and should care, about the importance of 'motivating' them in the right way, taking note, for example, of their race, gender, or social origin.

A brief conclusion

In these pages, I have tried to demonstrate the importance we attribute to the fact of having 'properly motivated' judges, even though our legal discourse tends to obscure that fact. I believe that we, as members of a legal community, are always trying to restrict judges' margins of discretion and 'orient' their decisions in certain directions. What seems clear is that in actual practice we apply ideas that we do not consistently defend in theory, namely that impartiality requires judges to be equally detached from all interests. Of course, to motivate judges in the 'proper way' is a very difficult task requiring serious theoretical reflection, and complex practical choices. We still do not know exactly how to guarantee the impartiality of judges. Moreover, we know that many of the attempts made to put judges on the 'right track' have already failed. My suggestion is, however, that – particularly during this constitutional process – we should not give up our efforts, in spite of the uncertainties we confront and our past failures. Significant institutional changes are still required at the level of the judiciary, if we want to honour our idea of living in a democratic community.

Conclusion

Andreas Follesdal and Lynn Dobson

Our chapters illustrate a point made often, but perhaps most eloquently by John Maynard Keynes over 50 years ago:

> the ideas of economists and political philosophers, both when they are right and when they are wrong, are more powerful than is commonly understood. Indeed the world is ruled by little else. I am sure that the power of vested interests is vastly exaggerated compared with the gradual encroachment of ideas ... soon or late, it is ideas, not vested interests, which are dangerous for good or evil.
>
> (Maynard Keynes 1953: 383–4)

His point of course is that the ideas of political philosophy are more powerful than is commonly understood. Many politicians and practitioners are hardly aware that they experience their worlds, goals and options on the basis of academics' speculations, often of years or generations back. But this might explain much in the Constitution – not least its endorsement of 'participatory democracy' in apparent disregard of both the conditions it would need in order to be practicable and the specific democratic goods it aims to secure.

The appropriate role of a constitution

Among the roles of a constitution is the securing of stability. The Constitution – if it goes ahead – will serve as the shared operating system of the Union, enabling longer-term commitments and plans. It will also provide a framework for continued deliberation, debate, agreement, disagreement, and negotiation about the legitimate ends and means of European public power. Acquiescence with normative principles supporting a particular constitution does not mean the end of politicking. Rather, it constrains conflict over ground rules: agreement on the central objectives and features of political co-existence helps provide citizens with trust in, and trustworthiness from, their institutions. Far from heralding the end of political processes, this convergence on constitutional rules – and on rules for effecting constitutional change – reinforces reliance on the future compliance of others with the results of such processes. On this view a legitimate constitution is not the triumph of deliberating over bargaining. Instead, while securing means for preference formation vis-à-vis the common good, it also specifies fair bargaining advantages within the political process (see Dahl 1956: 157), including human rights constraints over legislators' and governments' day-to-day decisions – and mechanisms for tracking fairness through informed discussion in, for example, civil society. To help stabilize legitimate normative expectations, the constitution must provide institutional mechanisms preventing unintentional and unexpected drastic changes in the political order or deviations from shared norms of legitimacy, while allowing that order to adjust to new circumstances and remain legitimate in the eyes of its citizens.

Such challenges are particularly daunting for quasi-federal political orders such as the EU. First, they tend to be marked by deep tensions from the outset. Federations typically arise when states come together, or a single state splits up, in circumstances where governments seek to maintain some common areas of action while allowing diversity in others. To maintain such a multi-level arrangement in the EU two risks must be avoided. The political order must neither unravel into completely independent units, nor must it centralize competences to such an extent that the EU becomes a unitary state whose units enjoy only powers delegated to them from the centre. Does the draft Constitutional Treaty move in directions securing such stability as a matter of institutional design, and at the same time foster sufficient support among elites and citizenry?

According to our authors, the glass is at best half full. The draft Constitution increases the empirical plausibility of describing the EU as a federation, in that it has a constitutionally entrenched division of competences between central and sub-unit political authorities. However, the large scope of 'shared' competences indicates that the EU may continue to be characterized by multi-level negotiated decision-making, typical of 'cooperative federalism' (Scharpf 1994) rather than cleanly demarcated allocations of competences – and attendant political responsibilities. This leads Schmitter to insist that new modes of accountability may also have to be developed.

Constitutional design contributes to political stability in several ways. Regarded as a nascent federation, McKay identified three salient issues for the EU: *constitutional design rules, constitutional principles and modes of representation.* Since a constitution is to be regarded largely as a co-ordination device, it should focus on the basic aspects of the relationships between institutions rather than address measures more appropriately dealt with by legislative and judicial bodies. The challenge is to foster the bargaining and coalition-building required for a flexible, self-sustaining political order. The draft Constitutional Treaty does include mechanisms that may prevent secessionist and centralizing tendencies, both for elites and for citizenry (McKay). Incentives to secede are limited by member states having influence over common decisions. The draft Constitution recognizes states' rights to block further transfers of competences and codifies the right to withdraw. At the same time, central authorities are constitutionally prevented from infringing on member states' competences – though we will only be able to assess the real degree of prevention once legal interpretations are made. Indeed, a stable federal future for the EU is at odds with the Preamble's claim that 'the peoples of Europe are determined, ... *united ever more closely*, to forge a common destiny.'[1] A federal structure can survive only so much unity before transforming into a unitary state.

One threat to long-term support for EU decisions is suspicion about variable implementation and compliance: even citizens and politicians prepared to follow legitimate rules may refrain if they doubt others' compliance. Schmitter, drawing on Tocqueville, notes that this risk remains as long as the EU lacks independent means for enforcement but must rely on member states' means of legal coercion. The representation of member states' political elites in EU decision-making bodies may help foster their 'overarching loyalty' to 'European interests', as some research indicates (Egeberg 1999). But elite socialization is not enough. The citizenry must also support European integration enough to accept the treaties, respect other Europeans and their interests sufficiently to comply with EU-based rules, and must not abuse their political power when electing politicians who will have to be capable of cooperating with their European colleagues. As Schmitter notes, an overarching identity among Europeans is rudimentary, at best. Would the Constitution, as drafted, facilitate and maintain a political culture conducive to adequate levels of trust between EU citizens and in their institutions? Optimists may draw support from Kraus's intimations of mediating mechanisms between diverse collective identities. Concretely, they may point to the expanding roles of the European Parliament and national parliaments in EU decisions. In this cross-arena activity and the increasing inter-parliamentary communication likely to follow may lie the beginnings of a European 'public sphere'. Pessimists may point to the Convention discussions that revealed deep disagreements concerning the popular value base and objectives of the Union (Olsen), indicating that there is some way to go before citizenry and elites find common ground.

While the draft Constitutional Treaty goes some distance in laying out the objectives of the Union, it is not clear that these articles give sufficient sense of direction and purpose to regulate political debates and foster general compliance with common decisions. Continued deep disagreements – exacerbated by asymmetries, as in the Euro-zone – may foster distrust and hence longer term instability. Agreements would help reduce the risks of abuse by majorities and veto players alike. If an important condition of general support for the EU's political order is a clearly agreed '*telos*', the constitutional process and the draft Constitutional Treaty seems unfinished.

The process of constitutionalization

A fundamental issue is why the EU should develop a written constitution by that name now. Schmitter points to several crucial challenges when trying to put the new political object that is the EU into the old conceptual shape of federalism. Agreement on the proper purposes of the political order is absent, hindering reasoned allocation of competences; the requisite trust in the efficacy of central-cum-member-state authorities is not evident, rendering variable implementation a real risk. A central question remains unanswered: if a written EU constitution by that name is the solution, what is the problem (see Follesdal 2002)? Nevertheless, a constitutional treaty is what we have before us. This raises questions about the genesis of the text.

First, what 'temper of mind' should motivate *conventionnels* (Mill 1958: Ch. 12)? How should they adjudicate between the interests of the institutions and electorate they 'represent' and the interests of other Europeans? Hard, fast, and allegedly exhaustive analytical oppositions between 'arguing', involving the giving of other-regarding reasons, versus 'bargaining', involving the conceding of self-interested goods, seems an unsatisfactory way to describe real exchanges, as well as being theoretically uninteresting (Elster 1998). And the customary normative evaluations of these – arguing better, bargaining worse – appear simply naïve in a setting like the EU where the bargaining 'self' is already collective, and the goods at stake are already normatively inscribed and lay claim (justifiable or not) to a normative defence.

As Bellamy and Schönlau explore in their chapter, such considerations may underdetermine the 'common good', the principles for assessing institutions to secure it, and also the particular arrangements satisfying such principles – so leaving much room for legitimate bargaining. The compromises witnessed in the Convention may not be regrettable sacrifices to the non-ideal real world of European politics but perfectly honourable modes of what is ultimately still cooperative activity. If so, more work is required in order to specify the proper and improper places of consensus and bargaining (and their alternatives) about and within institutions and constitutions. Bellamy and Schönlau supplement Dahl: as well as an agreed frame within which bargaining can occur, a constitution also supplies the setting for ongoing compromises concerning the rules of the game themselves. Empirical and normative analyses of EU constitutionalization must therefore heed both its social structural conditions and its temporality. It may well be, as Schmitter suggests, that only a more protracted and fitful process that succeeds in engaging special interests and citizens at various stages will assure a legitimate constitutionalization of the EU. On this reading the current Constitution is better seen as an important landmark in the journey than its terminus.

That journey may have to countenance the revisiting of issues deemed too contentious to acknowledge, as well as those embraced in an incautious rush of enthusiasm – as the chapters by Bellamy and Schönlau, Dobson, McKay, Naurin, Olsen, Smismans, and Tsakatika illustrate in one way or another. When the prevailing norm mandates consensus, on issues where consensus is plainly not to be had it may be difficult to switch to modes of behaviour oriented to sub-optimal outcomes. The result may then turn out to be silence on an issue, in the hope it will go away of its own accord.

The relatively high transparency of the Convention's workings has been regarded as potentially helpful to legitimacy. As commentators and analysts we should be careful to examine how and when the transparency of political exchanges – however exchanges are characterized – is normatively optimal, and under what conditions it is not. 'Purifying' effects on policy outputs are heavily contingent on institutional intricacies in general, and quite possibly for the Convention in particular. Naurin suggests that the 'cleansing' effect of transparency depends on the extent of a collective identity with shared norms and conceptions of the common good, and also the extent of conflicting institutional loyalties – indicating that Council transparency and Commission transparency may have quite different effects. In the absence of a clear European identity and well-functioning accountability mechanisms, transparency may foster divisive politicization and diminish problem-solving abilities.

Other transparency effects are noted by Tsakatika in relation to the open method of coordination's fate in the Convention. First, discussions may be more or less transparent to different audiences: sometimes only elites are able to actually comprehend and interpret the process. Second, transparency may offer a cheap way for participants to be seen to be doing something with an issue without actually resolving anything. Another effect of transparency, witnessed in the Convention, is to drive weighty decisions elsewhere. Though plenary and working group meetings and documents were public, the crucial discussions within the Praesidium on how to structure deliberations and incorporate conflicting views into drafts were not. The indiscriminate pursuit of transparency in all circumstances may mean throwing out the baby with the bathwater.

The various values expressed in the Constitution

Though it is now agreed that the differences between liberal and communitarian conceptions of justice and legitimacy are by no means as stark as once assumed, their commonalities should not overshadow important differences in detail between various thinkers on the roles of shared values in a common political order. That the basic operational capacity and stability of any common political order requires some, albeit parsimonious, values on which citizens can at least converge seems indisputable. But beyond that, we may ask whether such values need to be or ought to be minimal or maximal, thick or thin, perfectionist or neutral, political or comprehensive, procedural or substantive (see Dobson, forthcoming). And these are large differences, from which flow very disparate conceptions of the political, social, and moral order of a polity. It cannot be said that the Convention decided these matters, though some of the fault-lines began to emerge, and the ranges over which disagreement and agreement will in future play hove just a little more clearly into view. So we have no final answers to questions, but contours for continuing debate.

The Union's values, as stated in Article 2, are: respect for human dignity, liberty, democracy, equality, the rule of law and respect for human rights.

Human dignity

The Convention was much exercised about whether to introduce a reference to God in the draft Constitution and give special recognition to the Christian tradition and the work of the churches as essential to European moral and societal life; or, alternatively, to hold that the equal dignity of all Europeans required the Union to maintain neutrality with respect to fundamental values among contested religious and philosophical views. The Convention arrived at what we may see as a 'pruned communitarianism', possibly consistent with plausible versions of liberalism, in which common values were posited as necessary for stability and articulated without any of their controversial premises: an overlapping consensus on surface values supported across diverging deeper values. This mix may well prove destabilizing once values have to be interpreted – as for instance in determining whether a member state is in risk of a serious breach in accordance with Article 58.

Liberty

The draft Constitutional Treaty secures a variety of liberties worth protecting and promoting. Dobson identifies at least three conceptions of these: non-interference, non-domination, and enhanced capability sets. The Constitution may secure non-interference by means including human rights constraints on member states and on the Union bodies, widely dispersed veto points, low thresholds for blocking coalitions, competences reserved for member states, and the conferral, subsidiarity, and proportionality principles. Non-domination, meaning freedom from structural potentials for arbitrary interference, is served by active citizenship and institutionally by the separation, checking, and mixing of institutional powers – for instance by providing national parliaments with watchdog functions and ensuring different kinds of representation. Individuals' interests in capabilities worth having are promoted by EU action in pursuit of shared objectives on the basis of qualified majority decision-making and effective parliamentary majoritarianism if appropriately linked to pan-EU majorities. Discrepancies between citizens' liberties and those of their governments require further analysis, as do the grounds and scope for claims to immunity for the 'internal affairs' of member states (and indeed legislative regions). Difficult trade-offs also remain between various kinds of liberty. One is how domination over some member states and citizens by others might be prevented, while joint action capacity to pursue commonly valued goals in areas where inaction or coordinated efforts are unavailing might, at the same time, be enabled. This is a tall order. It recalls an old tension in democratic theory, with interesting added twists noted in the literature on federalism. Thus Stepan (1999, 2001) observes that 'coming together' federations among previously sovereign polities typically have constitutions that seek to *constrain* the use of public power, protecting individuals and sub-units from abuse by the centre. Federations emerging from unitary states, on the other hand, typically have constitutions seeking to maintain the capacities for common action. Such 'demos-enabling' arrangements typically rely more on majority rule. It remains to be seen whether the Constitution supplies the right mix of liberties, for individuals and member states, for the Union to succeed.

Democratic equality

Title VI of the draft Constitutional Treaty endorses three principles of democratic rule, namely democratic equality (Art. 44), representative democracy (Art. 45) and participatory democracy (Art. 46). Unfortunately, the draft provides little guidance when it comes to managing the tensions between these three. With regard to the first two, the draft does little to justify why citizens enjoy differently weighted representation at the Union level depending on the population size of their state. Small member states are over-represented in the European Parliament, and their votes are weighted disproportionately in the European Council and the Council of Ministers. This seems on the face of it a blatant violation of the principle of 'one person, one vote'. Arguments defending this as vital for rough equality regarding promotion of the interests of each citizen incorporate unwarranted assumptions that state borders also delineate populations with significantly different interests and concerns (Follesdal 1997, Kraus, this volume).

As to tensions between the principle of participatory democracy and the two other democratic principles, the draft Constitutional Treaty simply fails to indicate how to adjudicate conflicts between them. Judging from past experience, it seems clear that while the Commission maintains formal equality of access and indeed goes out of its way to recruit under-privileged groups, access depends heavily on actors' organizational resources, and these are heavily skewed toward some kinds of actors (Streeck and Schmitter 1991). The draft Constitution identifies the social partners, churches and non-confessional organizations as participants in participatory democracy, but it remains to be seen which other organizations will be included and also whether non-organized citizens with pressing interests will be able to make their voices heard as political equals through such 'participation'. Smismans argues that one reason for the unresolved tensions is vagueness concerning what makes participation – and dialogue – particularly democratic or otherwise respectable. It might also be said the Commission's understanding of 'representation' is at variance with that in the main traditions of Anglophone political philosophy, which by contrast are generally hostile to the notion of bureaucrats, enlisted experts, and special interests claiming representative authority on behalf of citizens at large. The ideals and standards of representative democracy are not themselves sufficiently well understood for a multi-level context, and adding participatory democracy as an ideal in this way will almost certainly import more confusion.

Rule of law and human rights

A constitution typically includes human rights clauses. In a quasi-federal arrangement, such rights may in principle play different roles – suggesting that the lists of rights should vary appropriately. One important role of an EU human rights catalogue would be to constrain member states' acts against their citizens, another would be to constrain EU institutions' impact on citizens, and a third function would be to protect member states' cultures – constitutional and otherwise – against encroachment by EU institutions. It is hard to see why these three roles are best served by a uniform schedule of rights. Attucci develops a fourth understanding of human rights standards as found in the Charter which may thereby serve as a framework for the constitutional politics of the EU and of the member states, seeking to maintain unity and diversity, universal principles and particularist practices – and universal practices and particularist principles. Thus, alleged conflicts between universal rights and particularist cultures merit revision. Her contribution also repeats a general lesson for normative political theory. The emergence of a new political order in Europe requires that established concepts be applied to yet another subject, but also requires a return to the fundamental issues of political theory, in order to understand better how – for example – human dignity might be best expressed in a new European order seeking to maintain unity in diversity.

Constitutions may provide the framework for continuing political jousting, they may secure the flexibility and space needed for inter-elite interaction and innovation, they may aim to distribute freedoms and powers and guarantee rights, but much that is politically consequential hangs not on their writing but on their reading. Central to constitutional legitimacy are: who interprets the Constitution? On what grounds do they base their interpretive strategies, and what are the consequences for inter-group balances of power? Gargarella reminds us of the risks involved in constitutional interpretation, which will surely arise regarding the constitution in general – whichever *de facto* constitution the EU ends up with – and the Charter on Fundamental Rights in particular. Should judges be the voice of powerless minorities, and should we find ways to ensure that judges reinforce democracy? What might that mean in the absence of consensus about democracy? Here, difficult and controversial issues emerge regarding the behaviour and values of judges in general and the behaviour and values of judges in multinational multi-level orders in particular. These are problems deserving more examination.

Final reflections

Some conclusions are germane to both EU politics and political theorists. For instance, many of the theoretical dichotomies that enjoy prominence in academic and political discussions – liberal versus communitarian, bargaining versus arguing, European interest versus national interest, rights versus values, universalism versus particularism – merit further refinement. Our papers show that though standard fare in normative political theory, once we try to understand them in a setting like the EU these distinctions are not so clear, so stable, nor so unidimensional, as sometimes portrayed. If we are to develop a sophisticated appreciation of normative issues in a multi-perspectival polity we may have to accept that our task lies less in specifying 'either/or' and more in specifying 'to what degree, in what combination, and in which circumstances', and defending our answers with clarity and rigour.

The Convention model, as we said in our Introduction, brought EU 'history-making' decisions (Peterson and Bomberg 1999) nearer to the 'ideal speech situation' or to mirroring arguments in a variant of an 'original position'. But naturally the Convention's workings departed significantly from either heuristic. *Conventionnels* were sometimes dealing with stakes perceived as so vital or commitments so profound that where the force of the better argument seemed against them, so much the worse for its unforced force. Nor could members continue deliberations until consensus was ultimately achieved – and some, no doubt, had everything to gain by holding out until time was up. As to the original position, *conventionnels* were far from standing behind a veil of ignorance as to their own positions, allegiances, and interests. This does not just mean they were unable to shuck off values; it means also they had a *status quo ante* to compare with prospective constitutional outcomes, and a *status quo* they could – and perhaps ought to – fall back to in the event that discussions became unprofitable. So we should temper our welcome of the Convention's qualities as a deliberative forum with acknowledgements of the limits both of deliberation and of the Convention.

Welcome, though, it deserves. The Convention was not the ideal speech community nor the meeting in the original position, but it was not Robinson Crusoe's state of nature, either. Members did not arrive with national values to stockade against predators or interests to trade as if they were cowrie shells. If the Constitutional Convention shows us anything, it surely shows us that the analytic and evaluative distinctions between self-regarding (bad) and other-regarding (good) motives and actions need something of an overhaul. And where *conventionnels* did appeal to European goods it seems they redefined, and shifted, interpretive emphases, not from self-regarding perspectives, but rather between different types of 'other-regardingness': from that of a confined 'other', to that of an enlarged 'other'. Any eventual EU Constitution, then, should not be expected to promulgate a schedule of perfectionist values we must from henceforth call 'the common good', though it might facilitate working agreements on specific goods in the common interest where EU citizens agree there manifestly is one. Another accomplishment beyond constitutional ambition is the suppression or negation of conflict: an uncontested democratic political order is an oxymoron as well as a chimera. What the Constitution might legitimately do is provide resources for managing conflicts so they do not spill their bounds and poison otherwise productive, worthwhile, and indefinitely extendable relationships. Our authors, then, have not explored the presumed ideal character of 'Europe'. Instead we addressed the important interplay between normative standards and institutional design, committed to detailed, creative, and informed normative scrutiny of institutions for democratic cooperation and contestation.

Notes

Introduction

1 Participating states comprised: 15 member states, 10 states that acceded to the Union in May 2004, and 3 (Bulgaria, Romania, and Turkey) that may form the next tranche of members.

2 There were some changes to the Convention's membership during its 15 month course but, since none of them seems to have substantially altered its composition, a 'snapshot' taken at any point in time gives a sufficiently accurate picture of the Convention overall. These figures derive from our analysis of the very useful 'Who's Who in the Convention on the Future of the European Union', 12 June 2003, an unofficial photo-album cum directory compiled on his own initiative by Ries Baeten (rbaeten@europarl.eu.int), whom we thank.

1 Is Euro-federalism a solution or a problem? Tocqueville inverted, perverted or subverted?

1 The initial indications suggest that it is much more likely that it will be 'watered down' rather than 'souped up' and, therefore, that its contribution to the federalizing of the Euro-polity will be even less than agreed upon by '*les conventionnels.*'

2 Tocqueville was, to put it mildly, not favourably impressed by the Swiss: 'As *un american*, I have developed such an utter disdain for the federal constitution of Switzerland, that I would unequivocally term it a league and not a federation. A government of that nature is certainly the weakest, the most impotent, the clumsiest and the least capable of leading its people anywhere except to anarchy, that one could imagine. I am also struck by the lack of any *vie politique* in its population. The Kingdom of England is a hundred times more republican than this republic.' (My translation from *Oeuvres Completes, Vol. XV*, 1: 70–1). This was written in 1836 after living several months there. Elsewhere, in a letter, he opined '[In Switzerland] power was exercised in the name of the people, but placed very far from it and handed over completely to executive authority . . . . The principle of the division of powers has been acknowledged by all *publicistes*, but it does not apply in Switzerland. Freedom of the press did not exist – neither in fact nor in law; the ability to form political associations was neither exercised nor recognized; and freedom of speech was restricted there within very strict limits . . . . Even if the Confederation had its own executive power, it would have been too impotent to make itself obeyed since it lacked the capacity to act directly and immediately upon the citizens' (*Oeuvres Complètes, Vol. XVI*: 203–20). This was written in 1848 shortly before the new Swiss constitution was ratified.

3 Note that I have not included the proviso that at least some of these *compétences* must be exclusive. In the oft-cited definition of William Riker, federalism is contingent upon a division of the activities of government 'in such a way that each kind of government has some activities on which it makes final decisions.' ('Federalism,' in F. Greenstein and N. W. Polsby (eds) *Handbook of Political Science*, Vol. 5, Reading, MA: Addison-Wesley, 1975: 101). This reflects a distinctively American view of the phenomenon. In European federations – whatever the formal provisions – the actual practice is more 'cooperative' in which the different levels interact both horizontally and vertically to produce policies.

4 'Federalism,' in *Handbook of Political Science*.

5 (2000) *How to Democratize the European Union . . . and Why Bother?* Lanham, MD: Rowman & Littlefield.

6 My hunch is that it is precisely the search for such an alternative basis of legitimacy that is behind the currently fashionable discussion of 'governance.' See my 'What is there to legitimize in the European Union . . . and how might this be accomplished?', in *Europe 2004 – Le Grand Debat. Setting the Agenda and Outlining the Options*, symposium proceedings 16 October 2001 (Brussels: Commission of the European Communities) – also published in C. Joerges, Y. Mény, J. H. H. Weiler (eds) *Mountain or Molehill? A Critical Appraisal of the Commission White Paper on Governance*, Jean Monnet Working Paper series, no. 6/01 of Harvard Law School.

7 Even the one case that had lasted the longest, Switzerland, Tocqueville dismissed on the grounds that the survival of that country's institutions was more a result of its neighbours' bungling than its citizens' virtues.

8 Tocqueville made the brilliant observation that Maine and Georgia were 4,000 kilometres apart and yet the social and cultural differences between their inhabitants were less than those that divided Normandy from Brittany, two French provinces that were only separated by a small brook. Leaving aside the fact that Tocqueville was not very well informed about the US Deep South and that Maine and Georgia did find themselves subsequently on different sides of a civil war, I wonder what he would say today about the differences between, say, Malmö and Madrid as compared to Minneapolis and Miami!

9 Which is precisely what Tocqueville regarded as one of the key weaknesses of the entire federalist project: 'As a rule, only simple propositions are capable of being grasped by popular imagination (*l'ésprit du peuple*) . . . and (in a federal system), everything is artificial and by convention.' (*Oeuvres Completes*, Vol. I, 1, 168–9).

10 The problem with the Convention is rather the reverse. It made extensive efforts via the Internet to keep its deliberations open and easily available to the citizens of Europe. Except for a select number of units of national and transnational civil society, the addressees of this effort showed very little interest in following what was going on in the Convention or in its eventual draft.

11 The fact that several of these constitutional drafts have come out of the European Parliament and that one of their most manifest objectives was to increase the powers of that very same institution suggests that 'institutional' – if not 'personal' – self-interest cannot be ruled out of the process.

12 Strategic choice in this domain is limited by one overriding 'peculiarity' of the EU, namely, its foundation in a series of international treaties. Any substantial change in rules would no doubt require not only the unanimous agreement of all members (although that might be finessed by leaving some out and moving ahead with a more compact 'core' group), but would have to go through a lengthy and uncertain process of ratification, first by national parliaments and second by national referenda (at least, in several member states). This intrinsic

cumbersome-ness places a considerable premium on coming up with reforms in the rules that, while democratic in nature, can still be implemented within the existing framework of treaties.

13 For an exploration of specific reforms in citizenship, representation and decision-making that might conduce to such an outcome, see my (2000) *Come democratizzare l'Unione Europea . . . e perché* (Bologna: Il Mulino), or (2000) *How to Democratize the European Union . . . and why bother?* (Lanham, MD: Rowman & Littlefield).

2 The EU as a self-sustaining federation: specifying the constitutional conditions

1 Indeed it is unhelpful to label the EU a confederation because it places the EU in the wrong analytic category. Comparing the EU with (say) the US under the Articles of Confederation, the early Swiss Confederation and other leagues and associations, tells us little because in all these cases the scope of central (federal) government power was so limited that unilateral state action, sometimes including secession, could go unpunished.

2 Although there may be variations according to whether member state governments were made up of coalitions or plurality administrations. Legislatures characterized by strong party discipline would presumably be more likely to act as delegates of incumbent governments.

3 The notable exception is, of course, the British Conservative Party, although no incumbent Conservative Government has been explicitly anti-EU.

4 In the Belgian case constitutional changes involving federal arrangements have actually increased the communal base of the main parties (see Fitzmaurice 1996).

5 These are the empirical cases used by Filippov *et al.* (Page nos refer to ms.) In addition these and other scholars tend to use the United States as the most relevant comparator state. Given the relatively centralized nature of the US Constitution, however, the utility of this comparison is limited.

6 To be fair these proposals involve not a centralization of taxes as such, but the imposition of central controls on the parameters available to national tax authorities.

7 The latter is unusual in federation, although for most of its history the Australian Labour Party supported the abolition of Australian federalism, mainly because it viewed federal arrangements as obstacles to centralized redistributive policies (see Holmes and Sharman 1977).

3 A union of peoples? Diversity and the predicaments of a multinational polity

1 For a stimulating picture of the impact of cultural pluralism on the societal configuration of Central Europe in the late Habsburg period see Csáky (1999).

2 See the largely converging assessments on the effects of different forms of pronounced cultural pluralism on democracies offered by Dahl (1971), Rustow (1975) or Stepan (2001). An orthodoxly liberal normative view of the problems of cultural pluralism is put forward by Sartori (2000).

3 'Our Constitution . . . is called a democracy because power is in the hands not of a minority but of the greatest number.' The European Convention, The Secretariat, July 2003: Draft Treaty establishing a Constitution for Europe, Preamble. http://european-convention.eu.int/docs/Treaty/cv00850.en03.pdf

4 Hallstein (1973: 112) – original text in German.

5 The 'identity strategies' worked out by European institutions during the last three decades are discussed in Dewandre and Lenoble (1994), García (1993) and in Stråth (2000).

6 Under Part Three (The Policies and Functions of the Union), Title III, Chapter V, Section 3, Article III-181.

7 See Delanty (1995) and Shore (2000) for critical evaluations of these initiatives.

8 At least, this is the impression one gets when studying the results of recent Eurobarometer surveys. According to the findings of Eurobarometer 54, published in April 2001 by the European Commission, the Union citizens conceiving of themselves as predominantly European are still a small minority. The overall identification with Europe does not seem to have been increasing during the last decade. Apparently, support for membership has even declined in some key member states, such as the FRG.

9 This section draws on Kraus (2004).

10 For instance, this message was one of the central components of the famous speech delivered by the German Minister of Foreign Affairs Joschka Fischer at Berlin's Humboldt University in May 2000; see Fischer (2000).

11 As is emphasized by the 'federation of nation-states' formula, that seems to have become the catchphrase in recent debates on the political perspectives of the EU; see the interview with Jacques Delors published in *Le Monde*, 19 January 2001.

12 A suggestive interpretation of the EU as a post-sovereign political community is presented by MacCormick (1999: 123–36); Preuß (1999) gives a similar account.

13 See the directly-deliberative polyarchy models put forward by Cohen and Sabel (1997) or Gerstenberg and Sabel (2002). In a volume devoted to the topic of deliberative democracy in the EU edited by Eriksen and Fossum (2000) the issue of the infrastructural preconditions of transnational communication, intimately linked to the whole complex of language politics in Europe, gets only scant attention.

14 A general overview of the different uses of the concept of subsidiarity in political theory can be found in Follesdal (1998).

15 The relevance of recognition for sustaining an open intercultural dialogue on constitutional issues is cogently elucidated in the work of James Tully (1995). See also Gagnon and Tully (2001) and Taylor (1994).

16 Honneth (2003), consequently, argues that recognition must be considered a central element of an emancipatory understanding of politics.

4 The Good, the Bad and the Ugly: the need for constitutional compromise and the drafting of the EU Constitution

1 Lijphart's (1984: 156–60) analysis of 21 stable democracies revealed only six as conforming to this pattern.

2 For the features conducive to deliberation, see Elster (1998).

3 Though as Shaw (2003a) notes, significant groups remained underrepresented. See also Dobson and Follesdal's Introduction, this volume.

5 Europe: united under God? Or not?

1 A theoretical example could be Rawls's (1972) two principles of justice, which are guidelines for the 'basic structure' of his liberal society, including its constitution. Another more concrete example could be Ackerman's (1991) 'dual

federalism'. A public philosophy could also be called the 'political theory' behind the constitution (Murphy 1993).

2 'What is supported gets modified by how it is supported; the nature of the justification affects what it is that is justified' (Gaus 1997: 223–4).

3 Bonde, Convention plenary, 27 February 2003.

4 Zieleniec (Parl, CZ, Civic Democrats), Convention plenary, 27 February 2003.

5 In this very broad definition of liberalism Habermas would fit even though he does not identify himself as a liberal (Habermas 1994).

6 Fini (Govt, IT) Convention plenary, 27 February 2003. See also Taylor (1989b).

7 See Habermas (1996a: Ch. 6) in which he outlines such a view of the constitution, which he calls 'republican'. I prefer 'communitarian'.

8 Haenel (Parl, FR, Groupe Union pour un Mouvement Populaire), Convention plenary, 27 February 2003.

9 Amato, vice president of the Praesidium, Convention plenary, 25 April 2003

10 The value article is supposed to take over the function of Art. 6.1 TEU.

11 In particular Hain (2003). See also the interventions by Kalniete (Govt, LV), Heathcoat-Amory (Parl, UK, Conservative), Kirkhope (EP, UK, EPP/ Conservative), Skaarup (Parl, DK), Hololei (Govt, EE) in the Convention plenaries on the 27 and 28 February 2003.

12 See e.g. Brok (EP, DE) *et al.* (2003), EPP Group in the Convention, and Fayot (Parl, LU, Socialist) in plenary debate, 27 February 2003.

13 Giscard D'Estaing, Convention plenary, 27 February 2003.

14 E.g. Kiljunen (Parl, FI, Social Democrat), Convention plenary, 25 April 2003.

15 E.g. Brok, Convention plenaries, 27 February 2003 and 25 April 2003 and Lobo Antunes, Convention plenary, 25 April 2003. See also Santer (Govt, LU, EPP) *et al.* (2003).

16 Zieleniec (Parl, CZ), Convention plenary, 7 November 2002.

17 See e.g. Fayot (Parl, LU), Meyer (Parl, DE, SPD), De Villepin (Govt, FR), Borrell Fontelles (Parl, ES, Socialist). Hjelm-Wallén (Govt, SE) in the Convention plenary, 27 February 2003. See Shaw (2003b) for background and discussion of the Working Group on Social Europe.

18 What was previously called the 'co-decision' procedure has been renamed 'the ordinary legislative procedure' and has been introduced in 46 new decision-making areas (policy areas), whereby this procedure applies in 75 per cent (81 policy areas) of all decision-making areas (total = 108). Likewise, the draft Constitution suggests that the Council moves from unanimity to qualified majority voting in 26 decision areas as well as in 12 completely new decision areas (Folketingets Europaudvalg 2003a, 2003b).

19 Baroness Scotland of Asthal (Govt, UK, Labour), Convention plenary, 27 February 2003

20 Rupel (Govt, SI), Brejc (Parl, SI) Convention plenary, 27 February 2003.

21 Duff *et al.* (2003), see Kiljunen, Convention plenaries, 27 February 2003 and 28 February 2003.

22 Convention plenary, 27 February 2003.

23 Tajani (EP, IT), Convention plenary, 27 February 2003.

24 Tajani (EP, IT), Convention plenary, 27 February 2003.

25 Follini (Parl, IT, Christian Democrats). Convention plenary, 27 February 2003, my translation.

26 Skaarup (Parl, DK) Convention plenary, 27 February 2003, my translation.

27 Paciotti (EP, IT), Convention plenary, 27 February 2003, my translation.

28 Kaufmann (EP, DE), Convention plenary, 27 February 2003.

29 De Rossa (Parl, IE), Convention plenary, 27 February 2003.

30 Haenel (Parl, FR), Convention plenary, 27 February 2003.

31 Haenel (Parl, FR), Convention plenary, 24 April 2003.
32 See Paciotti (EP, IT), Convention plenary, 6 June 2003, and De Rossa (Parl, IE) (2003).

7 Conceptions of freedom and the European Constitution

1 Thanks to ECPR workshop participants, staff and research students of the Department of Politics at Edinburgh, and Richard Bellamy, Andreas Follesdal, and Myrto Tsakatika, for comments.
2 This distinction has been criticized in the theoretical literature, most trenchantly by MacCallum (1967). Berlin's account would need to be severely scrutinized in any extended theoretical treatment of the concept of freedom *simpliciter*, but since this chapter is not such and his essay remains the most cited in the literature, I take it as read here.
3 I have drawn here not only on Hayek's work but also that found in Vanberg and Wagner (eds, 1996).
4 Notwithstanding some commentators' pessimism about the likelihood of transposing social democracy to the supranational level.
5 Speech given by Sir John Kerr, Secretary General of the European Convention, at the University of Edinburgh, 19 November 2003.

8 The constitutional labelling of 'the democratic life of the EU': representative and participatory democracy

1 I would like to thank Lynn Dobson, Andreas Follesdal and Peter Bonnor for useful comments and Kristin de Peyron for some 'insider information' on the Convention. The usual disclaimer applies.
2 Articles 7 and 308. The Council may decide to suspend certain of the rights deriving from the application of the Treaty to the Member States in question, including its voting rights in the Council. Yet, as Verhoeven (1998b: 224) argues, the *raison d'être* of such a sanction mechanism is comparable to that of atomic bombs: it is the deterrent effect that counts.
3 Also, the Charter of Fundamental Rights does not specify democracy. Like the EU Treaty, its Preamble mentions that the Union is based on the principles of democracy and the rule of law. It does not provide a further definition of the principles of democracy, although its title V dealing with 'citizens' rights' formulates rights such as the right to vote and to stand as candidate at elections to the EP and at municipal elections, right to good administration, right to refer to the Ombudsman, access to documents, and right to petition the EP.
4 Case 194/83 *Parti Ecologiste Les Verts* v *European Parliament* [1986] ECR 1339.
5 Case 9/56, *Meroni* v. *High Authority* [1957 and 1958] ECR 133, at 152.
6 Case 70/88 *Parliament* v *Council* [1990] ECR I-2041.
7 The basic idea is that the procedures, rituals, ideology, and substantive decisions of legal institutions, particularly judicial institutions, shape popular beliefs in the legitimacy of the polity. For the popularity of this idea in American legal theory, and for a critique, see Alan Hyde (1983).
8 Case 138/79, *Roquette Frères* v. *Council* [1980] ECR 3333, at para. 33. Also Case C-300/89 *Commission* v. *Council* [1991] ECR I-2867, para. 20; and Case T-135/96 *UEAPME* v. *Council* [1998] ECR II-2335.
9 See, for instance, Case T-135/96 *UEAPME* v. *Council* [1998] ECR II-2335. While the UEAPME case is 'the exception to the rule' by accepting that social partners' participation can 'replace' the democratic involvement of the parliament, the ruling is traditional in its stress on the need to respect the

institutional balance while not recognizing democratic representative features of institutions other than the EP (or social partners 'taking its place').

10 So too with the introduction by the Treaty of Nice of an article on political parties at the European level. They are said to 'contribute to forming a European awareness and to expressing the political will of the citizens of the Union', whereas the Council is asked to lay down the regulations governing these political parties, in particular regarding funding (article 191 TEC).

11 For instance, at the 1996 IGC, which placed the issue of EU legitimacy at the centre of debate, only Italy and Austria attempted to place the issue of direct democracy on the agenda with the idea of public petitions (Nentwich and Falkner 1997: 17). The European Parliament argued instead for a referendum to be held Union-wide or at national level to ratify any Treaty provisions (see EP 1995).

12 The EESC more openly expresses its doubts on an interpretation of participatory democracy that would try to involve individuals directly through information technology without the intermediary role of civil society organizations. See EESC (2001), para. 3.5.3.

13 Compare with the definition of participatory democracy provided by the EESC (2000), quoted above, and EESC (2002: para. 3.1).

14 For a recent attempt to place 'participation' centre-stage of democratic theory while building bridges with the literature on deliberation and the role of associations, see the model of 'empowered participatory governance' proposed by A. Fung and E.O. Wright (2003).

15 'The correctness of risk decisions cannot be guaranteed by unmediated recourse to interest or their negotiation – or in legal terms, by extending corresponding participation rights and veto positions (. . .). By virtue of its feedback links to Member States [cf. Member States representatives in comitology committee], comitology can, in principle, take all social concerns and interests into account while, at the same time, links with science (seen as a social body) can be shaped so as to allow for the plurality of scientific knowledge to be brought to bear' (Joerges 1999: 334).

16 A Declaration added to the Nice Treaty urged the European Council at its meeting in Laeken in December 2001 to present a declaration containing appropriate initiatives for further institutional reform of the Union. It should in particular tackle the delimitation of competencies between the European Union and the member states, the status of the Charter of Fundamental Rights of the European Union, a simplification of the treaties, and the role of national parliaments in the European architecture.

17 The minimum number of 1 million citizens had not been fixed in Meyer's proposal.

18 Petitions received by the Parliament are forwarded to its 'Committee on Petitions' that decides whether further action is taken; this can take the form of asking the European Commission to provide information, taking account of the petition in the Parliament's legislative activities, submitting a report to be voted in the plenary, or drawing up an opinion and asking the Council and/or Commission to take action.

9 Transparency and legitimacy

1 The concept of 'laundering', which is often used by deliberative theorists, comes so far as I know from Goodin (1986). What Goodin was focusing on in that article, however, was neither arguments, positions or decisions, which are the dependent variables in the discussion on output-effects of transparency, but

preferences. To what extent transparency may promote laundered preferences is a question beyond this chapter, but see for example Elster (1999).

2 For empirical support of how 'rhetorical action' matters, in the way that Elster reasons, by entrapping actors and forcing them to remain consistent in deeds with what they have conceded in words, see Risse (2000) (on human rights) and Schimmelfennig (2001) (on the eastern enlargement of the EU).

3 For a more in-depth analysis and critique of the logic of this causal chain from transparency to policy decisions more in line with the public interest, see Naurin (2003).

4 For an analysis of the question of how 'an institutional frame for transnational communication [can] be created that allows to "transcend" cultural differences without negating them', see Peter Kraus's contribution to this volume.

5 The terminology varies. Fisher *et al.* (1999) speak of 'negotiation on the merits' and 'positional bargaining', Lax and Sebenius (1986) of 'creating value' and 'claiming value', Elgström and Jönsson (2000) of 'problem-solving' and 'bargaining'.

6 In my dissertation I study the effects of transparency on the content of industry lobbyists' 'pressure' on officials in the European Commission and the Swedish government ministries. The dissertation will be finished in 2004.

10 An institutional dialogue on common principles: reflections on the significance of the EU Charter of Fundamental Rights

1 I take the term, though using it in a different context, from Beck (1998: 141–7): see Attucci (2001).

2 See, for example, the right to found a family, Article 9, which does not outlaw, nor demand recognition of, same-sex families.

3 It has been argued that it is rather naïve to expect the current status to remain (e.g. de Búrca 2001a). While I also believe that the Charter will foster an extension of EU competence, this should not follow *de jure*, but from the political and social changes that the Charter can trigger. A shift in the competence of the EU should be seen as the creation of new objectives of the EU (the promotion of human rights) and thus as a new common goal of the member states. While desirable, we need not assume that this simply consists in a transfer of ultimate authority to the ECJ to decide disputed issues concerning human rights.

4 The right to conduct a business (Art. 16), and other rights, including in the Chapter on Solidarity, that would raise doubts were they proclaimed as disentangled from their social structure. As argued elsewhere (Attucci 2001), they may still be rights of the person independently of their legal status or, even less, their citizenship.

5 Cf. Walzer's idea of 'reiterative universalism' as opposed to the traditional 'covering-law universalism' (Walzer 1990).

6 This is often presented as the question of the identity of the EU. I prefer, however, to avoid this terminology, for the idea of political identity is probably still too closely connected with nation-states – see Cerutti (1996, 2001), and Cerutti and Rudolph (2001).

7 I attach a constitutive role to the overlapping consensus, emphasizing the constructivist approach of Rawls's political liberalism, even though Rawls might not have agreed – see Rawls (2001: 188ff). Otherwise other criticisms against dogmatic universalistic assumptions would apply.

8 I cannot discuss here the application of Rawls's idea of political liberalism to states rather than to persons, as in Rawls (1993, 1999). The latter work allows an overlapping consensus in a more extended way than the former.

9 This does not deny that there may be essential needs or functions common to all human beings as the foundation of universal positive human rights but only that they may not exhaust what may be relevant for imposing obligations on another.

10 Nothing of what follows suggests that principles are less important than rights – indeed, they need at some level to be enforced through the definition of a right. On abstract principles in the Charter, see also Walker (2002).

11 Abstract principles still need to be accompanied by enforceable rights. I am only suggesting that institutional common goals may indicate the extent to which the definition of specific rights ought to be transferred at EU level, or even at global level, or remain at national or even subnational level.

12 The principle of non-discrimination is very abstract, but it is not weak, even though it may generate a very different kind of rights. More problematic examples are those provided by those principles that hide within their definition a substantive disagreement that leads to controversy in their translation into rights, such as the right to marriage and to found a family (Art. 9). A harmonized definition of this right at EU level would require a profound transformation of the *finalité* of the EU. The Charter may indeed foster such shift, but I suspect it should not impose it *de jure*, for this would raise dangerous tensions. On the possibility that the Charter expands EU competences and its *finalité*, see de Búrca (2001a).

13 This idea of abstract principles is inspired by Sunstein's idea of incompletely theorized agreement. See Sunstein (1996: 35ff). Similar considerations are put forward by Besson (forthcoming).

14 This comes close to the idea of universalism as a regulative principle, as opposed to the minimum threshold, suggested by Parekh (1999).

15 In many cases the text of the treaties and ordinary legislation may be more appropriate places for this.

16 Though such a view does not dismiss the fact that more precise rights need to be defined in many areas of EU law.

11 Motivating judges: democracy, judicial discretion, and the European Court of Human Rights

1 In the *Golder* case (21 Feb. 1975, n. 18, 1 E.H.R.R. 524), the Court tried to clarify its interpretative position referring to the guidelines for interpretation already established by the Vienna Convention of 1969. Now, those suggestions are tricky in themselves, and in need of their own interpretation and justification.

2 The following examples are taken from Merrills (1993).

3 These cases were about the possibility of invoking human rights in a process before the Court.

Conclusion

1 Emphasis added.

Bibliography

Official sources

The draft Constitution

European Convention (2003) (CONV 850/03) 'Draft Treaty Establishing a Constitution for Europe, adopted by consensus by the European Convention on 13 June and 10 July 2003, submitted to the President of the European Council in Rome 18 July 2003', Brussels: 18 July 2003. Online. Available at: http://www.europa.eu.int/futurum/constitution/index_en.htm (accessed July 2003).

Other documents

Bonde, J.P. *et al.* (2003) 'Amendment for Article 1: Establishment of the European Union', Brussels: European Convention. Online. Available at: http://european-convention.eu.int/amendemTrait.asp?lang=EN (accessed 31 October 2003).

Brok, E. *et al.* (2003) 'Amendment for Article 1: Establishment of the European Union', Brussels: European Convention. Online. Available at: http://european-convention.eu.int/amendemTrait.asp?lang=EN (accessed 31 October 2003).

Cisneros, G.L. (2003) 'Amendment for Preamble', Brussels: European Convention. Online. Available at: http://european-convention.eu.int/amendemTrait.asp?lang=EN (accessed 31 October 2003).

Commission of the European Communities (2001) (COM 428 final) 'White Paper on European Governance', 25 July.

—— (2001) (COM 387 final) 'Communication from the Commission to the Council and the European Parliament', Brussels, 11 July.

—— (2001) (COM 710 final) 'Communication from the Commission to the Council and the European Parliament. On the Common Asylum Policy, Introducing an Open Co-ordination Method', Brussels, 28 November.

—— (2000) (COM 11 final) 'The Commission and Non-Governmental Organisations: Building a Stronger Partnership', Discussion Paper, 18 January.

Committee of the Regions (2002) (Cdr 103/2001 final) 'Opinion on the White Paper on European Governance and the Communication on a New Framework for Cooperation on Activities Concerning the Information and Communication Policy of the European Union', 13 March.

—— (2001) (Cdr 430/2000 final) 'Resolution on the Outcome of the 2000 Intergovernmental Conference and the Discussion on the Future of the European Union', 4 April.

—— (2001) (Cdr 436/2000) 'Report on Proximity', 6 November.

De Rossa, P. (2003) 'Amendment for Preamble', Brussels: European Convention. Online. Available at: http://european-convention.eu.int/amendemTrait.asp?lang=EN (accessed 31 October 2003).

Duff, A. *et al.* (2003) 'Amendment for Article 2: The Union's Values', Brussels: European Convention. Online. Available at: http://european-convention.eu.int/amendemTrait.asp?lang=EN (accessed 31 October 2003).

European Convention (2003) (CONV 674/03) 'Summary Report of the Additional Plenary Session Brussels, 26 March 2003', Brussels, 8 April.

—— (2003) (CONV 724/03) 'Draft Constitution, Volume I – Revised Text of Part One', 26 May.

—— (2003) (CONV 670/03) 'Summary Sheet of the Proposals for Amendments relating to the Democratic Life of the Union: Draft Articles for Part One of the Constitution, Title VI (Articles 33 to 37)', 15 April.

—— (2003) (CONV 650/03) 'Title VI: The Democratic life of the Union', Brussels, 2 April.

—— (2003) (CONV 648/03) 'Title X: Union Membership', Brussels, 2 April.

—— (2003) (CONV 601/03) 'Summary Report on the Plenary Session – Brussels, 27 and 28 February 2003', Brussels, 11 March.

—— (2003) (CONV 574/1/03 REV 1) 'Reactions to Draft articles 1 to 16 of the Constitutional Treaty – Analysis', Brussels, 26 February.

—— (2003) (CONV 528/03) 'Draft of Articles 1 to 16 of the Constitutional Treaty', Brussels, 6 February.

—— (2003) (CONV 516/1/03, REV 1) The Secretariat, 'Final Report of Working Group XI on Social Europe', Brussels, 4 February.

—— (2003) (WG XI/042 REV 1) The Secretariat, 'Comments on the Preliminary Draft Report, Working Group on Social Europe', Brussels, 24 January.

—— (2002) (CONV 424/02) The Secretariat, 'Final Report of Working Group XI on Simplification, WG IX/13', Brussels, 29 November.

—— (2002) (CONV 375/1/02 REV 1) The Secretariat, 'Final Report of Working Group V on Complementary Competencies, WGV/14', Brussels, 4 November.

—— (2002) (CONV 369/02) 'Preliminary Draft Constitutional Treaty', 28 October.

—— (2002) (CONV 357/02) The Secretariat, 'Final Report of Working Group VI on Economic Governance, WG VI/17', Brussels, 21 October.

—— (2002) (CONV 354/02), WG II/16 and Annex, Brussels 22 October.

—— (2002) (CONV 60/02) The Secretariat, 'Note on the Plenary Meeting', Brussels, 29 May.

—— (2002) (WG XI/06) The Secretariat, 'Comments to Points 4, 5, 6 and 7 of the Mandate, Working Group on Social Europe', Brussels, 19 December.

—— (2002) (WG XI/01) The Secretariat, 'Comments to Points 1, 2 and 3 of the Mandate, Working Group on Social Europe', Brussels, 10 December.

—— (2002) (WG VI/014) The Secretariat, 'Report to the Convention by the Working Group on Economic Governance, Working Group on Economic Governance', Brussels, 16 September.

—— (2002) (WG VI/09) The Secretariat, 'Meeting of 17 July 2002: Members' Contributions, Working Group on Economic Governance', Brussels, 16 July.

—— (2002) (WG VI/08) The Secretariat, 'First Draft for Possible Conclusions of the Working Group on the Basis of the Discussion at the Meetings of the Group on 10 July 2002, Working Group on Economic Governance', Brussels, 15 July.

—— (2002) (WG VI/07) The Secretariat, 'Meeting of 10 July 2002: Members' Contributions, Working Group on Economic Governance', Brussels, 8 July.

—— (2002) (WG VI/05) The Secretariat, 'First Draft for Possible Conclusions of the Working Group on the Basis of the Discussion at the Meetings of the Group on 20 and 24 June, Working Group on Economic Governance', Brussels, 4 July.

—— (2002) (WG VI 3 rev.) The Secretariat, 'Meeting of 20 June 2002: Members' Contributions, Working Group on Economic Governance', Brussels, 19 June.

European Council (2001), 'Declaration on the Future of the European Union', Annex I to 'Conclusions of the Presidency', Laeken, 14 and 15 December.

—— (2000) 'Conclusions of the Presidency', Lisbon, 23 and 24 March, 24/03/00, SN 100/1/00. Online. Available at: http://ue.eu.int/en/Info/eurocouncil/index.htm (accessed March 2002).

—— (1999) 'Conclusions of the Presidency', Cologne, 3 and 4 June, Annex IV.

—— (1991) 'Conclusions of the 1991 Maastricht European Council', Bull. EC 12.

European Economic and Social Committee (2002) 'Resolution Addressed to the European Convention', 19 September.

—— (2001) 'Opinion on the Organised Civil Society and European Governance: The Committee's Contribution to the White Paper', 25 April.

—— (2000) 'Opinion on the Commission Discussion Paper "The Commission and Non-governmental Organisations: Building a Stronger Partnership"', OJ 268/67, 19/9/2000.

—— (1999) 'Opinion on the Role and Contribution of Civil Society Organisations in the Building of Europe, 22 September 1999', OJ C 329, 17/11/99.

European Parliament (2001) 'Resolution on the Commission White Paper on European Governance (COM(2001) 428 – C5–0454/2001 – 2001/2181 (COS)), A5–0933/2001'.

—— (2000) 'Resolution of 26.10.2000 on the Commission Reports to the European Council: Better Lawmaking – A Shared Responsibility (COM (1998) 715 – C5–0266/2000 – 1999/2197(COS)) and Better Lawmaking 1999 (COM (1999) 562 – C5–0279/1999 – 1999/2197 (COS)), OJ. C 197, 12.7.2001'.

—— (1995) 'Resolution on the Function of the Treaty on European Union with a view to the 1996 Intergovernmental Conference – Implementation and Development of the Union', A4–0102/95.

Folketingets Europaudvalg (2003a) (I 322)'EU-forfatningstraktat styrker Europa-Parlamentets lovgivningsbeføjelser', Info note I 322, Copenhagen 14 July 2003. (The Danish Parliament's European Committee, 'EU Constitutional Treaty Strengthens the Legislative Competence for the European Parliament'.)

—— (2003b) (I 352)'Væsentlige nyskabelser I Konventets udkast til forfatningstraktat', Info note I 352, Copenhagen 29 October 2003. (The Danish Parliament's European Committee, 'Substantial Innovations in the Convention's Draft for a Constitutional Treaty'.)

Hain, P. (2003) 'Amendment for Article 1: Establishment of the European Union', Brussels: European Convention. Online. Available at: http://european-convention.eu.int/amendemTrait.asp?lang=EN (accessed 31 October 2003).

Hjelm-Wallen, L. *et al.* (2003) 'Amendment for Article 1: Establishment of the European Union', Brussels: European Convention. Online. Available at:

http://european-convention.eu.int/amendemTrait.asp?lang=EN (accessed 31 October 2003).

House of Commons (2003a) (03/58) 'The Draft Treaty Establishing a European Constitution: Parts II and III', Library Research Paper 7 July 2003, London. Online. Available at: http://www.parliament.uk (accessed August 2003).

—— (2003b) (03/60) 'The Draft Treaty Establishing a European Constitution: Technical and Constitutional Issues in Parts I and IV', Library Research Paper 7 July 2003, London. Online. Available at: http://www.parliament.uk (accessed August 2003).

House of Lords (2003a) (35th Report) 'The Future of Europe – Progress Report on the Draft Constitutional Treaty and the IGC', Select Committee on the European Union, 18 July 2003, London. Online. Available at: http://www.parliament.the-stationery-office.co.uk/pa/ld/ldeucom.htm (accessed August 2003).

—— (2003b) (41st Report) 'The Future of Europe – The Convention's Draft Constitutional Treaty', Select Committee on the European Union, 21 October 2003, London. Online. Available at: http://www.parliament.the-stationery-office.co.uk/pa/ld/ldeucom.htm (accessed November 2003).

Santer, J. *et al.* (2003) 'Amendment for Article 59 (ex. 46): Voluntary Withdrawal from the Union', Brussels: European Convention. Online. Available at: http://european-convention.eu.int/amendemTrait.asp?lang=EN (accessed 31 October 2003).

Szajer, J. (2003) 'Amendment for Article 1: Establishment of the European Union', Brussels: European Convention. Online. Available at: http://european-convention.eu.int/amendemTrait.asp?lang=EN (accessed 31 October 2003).

Teufel, E. (2003) 'Amendment for Preamble', Brussels: European Convention. Online. Available at: http://european-convention.eu.int/amendemTrait.asp?lang=EN (accessed 31 October 2003).

Other sources

Ackerman, B. (1991) *We The People*, Cambridge, MA: The Belknap Press of Harvard University Press.

Ackerman, B. (1984) 'The Storrs Lectures: Discovering the Constitution', *Yale Law Journal*, 93: 1013–72.

Amitsis, G., Berghmann, J., Hemerijck, A., Sakellaropoulos, T., Stergiou, A. and Stevens, Y. (2003) 'Connecting Welfare Diversity within the European Social Model', Background Report, International Conference of the Hellenic Presidency of the European Union, 'The Modernisation of the European Social Model', Ioannina, Greece, 20–21 May.

Ardy, B. and Begg, I. (2001) 'The European Employment Strategy: Policy Integration by the Back Door?', South Bank European Papers, 4.

Arneson, R.J. (1992) 'Introduction', in R.J. Arneson (ed.) *Liberalism*, vol. III, Aldershot: Edward Elgar Publishing Ltd.

Attucci, C. (2001) 'Identità e diritti. Prospettive filosofiche per la cittadinanza nell'epoca della globalizzazione', in D. D'Andrea and E. Pulcini (eds) *Filosofie della Globalizzazione*, Pisa: ETS.

Avineri, S. and De-Shalit, A. (1992) 'Introduction', in S. Avineri and A. De-Shalit (eds) *Communitarianism and Individualism*, Oxford: Oxford University Press.

Baeten, R. (2003) 'Who's Who in the Convention on the Future of the European Union', unpublished directory, apply to author at the European Parliament (rbaeten@europarl.eu.int).

Baldwin, R. and Widgren, M. (2003) 'Decision-Making and the Constitutional Treaty: Will the IGC Discard Giscard?', Centre for European Policy Studies, CEPS Policy Brief, 37. Online. Available at: http://www.ceps.be (accessed September 2003).

Barber, B. (1984) *Strong Democracy: Participatory Politics for a New Age*, Berkeley: University of California Press.

Barry, B. (2001) *Culture and Equality: An Egalitarian Critique of Multiculturalism*, Cambridge: Polity Press.

Barry, B. (1995) *Justice as Impartiality: A Treatise on Social Justice, vol. II*, Oxford: Clarendon Press.

Barry, B. (1991) *Democracy and Power: Essays in Political Theory I*, Oxford: Clarendon Press.

Barry, B. (1989) *Theories of Justice. A Treatise on Social Justice, 1.*, Berkeley: University of California Press.

Baviera, S. (2001) 'Les pétitions au Parlement européen et le médiateur européen', *Revue du Marché Commun et de l'Union européene*, no. 445, pp. 129–35.

Beck, U. (1998) *Was ist Globalisierung?*, Frankfurt: Suhrkamp.

Bednar, J., Ferejohn, J. and Garrett, G. (1996) 'The Politics of European Federalism', *International Review of Law and Economics*, 16: 279–94.

Bednar, J., Eskridge, W.N. and Ferejohn, J. (2001) 'A Political Theory of Federalism,' in J. Ferejohn, J.N. Rakove and R. Riley (eds), *Constitutional Culture and Democratic Rule*, Cambridge and New York: Cambridge University Press.

Begg, I. and Berghman, J. (2002) 'Introduction: EU Social (Exclusion) Policy Revisited?', *Journal of European Social Policy*, 12, 3: 179–94.

Bellamy, R. (forthcoming) 'Sovereignty, Post-Sovereignty and Pre-Sovereignty: Reconceptualising the State, Rights and Democracy in the EU?', in N. Walker (ed.) *Sovereignty in Transition*, Portland, Oregon: Hart.

Bellamy, R. (1999) *Liberalism and Pluralism: Towards a Politics of Compromise*, London: Routledge.

Bellamy, R. and Castiglione, D. (2002) 'Beyond Community and Rights: European Citizenship and the Virtues of Participation', *Quaderni Fiorentini*, 31, 1: 349–80.

Bellamy, R. and Castiglione, D. (1999) 'Between Cosmopolis and Community: Three Models of Rights and Democracy within the European Community', in D. Archibugi, D. Held and M. Köhler (eds) *Re-imagining Political Community*, Cambridge: Polity Press.

Bellamy, R. and Schönlau, J. (forthcoming) 'The Normality of Constitutional Politics: An Analysis of the Drafting of the EU Charter of Fundamental Rights', *Constellations*, 11, 1.

Berlin, I. (1990) 'The Pursuit of the Idea', in I. Berlin (ed.) *The Crooked Timber of Humanity*, London: John Murray Publishers.

Berlin, I. (1969) 'Two Concepts of Liberty', in I. Berlin (ed.) *Four Essays on Liberty*, Oxford: Oxford University Press.

Besselink, L. (1998) 'Entrapped by the Maximum Standard. On Fundamental Rights, Pluralism and Subsidiarity in the European Union', *Common Market Law Review*, 35, 3: 629–80.

Besson, S. (forthcoming) *Reasonable Disagreement and the Law*, Oxford: Hart Publishing.

Betten, L. (1998) 'The Democratic Deficit of Participatory Democracy in Community Social Policy', *European Law Review*, 23: 20–36.

Bickel, A. (1978) *The Least Dangerous Branch*, Indianapolis: Bobbs-Merrill Educational Publishing.

Bohman, J. (1996) *Public Deliberation: Pluralism, Complexity and Democracy*, Cambridge, Mass: The MIT Press.

Bohman, J. and Rehg, W. (eds) (1997) *Deliberative Democracy: Essays on Reason and Politics*, Cambridge, Mass: The MIT Press.

Bonjour, E., Offler, H.S. and Potter, G.R. (1952) *A Short History of Switzerland*, Oxford: Oxford University Press.

Bork, R. (1990) *The Tempting of America*, New York: Simon and Schuster.

Boyer, R. (2000) 'The Unanticipated Fallout of European Monetary Union: The Political and Institutional Deficits of the Euro', in C. Crouch (ed.) *After the Euro: Shaping Institutions for Governance in the Wake of European Monetary Union*, Oxford: Oxford University Press.

Brown, T. (2003) 'Economic and Social Governance at the Convention on the Future of Europe', Constitutional Online Paper No. 21/03, July 2003, The Federal Trust for Education and Research. Online. Available at: http://www.fedtrust.org/eu_constitution (accessed August 2003).

Buiter, W.H. (1999) 'Alice in Euroland,' *Journal of Common Market Studies*, 37: 181–209.

Buiter, W.H. (1998) 'Alice in Euroland', speech before the South Bank University, November.

Burgess, M. (2000) *Federalism and European Union*, London: Routledge.

Business Week (2003) 'Germany's Budget Gap Sets a Bad Example', 25 November, p. 2.

Calmfors, L. *et al.* (2003) 'Report on the European Economy', European Advisory Group at CES, Institute for Economic Research, Munich.

Carrió, G.A. (1968) *Notas sobre derecho y lenguaje*, Buenos Aires: Abeledo Perrot.

Cassese, A., Clapham, A. and Weiler, J. (eds) (1991) *Human Rights and the European Community*, Baden Baden: Nomos.

Castiglione, D. (1996) 'The Political Theory of the Constitution', in R. Bellamy and D. Castiglione (eds) *Constitutionalism in Transformation: European and Theoretical Perspectives*, Oxford: Blackwell.

Cerutti, F. (2001) 'Towards the Political Identity of the Europeans. An Introduction', in F. Cerutti and E. Rudolph (eds) *A Soul for Europe, Vol. I. A Reader*, Leuven: Peeters.

Cerutti, F. (1996) 'Identità e Politica', in F. Cerutti (ed.), *Identità politica*, Roma-Bari: Laterza.

Cerutti, F. and Rudolph, E. (eds) (2001) *A Soul for Europe, Vol. I. A Reader*, Leuven: Peeters.

Closa, C. (2003) 'Improving EU Constitutional Politics? A Preliminary Assessment of the Convention', Constitutionalism Web Papers, ConWEB, 1, 03. Online. Available at: http://www.qub.ac.uk/ies/onlinepapers/const.html (accessed October 2003).

Cohen, J. and Sabel, C.F. (2003) 'Sovereignty and Solidarity: EU and US', in J. Zeitlin and D. Trubek (eds) *Governing Work and Welfare in a New Economy: European and American Experiments*, Oxford: Oxford University Press.

Cohen, J. and Sabel, C. (1997) 'Directly-Deliberative Polyarchy', *European Law Journal*, 3: 313–40.

Coulmas, F. (1991) 'European Integration and the Idea of the National Language. Ideological Roots and Economic Consequences', in F. Coulmas (ed.) *A Language Policy for the European Community. Prospects and Quandaries*, Berlin: Mouton de Gruyter.

Craig, P. (2003) 'When is the Time Right? Historical Big Bangs and Peaceful Reform', in K. Nicolaidis and S. Weatherill (eds) *Whose Europe? National Models and the Constitution of the European Union*, Papers of a Multi-Disciplinary Conference held in Oxford in April 2003, Oxford: Oxford University Press.

Craig, P. (1999) 'The Nature of the Community: Integration, Democracy, and Legitimacy', in P. Craig and G. de Búrca (eds) *The Evolution of EU Law*, Oxford: Oxford University Press.

Craig, P. (1997) 'Democracy and Rule-making Within the EC: An Empirical and Normative Assessment', *European Law Journal*, 3: 105–30.

Csáky, M. (1999) 'Pluralistische Gemeinschaften: Ihre Spannungen und Qualitäten am Beispiel Zentraleuropas', in E. Blau and M. Platzer (eds) *Mythos Großstadt. Architektur und Stadtbaukunst in Zentraleuropa 1890–1937*, München: Prestel.

Curtin, D. (2001) 'The Commission as Sorcerer's Apprentice? Reflections on EU Public Administration and the Role of Information Technology in Holding Bureaucracy Accountable', in C. Joerges, Y. Mény and J.H.H. Weiler (eds) 'Mountain or Molehill? A Critical Appraisal of the Commission White Paper on Governance', Jean Monnet Working Paper 6/01, Harvard. Online. Available at: http://www.iue.it/RSC/Governance (accessed April 2002).

Curtin, D. (1997) *Postnational Democracy. The European Union in Search of a Political Philosophy*, The Hague: Kluwer Law International.

Curtin, D. (1996) 'Betwixt and Between: Democracy and Transparency in the Governance of the European Union', in J.A. Winter, D.M. Curtin, A.E. Kellermann and B. De Witte (eds) *Reforming the Treaty on European Union. The Legal Debate*, The Hague: Kluwer Law International.

Dahl, R.A. (1971) *Polyarchy. Participation and Opposition*, New Haven: Yale University Press.

Dahl, R.A. (1956) *A Preface to Democratic Theory*, Chicago: University of Chicago Press.

de Búrca, G. (2003) 'The Constitutional Challenge of New Governance in the European Union', paper presented at the Workshop on New Governance and Law in EU, Minda de Gunzburg Center for European Studies, Harvard University, 28 February 2003.

de Búrca, G. (2001a) 'Human Rights, the Charter and Beyond', Jean Monnet Working Paper 10:01, New York University School of Law.

de Búrca, G. (2001b) 'The Drafting of the EU Charter of Fundamental Rights', *European Law Review*, 26, 2: 126–38.

de Búrca, G. (1999) 'The Institutional Development of the European Union: A Constitutional Analysis', in P. Craig and G. de Búrca (eds), *The Evolution of EU Law*, Oxford: Oxford University Press.

de Búrca, G. (1996) 'The Quest for Legitimacy in the European Union', *The Modern Law Review*, 59: 349–76.

de Búrca, G. and Zeitlin, J. (2003) 'Constitutionalising the Open Method of Coordination: What Should the Convention Propose?', Centre for European

Policy Studies Policy Brief. Online. Available at: http://www.ceps.be (accessed 27 May 2003).

Deckmyn, V. (2002) *Increasing Transparency in the European Union?*, Maastricht: European Institute of Public Administration.

Dehousse, R. (2002) 'The Open Method of Coordination: A New Policy Paradigm?', paper presented at the First Pan-European Conference on European Union Politics, 'The Politics of European Integration: Academic Acquis and Future Challenges', Bordeaux, 26–28 September 2002.

Dehousse, R. (1998) 'European Institutional Architecture after the Amsterdam Treaty: Parliamentary or Regulatory Structure?', *Common Market Law Review*, 35: 598–619.

Delanty, G. (1995) *Inventing Europe. Idea, Identity, Reality*, Houndmills: Macmillan.

de la Porte, C., Pochet, P. and Room, G. (2001) 'Social Benchmarking, Policy Making and New Governance in the EU', *Journal of European Social Policy*, 11, 4: 291–307.

de la Porte, C. and Pochet, P. (2002) 'Introduction', in C. de la Porte and P. Pochet (eds) *Building Social Europe through the Open Method of Co-ordination*, Brussels: PIE – Peter Lang.

De Schutter, O. (2002) 'Europe in Search of its Civil Society', *European Law Journal*, 8: 198–217.

De Tocqueville, A. (1989) *Oeuvres complètes: Tom. 16, Mélanges* (ed.) F. Mélonio, Paris: Édition Gallimard.

—— (1983) *Oeuvres complètes: Tom. 15, Correspondance d'Alexis de Tocqueville et de Francisque de Corcelle; correspondance d'Alexis de Tocqueville et de Madame Swetchine* (ed.) P. Gibert, Paris: Édition Gallimard.

—— (1951) *Oeuvres complètes: oeuvres, papiers et correspondences. Vol 1, De la democratie en Amerique*, (ed.) J.-P. Mayer, Paris: Librarie de Médicis.

Dewandre, N. and Lenoble, J. (eds) (1994) *Projekt Europa. Postnationale Identität: Grundlage für eine europäische Demokratie?*, Berlin: Schelzky and Jeep.

Dobson, L. (forthcoming) *Supranational Citizenship*, Manchester: Manchester University Press.

Dougan, M. (2003) 'The Convention's Draft Constitutional Treaty: A "Tidying-Up Exercise" that needs some Tidying-up of its Own', Constitutional Online Paper No. 27/03, August 2003, The Federal Trust for Education and Research. Online. Available at: http://www.fedtrust.org/eu_constitution (accessed August 2003).

Dworkin, R. (1996) *Freedom's Law: The Moral Reading of the American Constitution*, Cambridge, Mass: Harvard University Press.

Dworkin, R. (1986) *Law's Empire*, Cambridge, Mass: Harvard University Press.

Dyson, K. (ed.) (2002) *European States and the Euro: Europeanization, Variation and Convergence*, Oxford: Oxford University Press.

Dyson, K. and Featherstone, K. (1999) *The Road to Maastricht: Negotiating Economic and Monetary Union*, Oxford: Oxford University Press.

Eberlein, B. and Kerwer, D. (2002) 'Theorising the New Modes of European Union Governance', *European Integration Online Papers*, 6, 5. Online. Available at: http://www.eiap.or.at/eiop/texte/2002–005a.htm (accessed 20 May 2003).

Egeberg, M. (1999) 'Transcending Intergovernmentalism? Identity and Role Perceptions of National Officials in EU Decision-Making', *Journal of European Public Policy* 6, 3: 456–74.

Eichengreen, B. and Wyplosz, C. (1998) 'The Stability Pact: More than a Minor Nuisance?', in D. Egg, J. Von Hagen, C. Wyplosz and K.F. Zimmerman (eds) *EMU: Prospects and Challenges for the Euro*, Oxford: Blackwell.

Ekengren, M. and Jacobsson, K. (2000) 'Explaining the Constitutionalisation of EU Governance – The Case of European Employment Cooperation', *SCORE Report*, 2000: 8.

Elazar, D.J. (2001) 'The United States and the European Union: Models for their Epochs', in K. Nicolaidis and R. Howse (eds) *The Federal Vision: Legitimacy and Levels of Governance in the United States and the European Union*, Oxford: Oxford University Press.

Elazar, D.J. (1987) *Exploring Federalism*, Tuscaloosa: University of Alabama Press.

Elgström, O. and Jönsson, C. (2000) 'Negotiating in the European Union', *Journal of European Public Policy*, 7, 5: 684–704.

Elster, J. (1999) *Alchemies of the Mind. Rationality and the Emotions*, Cambridge: Cambridge University Press.

Elster, J. (1998) 'Deliberation and Constitution Making', in J. Elster (ed.) *Deliberative Democracy*, Cambridge: Cambridge University Press.

Elster, J. (1997) 'The Market and the Forum: Three Varieties of Political Theory' in J. Bohman and W. Rehg (eds) *Deliberative Democracy: Essays on Reason and Politics*, Cambridge, MA: The MIT Press.

Elster, J. (1996) *Argomentare e negoziare*, Milan: Anabasi.

Elster, J. (1995) 'Strategic uses of arguments', in K. Arrow *et al.* (eds) *Barriers to Conflict Resolution*, New York: Norton.

Elster, J. (1986) 'The Market and the Forum: Three Varieties of Political Theory', in J. Elster and A. Hylland (eds) *Foundations of Social Choice Theory*, Cambridge: Cambridge University Press.

Ely, J. (1980) *Democracy and Distrust*, Cambridge: Harvard University Press.

Eriksen, E.O. and Fossum, J.E. (eds) (2000) *Democracy in the European Union. Integration through Deliberation?*, London: Routledge.

Eriksen, E.O., Fossum, J.E. and Menéndez, A.J. (2003) *The Chartering of Europe*, Baden Baden: Nomos.

Eriksen, E.O., Fossum, J.E. and Menéndez, A.J. (2002) 'Constitution Making and Democratic Legitimacy', ARENA Report 5/2002.

Eriksen, E.O., Fossum, J.E. and Menéndez, A.J. (eds) (2001) 'The Chartering of Europe. The Charter of Fundamental Rights in Context', ARENA Report 8/2001.

Eskridge, W. (1987) 'Dynamic Statutory Interpretation', *University of Pennsylvania Law Review*, 135: 1479–97.

Everson, M. (1999) 'The Constitutionalisation of European Administrative Law: Legal Oversight of a Stateless Internal Market', in C. Joerges and E. Vos (eds) *EU Committees: Social Regulation, Law and Politics*, Oxford: Hart Publishing.

Fabre, C. (2000) *Social Rights under the Constitution*, Oxford: Oxford University Press.

Farrand, M. (ed.) (1937) *The Records of the Federal Convention*, New Haven, Conn.: Yale University Press.

Ferrera, M., Matsaganis, M. and Sacchi, S. (2002) 'Open Co-ordination Against Poverty: The New EU "Social Inclusion" Process', *Journal of European Social Policy*, 12, 3: 227–39.

Filippov, M., Ordeshook, P.C. and Shvetsova, O. (forthcoming) *Federal Institutional*

Design: A Theory of Self Sustainable Federal Government, Cambridge and New York: Cambridge University Press.

Fischer, J. (2000) 'Vom Staatenverbund zur Föderation: Gedanken über die Finalität der europäischen Integration', in C. Joerges, Y. Mény and J.H.H. Weiler (eds) *What Kind of Constitution for What Kind of Polity? Responses to Joschka Fischer,* Florence: Robert Schuman Centre for Advanced Studies/European University Institute.

Fisher, R., Ury, W. and Patton, B. (1999) *Getting to Yes. Negotiating an Agreement Without Giving in,* 2nd edn, London: Random House.

Fiss, O. (1999) 'A Community of Equals', in J. Cohen and J. Rogers (eds) *A Community of Equals. The Constitutional Protection of New Americans,* Boston: Beacon Press.

Fiss, O. (1976) 'Groups and the Equal Protection Clause', *Philosophy and Public Affairs,* 5, 2: 107–77.

Fitzmaurice, J. (1996) *The Politics of Belgium: A Unique Federalism,* Boulder CO: Westview Press.

Follesdal, A. (2003) 'The Political Theory of the White Paper on Governance: Hidden and Fascinating', *European Public Law,* 9: 1.

Follesdal, A. (2002) 'Drafting a European Constitution: Challenges and Opportunities', Constitutionalism Web Papers, University of Manchester School of Law. ConWEB, 4. Online. Available at: http://www.les1.man.ac.uk/conweb/papers/conweb4–2002.pdf (accessed June 2003).

Follesdal, A. (2001) 'Union Citizenship: Unpacking the Beast of Burden', *Law and Philosophy,* 20, 3: 313–43.

Follesdal, A. (1998) 'Subsidiarity', *Journal of Political Philosophy,* 6: 231–59.

Follesdal, A. (1997) 'Democracy and Federalism in the EU: A Liberal Contractualist Perspective', in A. Follesdal and P. Koslowski (eds) *Democracy and the European Union: Studies in Economic Ethics and Philosophy,* Berlin: Springer; and also in ARENA reprint 98/9.

Franck, T.M. (1968) *Why Federations Fail,* New York: New York University Press.

Friese, H. and Wagner, P. (2002) 'The Nascent Political Philosophy of the European Polity', *Journal of Political Philosophy,* 10, 3: 342–64.

Fung, A. and Wright, E.O. (eds) (2003) *Deepening Democracy. Institutional Innovations in Empowered Participatory Governance,* London: Verso.

Gagnon, A.G. and Tully, J. (eds) (2001) *Multinational Democracies,* Cambridge: Cambridge University Press.

García, S. (ed.) (1993) *European Identity and the Search for Legitimacy,* London: Pinter.

Gaus, G. (1997) 'Reason, Justification and Consensus: Why Deliberative Democracy Can't Have It All', in J. Bohman and W. Rehg (eds) *Deliberative Democracy: Essays on Reason and Politics,* Cambridge, MA: The MIT Press.

Gerstenberg, O. and Sabel, C.F. (2002) 'Directly Deliberative Polyarchy: An Institutional Ideal for Europe?', in C. Joerges and R. Dehousse (eds) *Good Governance in Europe's Integrated Market,* Oxford: Oxford University Press.

Goetschy, J. (2001) 'The European Employment Strategy from Amsterdam to Stockholm: Has it Reached its Cruising Speed?', *Industrial Relations Journal,* 32, 5: 401–18.

Goetschy, J. (2000) 'The European Employment Strategy', in M. Rhodes, J. Goetschy and J. Mosher (eds) 'The Lisbon European Council and the Future of European Economic Governance', *ECSA Review,* 13, 3: 2–7.

Goldsmith, Lord Q.G. (2001) 'A Charter of Rights, Freedoms and Principles', *Common Market Law Review*, 38: 1201–16.

Goodin, R.E. (1995) *Motivating Political Morality*, Cambridge, MA: Blackwell.

Goodin, R.E. (1986) 'Laundering Preferences', in J. Elster and A. Hylland (eds) *Foundations of Social Choice Theory*, Cambridge: Cambridge University Press.

Gray, T. (1991) *Freedom*, Basingstoke and London: Macmillan Press.

Grimm, D. (1995) 'Does Europe Need a Constitution?', in *European Law Journal*, 1: 282–302.

Gustavsson, S. (2002) 'Double Asymmetry and its Alternatives', paper presented at the First Pan-European Conference on European Union Politics, 'The Politics of European Integration: Academic Acquis and Future Challenges', Bordeaux, 26–28 September.

Gutmann, A. and Thompson, D. (1996) *Democracy and Disagreement. Why Moral Conflict Cannot be Avoided in Politics, and What Should be Done about it*, Cambridge, MA: The Belknap Press of Harvard University Press.

Habermas, J. (2001a) *Zeit der Übergänge*, Frankfurt: Suhrkamp.

Habermas, J. (2001b) 'Why Europe Needs a Constitution', *New Left Review* 11: 5–26.

Habermas, J. (1999) *Die Postnationale Konstellation. Politische Essays*, Frankfurt: Suhrkamp.

Habermas, J. (1996a) *Between Facts and Norms: Contributions to a Discourse Theory of Law and Democracy*, W. Rehg (trans.), Cambridge: Polity Press.

Habermas, J. (1996b) 'The European Nation State. Its Achievements and its Limitations. On the Past and Future of Sovereignty and Citizenship', *Ratio Juris* 9, 2: 125–37.

Habermas, J. (1994) 'Three Normative Models of Democracy', *Constellations*, 1, 1: 1–10.

Habermas, J. (1990) 'Discourse Ethics: Notes on a Program of Philosophical Justification', in *Moral Consciousness and Communicative Action*, Cambridge: Polity Press.

Hallstein, W. (1973) *Die Europäische Gemeinschaft*, Düsseldorf: Econ.

Hamilton, A., Madison, J. and Jay, J. (1989) *The Federalist Papers*, G. Wills (ed.), New York: Bantam Classics.

Harlow, C. (2002) *Accountability in the European Union*, Oxford: Oxford University Press.

Hart, H. (1961) *The Concept of Law*, Oxford: Clarendon Press.

Hayek, F.A. (1979) *Law, Legislation and Liberty, Vol. 3: The Political Order of a Free People*, London and Henley: Routledge and Kegan Paul.

Heringa, A.W. and Verhey, L. (2001) 'The EU Charter: Text and Structure', *Maastricht Journal of European and Comparative Law*, 8, 1: 11–32.

Héritier, A. (2002) 'New Modes of Governance in Europe: Policy Making without Legislating?', in A. Héritier (ed.) *Common Goods: Reinventing European and International Governance*, Boulder, CO: Rowman and Littlefield.

Hirschman, A. (1994) 'Social Conflict as Pillars of Democratic Market Society', *Political Theory*, 22: 203–18.

Hix, S. (1999) *The Political System of the European Union*, New York, NY: St. Martin's Press.

Hobbes, T. (1968 [1651]) *Leviathan*, C.B. Macpherson (ed.), Middlesex: Penguin Books.

Hodson, D. and Maher, I. (2001) 'The Open Method as a New Mode of Governance: The Case of Soft Economic Policy Co-ordination', *Journal of Common Market Studies*, 39, 4: 719–46.

Hoffmann, L. and Vergés-Bausili, A. (2003) 'The Reform of Treaty Revision Procedures: The European Convention on the Future of Europe', in T.A. Börzel and R.A. Cichowski (eds) *The State of the European Union: Law, Politics, and Society*, Oxford: Oxford University Press.

Holmes, S. (1998) 'Gag Rules or the Politics of Omission', in J. Elster and R. Slagstad (eds) *Constitutionalism and Democracy*, Cambridge: Cambridge University Press.

Holmes, S. (1995) *Passions and Constraint: On the Theory of Liberal Democracy*, Chicago: Chicago University Press.

Holmes, J. and Sharman, C. (1977) *The Australian Federal System*, Sydney and London: Allen and Unwin.

Honneth, A. (2003) 'Umverteilung als Anerkennung. Eine Erwiderung auf Nancy Fraser', in N. Fraser and A. Honneth *Umverteilung oder Anerkennung?*, Frankfurt: Suhrkamp.

Hooghe, L. and Marks, G. (2001) *Multi-Level Governance and European Integration*, Lanham: Rowman and Littlefield.

Hoskyns, C. (2000) 'Democratizing the EU: Evidence and Argument', in C. Hoskyns and M. Newman (eds) *Democratizing the European Union. Issues for the Twenty-First Century*, Manchester: Manchester University Press.

Hughes, K. (2003) 'A Dynamic and Democratic EU or Muddling Through Again? Assessing the EU's draft Constitution', EPIN Working Paper No. 8, European Policy Institutes Network, July 2003. Online. Available at: http://www.ceps.be (accessed August 2003).

Hughes, K. (2001) 'The "Open Method" of Co-ordination: Innovation or Talking Shop?', Centre for European Reform Bulletin, Issue 15, December 2000–January 2001. Online. Available at: http://www.cer.org.uk/articles/issue 15_hughes.html (accessed 5 June 2002).

Hüglin, T.O. (1991) *Sozietaler Föderalismus. Die politische Theorie des Johannes Althusius*, Berlin: de Gruyter.

Hyde, A. (1983) 'The Concept of Legitimation in the Sociology of Law', *Wisconsin Law Review*, 1: 379–426.

Ipsen, H.P. (1972) *Europäisches Gemeinschaftsrecht*, Tübingen: Mohr.

Jacobsson, K. (2001) 'Innovations in EU Governance: The Case of Employment Policy Co-ordination', *SCORE Report*, 2001: 12.

Jacobsson, K. and Schmid, H. (2002) 'The European Employment Strategy at the Crossroads: Contributions to the Evaluation', paper presented at the Nordic Sociology Conference, Reykjavik 15–17 August 2002.

Janis, M., Kay, R. and Bradley, A. (2000) *European Human Rights Law*, Oxford: Oxford University Press.

Jászi, O. (1961) [1929] *The Dissolution of the Habsburg Monarchy*, Chicago: University of Chicago Press.

Jayal, N.G. (2001) *Democracy in India*, Delhi and Oxford: Oxford University Press.

Joerges, C. (1999) '"Good Governance" Through Comitology?', in C. Joerges and E. Vos (eds) *EU Committees: Social Regulation, Law and Politics*, Oxford: Hart Publishing.

Joerges, C. and Neyer, J. (1997) 'From Intergovernmental Bargaining to Deliberative Political Processes: The Constitutionalisation of Comitology', *European Law Journal*, 3: 273–99.

Karlsson, C. (2001) *Democracy, Legitimacy and the European Union*, Uppsala: Acta Universitatis Upsaliensis.

Keiser, R. and Prange, H. (2002) 'A New Concept of Deepening European Integration? – The European Research Area and the Emerging Role of Policy Coordination in a Multi-level Governance System', *European Integration Online Papers*, 6, 18. Online. Available at: http://eiop.or.at/eiop/texte/2002–018a.htm (accessed January 2003).

Kendall, J. and Anheier, H.K. (1999) 'The Third Sector and the European Union Policy Process: An Initial Evaluation', *Journal of European Public Policy*, 6: 283–307.

Keynes, J.M. (1953) *The General Theory of Employment, Interest, and Money*, San Diego: Harcourt Brace Jovanovich.

Kohler-Koch, B. (2001) 'The Commission White Paper and the Improvement of European Governance', in C. Joerges, Y. Mény, and J.H.H. Weiler (eds) 'Mountain or Molehill? A Critical Appraisal of the Commission White Paper on Governance', Jean Monnet Working Paper 6/01, Harvard. Online. Available at: http://www.iue.it/RSC/Governance (accessed April 2002).

Korsten, A.F.A. (1979) *Het spraakmakende bestuur*, 's-Gravenhage: VUGA-Boekerij.

Kraus, P.A. (2004) '"Transnationalism" or "renationalization"? The politics of cultural identity in the EU', in A.G. Gagnon, M. Guibernau and F. Rocher (eds) *Conditions of Diversity in Multinational Democracies*, Montreal: McGill-Queen's University Press.

Kraus, P.A. (2003) 'Cultural Pluralism and European Polity-Building: Neither Westphalia nor Cosmopolis', *Journal of Common Market Studies*, 41, 4: 665–86.

Kraus, P.A. (2000) 'Political Unity and Linguistic Diversity in Europe', *Archives Européennes de Sociologie/European Journal of Sociology*, XLI, 1: 138–63.

Kymlicka, W. (1995) *Multicultural Citizenship*, Oxford: Clarendon Press.

Lamfalussy, A. *et al.* (2001) 'Final Report of the Committee of Wise Men on the Regulation of European Securities Markets', Brussels.

Lax, D.A. and Sebenius, J.K. (1986) *The Manager as Negotiator: Bargaining for Co-operation and Competitive Gain*, New York: Free Press.

Le Galès, P. (2002) *European Cities: Social Conflicts and Governance*, Oxford: Oxford University Press.

Lenaerts, K. (1993) 'Regulating the Regulatory Process: "Delegation of Powers" in the European Community', *European Law Review*, 18: 23–49.

Lenaerts, K. and de Smijter, E. (2001) 'A "Bill of Rights" for the European Union', *Common Market Law Review*, 38, 2: 273–300.

Lenaerts, K. and Verhoeven, A. (2002) 'Institutional Balance as a Guarantee for Democracy in EU Governance', in C. Joerges and R. Dehousse (eds) *Good Governance in Europe's Integrated Market*, Oxford: Oxford University Press.

Lijphart, A. (1996) 'The Puzzle of Indian Democracy', *American Political Science Review*, 90: 258–68.

Lijphart, A. (1984) *Democracies*, New Haven: Yale University Press.

Lijphart, A. (1977) *Democracy in Plural Societies*, New Haven: Yale University Press.

Lijphart, A. (1968) *The Politics of Accommodation: Pluralism and Democracy in the Netherlands*, Berkeley: University of California Press.

Lindberg, L.N. and Scheingold, S.A. (1970) *Europe's Would-Be Polity: Patterns of Change in the European Community*, Englewood Cliffs: Prentice Hall.

Linz, J.J. (1999) 'Democracy, Multinationalism and Federalism', in W. Busch and A. Merkel (eds) *Demokratie in Ost und West*, Frankfurt: Suhrkamp.

Lodge, J. (1994) 'Transparency and Democratic Legitimacy', *Journal of Common Market Studies*, 32: 343–68.

Lord, C. (1998) *Democracy in the European Union*, Sheffield: Sheffield Academic Press.

MacCallum, G.C. Jr. (1967) 'Negative and Positive Freedom', *The Philosophical Review*, 76: 312–34.

MacCormick, N. (1999) *Questioning Sovereignty. Law, State, and Nation in the European Commonwealth*, Oxford: Oxford University Press.

McKay, D. (2002) 'Fiscal Policy Under Monetary Union', in K. Dyson (ed.) *The European State and the Euro: Europeanization, Variation and Convergence*, Oxford: Oxford University Press.

McKay, D. (2001) *Designing Europe: Comparative Lessons for the European Union*, Oxford: Oxford University Press.

McKay, D. (1999) 'The Political Sustainability of European Monetary Union', *British Journal of Political Science*, 29: 519–41.

McKinnon, R.I. (1997) 'EMU as a Device for Collective Fiscal Responsibility', *American Economic Review*, 87: 227–9.

McRoberts, K. (1997) *Misconceiving Canada: The Struggle for National Unity*, Toronto and Oxford: Oxford University Press.

Madison, J., Hamilton, A. and Jay, J. (1987 [1788]), I. Kramnick (ed.) *The Federalist Papers*, Harmondsworth, Middlesex: Penguin Books.

Magnette, P. (2004) 'Deliberation vs Bargaining: Coping with Constitutional Conflicts in the Convention on the Future of Europe', in E.O. Eriksen and J. Fossum (eds) *Developing a European Constitution*, London: Routledge.

Magnette, P. (2003) 'Will the EU be More Legitimate after the Convention?', in J. Shaw, P. Magnette, L. Hoffman and A. Vergés Bausili (eds) *The Convention on the Future of Europe: Working Towards an EU Constitution*, London: The Federal Trust for Education and Research.

Magnette, P. (2001) 'European Governance and Civic Participation: Can the European Union be politicised?', in C. Joerges, Y. Mény, and J.H.H. Weiler (eds) 'Mountain or Molehill? A Critical Appraisal of the Commission White Paper on Governance', Jean Monnet Working Paper 6/01, Harvard. Online. Available at: http://www.iue.it/RSC/Governance (accessed April 2002).

Majone, G. (1996) *Regulating Europe*, London: Routledge.

Mancini, F.G. (1998) 'Europe: The Case for Statehood', *European Law Journal*, 4: 29–42.

Marks, G., Hooghe, L. and Blank, K. (1996) 'European Integration from the 1980s: State-centric vs Multi-level Governance', *Journal of Common Market Studies*, 34, 3: 341–78.

Maurer, A. (2003) 'Schließt sich der Kreis? Der Konvent, nationale Vorbehalte und Regierungskonferenz', Berlin: Stiftung Wissenschaft und Politik Arbeitspapier.

May, K. (1952) 'A Set of Independent Necessary and Sufficient Conditions for Simple Majority Decision', *Econometrica* 10: 680–4.

Maynor, J. (2003) *Republicanism in the Modern World*, Cambridge: Polity Press.

Merrills, J. (1993) *The Development of International Law by the European Court of Human Rights*, Manchester: Manchester University Press.

Mill, J.S. (1972) [1861] 'Considerations on Representative Government', in J.S. Mill (H.C. Acton, ed.) *Utilitarianism. Liberty. Representative Government*, London: Dent.

Mill, J.S. (1958) [1861] *Considerations on Representative Government*. New York: Liberal Arts Press.

Miller, D. (1992) 'Deliberative Democracy and Social Choice', in D. Held (ed.) *Prospects for Democracy: North, South, East, West*, Oxford: Polity Press.

Modood, T. (1993) 'Kymlicka on British Muslims', *Analyse und Kritik*, 15: 87–91.

Moravcsik, A. (2003) 'The EU ain't Broke', *Prospect*, March: 38–45.

Moravcsik, A. (2001) 'Federalism in the European Union: Myth and Reality, in K. Nicolaidis and R. Howse (eds) *The Federal Vision: Legitimacy and Levels of Governance in the European Union*, Oxford: Oxford University Press.

Moravcsik, A. (1994) 'Why the European Community Strengthens the State: Domestic Politics and International Cooperation', Harvard University Center for European Studies Working Paper Series, 52.

Morriss, P. (2002) *Power: A Philosophical Analysis,* 2nd edn, Manchester and New York: Manchester University Press.

Mosher, J. (2000) 'Open Method of Co-ordination: Functional and Political Origins', in M. Rhodes, J. Goetschy and J. Mosher (eds) 'The Lisbon European Council and the Future of European Economic Governance', *ECSA Review*, 13, 3: 2–7.

Murphy, W. (1993) 'Constitutions, Constitutionalism, and Democracy', in D. Greenberg *et al.* (eds.) *Constitutionalism and Democracy*, Oxford: Oxford University Press.

Naurin, D. (2003) 'Does Publicity Purify Politics?', *Journal of Information Ethics*, 12, 1.

Nentwich, M. (1996) 'Opportunity Structures for Citizens' Participation: The Case of the European Union', *European Integration Online Papers (EIoP)*, 0, 1. Online. Available at: http://eiop.or.at/eiop/texte/1996-001.htm.

Nentwich, M. and Falkner, G. (1997) 'The Treaty of Amsterdam: Towards a New Institutional Balance', *European Integration Online Papers (EIoP)*, 1, 15. Online. Available at: http://eiop.or.at/eiop/texte/1997-015a.htm.

Neunreither, K. (2001) 'The European Union in Nice: A Minimalist Approach to a Historic Challenge', *Government and Opposition*, 36, 2: 184–208.

Neyer, J. (2003) 'Discourse and Order in the EU', *Journal of Common Market Studies*, 41, 4: 687–706.

Nicolaidis, K. and Howse, R. (eds) (2001) *The Federal Vision: Legitimacy and Levels of Governance in the European Union*, Oxford and New York: Oxford University Press.

Nozick, R. (1975) *Anarchy, State and Utopia*, Oxford: Basil Blackwell.

Obradovic, D. (1996) 'Policy Legitimacy and the European Union', *Journal of Common Market Studies*, 34: 191–221.

O'Neill, O. (1988) 'Ethical Reasoning and Ideological Pluralism', *Ethics*, 98, 4: 705–22.

Ordeshook, P.C. and Shvetsova, O. (1997) 'Federalism and Constitutional Design', *Journal of Democracy*, 8: 27–42.

Palombella, G. (2002) *L'autorità dei diritti*, Roma-Bari: Laterza.

Parekh, B. (2000) *Rethinking Multiculturalism – Cultural Diversity and Political Theory*, London: Macmillan Press Ltd.

Parekh, B. (1999) 'Non-ethnocentric Universalism', in T. Dunne and N. Wheeler (eds) *Human Rights in Global Politics*, Cambridge: Cambridge University Press.

Parekh, B. (1997) 'Cultural Diversity and the Modern State', in M. Doornbos and

S. Kaviraj (eds) *Dynamics of State Formation. India and Europe Compared*, New Delhi: Sage.

Parmar, S. (2001) 'International Human Rights and the EU Charter', *Maastricht Journal of European and Comparative Law*, 8, 4: 351–70.

Pateman, C. (1970) *Participation and Democratic Theory*, Cambridge: Cambridge University Press.

Peers, S. (2003a) 'EU Constitution: Decision-making', *Statewatch*. Online. Available at: http://www.statewatch.org/news/2003/aug/constitution.htm (accessed August 2003).

Peers, S. (2003b) 'EU Constitutional Annotation no. 1: Part I, Draft EU Constitution', *Statewatch*. Online. Available at: http://www.statewatch.org/news/2003/aug/constitution.htm (accessed August 2003).

Peers, S. (2003c) 'The EU Constitution and Justice and Home Affairs: The Accountability Gap', *Statewatch*. Online. Available at: http://www.statewatch.org/news/2003/aug/constitution.htm (accessed August 2003).

Peterson, J. and Bomberg, E. (1999) *Decision-Making in the European Union*, London and New York: Palgrave.

Pettit, P. (2001) *A Theory of Freedom: from the Psychology to the Politics of Agency*, Cambridge: Polity Press.

Pettit, P. (1999) 'Republican Freedom and Contestatory Democratization', in I. Shapiro and C. Hacker-Cordón (eds) *Democracy's Value*, Cambridge: Cambridge University Press.

Pettit, P. (1997) *Republicanism: A Theory of Freedom and Government*, Oxford: Oxford University Press.

Pettit, P. (1993) 'Negative Liberty, Liberal and Republican', *European Journal of Philosophy*, 1, 1: 15–38.

Phillips, A. (1995) *The Politics of Presence*, Oxford: Clarendon Press.

Preuß, U.K. (1999) 'Auf der Suche nach Europas Verfassung', *Transit*, 17: 154–74.

Rabushka, A. and Shepsle, K.A. (1972) *Politics in Plural Societies: A Theory of Democratic Instability*, Columbus, Ohio: Bobbs-Merrill.

Radaelli, C.M. (2003) 'The Open Method of Co-ordination: A New Governance Architecture for the European Union?', Preliminary Report, March 2003, SIEPS. Online. Available at: http://www.sieps.su.se (accessed 30 May 2003).

Rae, J. (1895) *Life of Adam Smith*, London and New York: Macmillan and Co.

Raveaud, G. (2003) 'The European Employment Policy: From Ends to Means?', in R. Salais and R. Villeneuve (eds) *Europe and the Politics of Capabilities*, Cheltenham: Edward Elgar.

Rawls, J. (2001) *Justice as Fairness. A Restatement*, E. Kelly (ed.), Cambridge, Mass: The Belknap Press of Harvard University Press.

Rawls, J. (1999) *The Law of Peoples*, Cambridge, Mass: Harvard University Press.

Rawls, J. (1993) *Political Liberalism*, Chicago: Chicago University Press.

Rawls, J. (1972) *A Theory of Justice*, Oxford: Oxford University Press.

Raz, J. (1994) 'Rights and Individual Well Being', *Ethics in the Public Domain*, Oxford: Clarendon Press.

Raz, J. (1986) *The Morality of Freedom*, Oxford: Clarendon Press.

Raz, J. (1979) *The Authority of Law*, Oxford: Clarendon Press.

Riker, W. (1975) 'Federalism', in F.I. Greenstein and N. Polsby (eds) *The Handbook of Political Science. Volume V: Government Institutions and Processes*, Reading, MA: Addison Wesley.

Riker, W. (1955) 'The Senate and American Federalism', *American Political Science Review*, 49: 452–69.

Risse, T. (2000) '"Let's Argue!" Communicative Action in World Politics', *International Organization*, 54, 1: 1–39.

Rousseau, J.-J. (1968) [1762] *The Social Contract*, M. Cranston (trans. and ed.), Harmondsworth, Middlesex: Penguin Books.

Roth, G. and Wittich, C. (eds) (1968) *M. Weber, Economy and Society: An Outline of Interpretative Sociology*, New York: Bedminster.

Rudolph, L.I. and Rudolph, S.H. (2001) 'Redoing the Constitutional Design: From an Interventionist to a Regulatory State', in A. Kohli (ed.) *The Success of India's Democracy*, Cambridge: Cambridge University Press.

Rustow, D.A. (1975) 'Language, Nations, and Democracy', in J.-G. Savard and R. Vigneault (eds) *Les États multilingues: problèmes et solutions*, Québec: Les Presses de l'Université Laval.

Sabel, C.F. and Zeitlin, J. (2003) 'Active Welfare, Experimental Governance, Pragmatic Constitutionalism: The New Transformation of Europe', prepared for the International Conference of the Hellenic Presidency of the European Union, 'The Modernisation of the European Social Model and EU Policies and Instruments', Ioannina, Greece, 21–22 May.

Sartori, G. (2000) *Pluralismo, multiculturalismo e estranei*, Milano: Rizzoli.

Sartori, G. (1987) *The Theory of Democracy Revisited*, Chantam/New Jersey: Chantham House Publishers.

Scalia, A. (1997) *A Matter of Interpretation*, Princeton: Princeton University Press.

Schaber, T. (1998) 'The Regulation of Lobbying at the European Parliament: The Quest for Transparency', in P.-H. Claeys, C. Gobin, I. Smets and P. Winand (eds) *Lobbying, Pluralism and European Integration*, Brussels: European Interuniversity Press.

Scharpf, F.W. (2003) 'Problem-Solving Effectiveness and Democratic Accountability in the EU', MPIfG Working Paper 03/1, February 2003.

Scharpf, F.W. (2002) 'The European Social Model: Coping With the Challenges of Diversity', *Journal of Common Market Studies*, 40, 4: 645–70.

Scharpf, F.W. (2001) 'European Governance: Common Concerns vs the Challenge of Diversity', in C. Joerges, Y. Mény and J.H.H. Weiler (eds) 'Mountain or Molehill? A Critical Appraisal of the Commission White Paper on Governance', Jean Monnet Working Paper 6/01, Harvard. Online. Available at: http://www.iue.it/RSC/Governance (accessed April 2002).

Scharpf, F.W. (1999) *Governing in Europe: Effective and Democratic?*, Oxford: Oxford University Press.

Scharpf, F.W. (1994) 'Community and Autonomy: Multi-Level Policy-Making in the European Union', *Journal of European Public Policy* 1, 2: 219–42.

Schattschneider, E.E. (1960) *The Semi-sovereign People. A Realist's View of Democracy in America*, New York: Holt, Rinehart and Winston.

Schimmelfennig, F. (2001) 'The Community Trap: Liberal Norms, Rhetorical Action, and the Eastern Enlargement of the European Union', *International Organization*, 55, 1: 47–80.

Schmitter, P. (2001) 'What is there to Legitimize in the European Union ... and how Might this be Accomplished?', in C. Joerges, Y. Mény and J.H.H. Weiler (eds) 'Mountain or Molehill? A Critical Appraisal of the Commission White

Paper on Governance', Jean Monnet Working Paper 6/01, Harvard. Online. Available at: http://www.iue.it/RSC/Governance (accessed April 2002).

Schmitter, P. (2000) *How to Democratize the European Union ... and Why Bother,* Lanham, MD: Rowman and Littlefield; also published as *Come democratizzare l'Unione Europea ... e perché,* Bologna: Il Mulino.

Schmitter, P.C. (1996) 'Imagining the Future of the Euro Polity with the Help of New Concepts', in G. Marks, F.W. Scharpf, P.C. Schmitter and W. Streeck (eds) *Governance in the European Union,* Thousand Oaks, CA and London: Sage Publications.

Schofield, N. (2000) 'Constitutional Political Economy: On the Possibility of Combining Rational Choice Theory and Comparative Politics', *Annual Review of Political Science,* 3: 277–303.

Schönlau, J. (2001) 'The EU Charter of Fundamental Rights: Legitimation through Deliberation?', unpublished PhD thesis, University of Reading.

Scott, J. and Trubek, D.M. (2002) 'Mind the Gap: Law and New Approaches to Governance in the European Union', *European Law Journal,* 8, 1: 1–18.

Sen, A. (1982) 'Rights and Agency', *Philosophy and Public Affairs,* 11, 1: 3–39.

Shapiro, I. (2003) *The State of Democratic Theory,* Princeton and Oxford: Princeton University Press.

Shaw, J. (2003a) 'Process, Responsibility and Inclusion in EU Constitutionalism', *European Law Journal,* 9, 1: 53–67.

Shaw, J. (2003b) 'A Strong Europe is a Social Europe', London: The Federal Trust for Education and Research. Online. Available at: http://www.cix.co.uk/ ~fedtrust/Media/Josocialeuorope.pdf (accessed 1 June 2003).

Shaw, J. (1999) 'Postnational constitutionalism in the European Union', *Journal of European Public Policy,* 6, 4: 579–97.

Shore, C. (2000) *Building Europe: The Cultural Politics of European Integration,* London: Routledge.

Simon, V. (1995) 'A Commentary on Article F of the Treaty on European Union', in V. Constantinesco, R. Kovar and D. Simon (eds) *Traité sur l'Union Européenne,* Paris: Economica.

Skinner, Q. (1998) *Liberty Before Liberalism,* Cambridge: Cambridge University Press.

Skinner, Q. (1986) 'The Paradoxes of Political Liberty', in S.M. McMurrin (ed.) *Tanner Lectures on Human Values, VII,* Salt Lake City: University of Utah Press; Cambridge: Cambridge University Press.

Skinner, Q. (1984) 'The Idea of Negative Liberty: Philosophical and Historical Perspectives', in R. Rorty, J.B. Schneewind and Q. Skinner (eds) *Philosophy in History: Essays on the Historiography of Philosophy,* Cambridge: Cambridge University Press.

Smismans, S. (2003) 'European Civil Society: Shaped by Discourses and Institutional Interests', *European Law Journal,* 9: 482–504.

Smismans, S. (2002) 'Institutional Balance as Interest Representation. A Comment on Lenaerts and Verhoeven', in C. Joerges and R. Dehousse (eds) *Good Governance in Europe's Integrated Market,* Oxford: Oxford University Press.

Smismans, S. (2000) 'The European Economic and Social Committee: Towards Deliberative Democracy via a Functional Assembly', *European Integration Online Papers (EIoP),* 4, 12. Online. Available at: http://eiop.or.at/eiop/texte/ 2000–012a.htm.

Smismans, S. (1999) 'An Economic and Social Committee for the Citizen, or a Citizen for the Economic and Social Committee?', *European Public Law*, 5: 556–81.

Smismans, S. (1998) 'The Role of National Parliaments in the European Decision-Making Process: Addressing the Problem at European Level?', ELSA Selected Papers on European Law, 9: 49–76. Online. Available at: http://www.elsa-online.org/pdf/spel_4.pdf.

Smith, G. and Wales, C. (2002) 'Citizens' Juries and Deliberative Democracy', in M. Passerin d'Entrèves (ed.) *Democracy as Public Deliberation. New Perspectives*, Manchester: Manchester University Press.

Spruyt, H. (1994) *The Sovereign State and its Competitors*, Princeton, NJ: Princeton University Press.

Stepan, A. (2001) *Arguing Comparative Politics*, Oxford: Oxford University Press.

Stepan, A. (1999) 'Federalism and Democracy: Beyond the U.S. Model', *Journal of Democracy*, 10: 19–34.

Stewart, J., Kendall, E. and Coote, A. (1994) *Citizens' Juries*, London: Institute of Public Policy Research.

Streeck, W. and Schmitter, P.C. (1991) 'From National Corporatism to Trans-national Pluralism: Organized Interests in the Single European Market', *Politics and Society* 19, 2: 133–64.

Streeck, W. and Schmitter, P.C. (1985) *Private Interest Government: Beyond Market and State*, London: Sage.

Stråth, B. (2000) 'Multiple Europes: Integration, Identity and Demarcation to the Other', in B. Stråth (ed.) *Europe and the Other and Europe as the Other*, Brussels: P.I.E.-Peter Lang.

Sunstein, C.R. (1999) *One Case at a Time. Judicial Minimalism on the Supreme Court*, Cambridge: Harvard University Press.

Sunstein, C.R. (1996) *Legal Reasoning and Political Conflict*, Oxford: Oxford University Press.

Tallberg, J. (2003) *European Governance and Supranational Institutions: Making States Comply*, London: Routledge.

Taylor, C. (1995) 'Liberal Politics and the Public Sphere', in A. Etzioni (ed.) *New Communitarian Thinking, Persons, Virtues, Institutions, and Communities*, Char-lottesville and London: University Press of Virginia.

Taylor, C. (1994) *Reconciling the Solitudes. Essays on Canadian Federalism and Nation-alism*, Montreal and Kingston: McGill-Queen's University Press.

Taylor, C. (1992) *Multiculturalism and 'The Politics of Recognition'*, Princeton, New Jersey: Princeton University Press.

Taylor, C. (1989a) 'Cross-Purposes: The Liberal-Communitarian Debate', in N.L. Rosenblum (ed.) *Liberalism and the Moral Life*, Cambridge, MA: Harvard University Press.

Taylor, C. (1989b) *Sources of the Self*, Cambridge: Cambridge University Press.

Taylor, C. (1985) 'Atomism', in C. Taylor (ed.) *Philosophy and The Human Sciences, Philosophical Papers 2*, Cambridge: Cambridge University Press.

Taylor, C. (1979) 'What's Wrong with Negative Liberty?' in A. Ryan (ed.) *The Idea of Freedom*, Oxford: Oxford University Press.

Telò, M. (2001) 'Governance and Government in the European Union. The Open Method of Co-ordination', in M. Rodriguez (ed.) *The New Knowledge Economy in Europe*, London: Elgar.

Temple Lang, J. (2003) 'The Convention on the Future of Europe – So Far', Constitutional Online Paper, 18/03, June, The Federal Trust for Education and Research. Online. Available at: http://www.fedtrust.org/eu_constitution (accessed July 2003).

Terry, M. and Towers, B. (2000) 'Editorial: Developing Social Policy in the EU: Prospects and Obstacles', *Industrial Relations Journal*, 31, 4: 242–6.

Tilly, C. (1990) *Coercion, Capital, and European States, AD 990–1990*, Oxford: Blackwell.

Tronti, L. (1999) 'Benchmarking Employment Performance and Labour Market Policies: The Results of the Research Project', *Transfer*, 5, 4: 1–14.

Trubek, D.M. and Mosher, J.S. (2003) 'New Governance, Employment Policy and the European Social Model', in J. Zeitlin, and D. Trubek (eds) *Governing Work and Welfare in a New Economy: European and American Experiments*, Oxford: Oxford University Press.

Trubek, D.M. and Trubek, L.G. (2003) 'Hard and Soft Law in the Construction of Social Europe', paper prepared for presentation at the SALTSA, OSE, UW Workshop on Opening the Open Method of Coordination, European University Institute, Florence, Italy, July.

Tsebelis, G. (1990) *Nested Games: Rational Choice in Comparative Politics*, Berkeley and Los Angeles: University of California Press.

Tully, J. (2001) 'Introduction', in A.-G. Gagnon and J. Tully (eds) *Multinational Democracies*, Cambridge: Cambridge University Press.

Tully, J. (2000) 'The Unfreedom of the Moderns in Comparison to their Ideals of Constitutionalism and Democracy', Constitutionalism Web Papers, ConWEB No. 6/2000. Online. Available at: http://www.qub.ac.uk/ies/onlinepapers/const.html (accessed October 2003).

Tully, J. (1999) 'The Agonic Freedom of Citizens', *Economy and Society*, 28, 2: 161–82.

Tully, J. (1995) *Strange Multiplicity. Constitutionalism in an Age of Diversity*, Cambridge: Cambridge University Press.

Vanberg, V. and Wagner, R. (eds) (1996) 'Special Issue: Europe: A Constitution for the Millenium' [*sic*], *Constitutional Political Economy*, 7, 4.

Vandenbroucke, F. (2003) 'Intervention', Expert Hearing, European Convention, Working Group XI, Social Europe, 21 January 2003.

Vandenbroucke, F. (2002) 'The EU and Social Protection: What Should the European Convention Propose?' MPIfG Working Paper 02/6, June.

Van Kersbergen, K. and Verbeek, B. (1994) 'The Politics of Subsidiarity in the European Union', *Journal of Common Market Studies*, 32: 225–47.

Van Parijs, P. (1999) 'Contestatory Democracy Versus Real Freedom for All', in I. Shapiro and C. Hacker-Cordón (eds) *Democracy's Value*, Cambridge: Cambridge University Press.

Van Parijs, P. (1997a) *Real Freedom for All: What (if Anything) can Justify Capitalism?*, Oxford: Clarendon Press.

Van Parijs, P. (1997b) 'Should the European Union Become More Democratic?', in A. Follesdal and P. Koslowski (eds) *Democracy and the European Union*, Berlin: Springer.

Verdun, A. (ed.) (2002) *The Euro: European Integration Theory and Economic and Monetary Union*, Boulder and Oxford: Rowman and Littlefield.

Verhoeven, A. (1998a) 'Europe beyond Westphalia: Can Postnational Thinking

Cure Europe's Democracy Deficit?', *Maastricht Journal of European and Comparative Law*, 5: 369–90.

Verhoeven, A. (1998b) 'How Democratic Need European Union Members Be? Thoughts After Amsterdam', *European Law Review*, 23: 217–34.

Vibert, F. (2001) *Europe Simple, Europe Strong: The Future of European Governance*, Cambridge: Polity Press.

Waldron, J. (1999) *Law and Disagreement*, Oxford: Oxford University Press.

Waldron, J. (1993) 'A Rights-based Critique of Constitutional Rights', *Oxford Journal of Legal Studies*, 13, 1: 18–51.

Waldron, J. (1989) 'Rights in Conflict', *Ethics*, 99, 3: 503–19.

Walker, N. (2002) 'The Charter of Fundamental Rights of the European Union: Legal, Symbolic and Constitutional Implications', in P. Cullen and P.A. Zervakis (eds) *The Post-Nice Process: Towards a European Constitution?* Baden Baden: Nomos.

Wallace, H. (2001) 'The Changing Politics of the European Union', *Journal of Common Market Studies*, 39, 4: 581–94.

Wallace, H. and Hayes-Renshaw, F. (1997) *The Council of Ministers*, Basingstoke: Macmillan.

Walton, R.E. and McKersie, R.B. (1965) *A Behavioral Theory of Labor Negotiations: An Analysis of a Social Interaction System*, Ithaca, New York: ILR Press.

Walzer, M. (1990) 'Nations and Universe', in G.B. Peterson (ed) *The Tanner Lectures on Human Values, Vol XI*, Salt Lake City: Utah University Press.

Ward, I. (1996) '(Pre)conceptions in European Law', *Journal of Law and Society*, 23: 198–212.

Weale, A. (2001) 'Trust and Political Constitutions', *Critical Review of International Social and Political Philosophy*, 4, 4: 69–83.

Weale, A. and Nentwich, M. (eds) (1998) *Political Theory and the European Union: Legitimacy, Constitutional Choice and Citizenship*, London: Routledge/ECPR.

Weatherill, S. (2002) 'Is Constitutional Finality Feasible or Desirable? On the Cases for European Constitutionalism and a European Constitution', Constitutionalism Web Papers, ConWEB No. 7/2002. Online. Available at: http://www.qub.ac.uk/ies/onlinepapers/const.html (accessed May 2003).

Weiler J.H.H. (2000) 'Editorial: Does the European Union Truly Need a Charter of Rights?', *European Law Journal*, 6, 2: 95–7.

Weiler, J.H.H. (1999) *The Constitution of Europe. Do the New Clothes have an Emperor?*, Cambridge: Cambridge University Press.

Weiler, J.H.H. (1997) 'The European Union Belongs to its Citizens: Three Immodest Proposals', *European Law Review*, 22: 150–6.

Westlake, M. (1995) 'The European, the National Parliaments and the 1996 Intergovernmental Conference', *The Political Quarterly*, 66: 59–73.

Williamson, P.J. (1989) *Corporatism in Perspective*, London: Sage.

Young, I.M. (1990) *Justice and the Politics of Difference*, Princeton, New Jersey: Princeton University Press.

Zeitlin, J. (2003) 'Introduction', in J. Zeitlin and D. Trubek (eds) *Governing Work and Welfare in a New Economy: European and American Experiments*, Oxford: Oxford University Press.

Index

References to tables are in *italic*.

accountability 15, 97–8, 176; and
    transparency 144–5
Ackerman, B. 166
agency shirking 139–40, 149
Althusius, Johannes 53
American federalism 11
Amitsis, G. 98
Amsterdam, Treaty of *see* Treaty of
    Amsterdam (1997)
Anheier, H.K. 127
anti-facism 86
anti-federalism 11–15
appellate resources 109
Ardy, B. 93, 96, 97, 98, 99
Arneson, R.J. 77
Articles 1–16: 80
Article 1.59: 34
Article 2: 89, 132, 180
Article 6: 116
Article 6 (EU Treaty) 122
Article 9: 116
Article 10.3: 38
Article 12: 70
Article 13: 70
Articles 14-15: 70
Article 16: 70
Article 17: 119
Article 17.1-3: 70
Article 21: 137
Article 22 (Charter of Rights) 48
Article 22 TEC 120
Article 23: 70
Article 23.4: 71
Article 24: 71, 118
Article 25: 71

Article 26: 71
Article 26.2: 71
Article 34: 132–4
Article 39: 117
Article 40.7: 117
Article 42: 117
Article 43: 73
Articles 44-51: 80
Article 46.1/4: 120
Article 49(2) 139
Article 51: 85, 88, 155
Articles 57-59: 80
Article 58: 180
Article 59: 82, 118
Article F TEU 122
Article I-3: 48
Article I-14.3: 73
Article I-22: 48
Article I-28–2: 173
Article I-45: 134–6
Article I-46: 134, 136, 137
Article I-47: 137
Article I-51: 137
Article II-47: 120
Articles III 2-5: 120
Articles III 88-90: 73
Articles III 91-96: 73
Article III-235: 119
Article III-270: 119
asylum 33
Attucci, Claudia ix, 8, 9, 182
Australia 28, 30
Austria 1, 3
Austro-Hungarian empire 40–1
autonomy 104, 106, 113–14

Avineri, S. 78

Baldwin, R. 116, 117
Barber, B. 128, 129
bargaining: compromises 60, *65*, 68, *69*,
    76; distributive 145–6; integrative 146
Barry, Brian 76, 77, 78, 110–11
Baviera, S. 137
Bednar, J. 24, 27, 28, 29, 32
Begg, I. 93, 96, 97, 98, 99
Belgium 3, 19
Bellamy, Richard ix, 7, 58, 59, 79, 87,
    112, 113, 158, 162, 178
Berger, Maria 136
Berghman, J. 97
Berlin, Isaiah 79, 104
Besselink, L. 156
Betten, L. 129
Bickel, A. 170
bills of rights 154
Blank, K. 93
Bohman, J. 59, 62, 79, 129
Bomberg, E. 183
Bonde, J.P. 77, 81
Bonjour, E. 23
Bork, R. 166
'bottom up' benchmarking 100
Boyer, R. 35
Britain 117; privacy rights 59
Broad Economic Policy Guidelines
    process 92
Brown, T. 120
Brussels summit (2003) xii
budgetary powers 118
Buiter, Wilhelm 35–6, 37
Bulgaria 3
Bundesrat 27
Burgess, M. 23

Calmfors, L. 24, 36
Canada 19, 28, 29, 32
Carrió, G.A. 165
Castiglione, D. 78, 79, 112
Catholic social doctrine 125
centralization 176–7
Chair of the European Council 70
Charter of Fundamental Human Rights
    xii, 2, 9, 33–4, 47–8, 58–9, 64, 87,
    119, 151–63; aim 151–2; common
    principles 156–9; concept of rights
    160–1; constraining function 153–6;

contents 72; indivisibility 159–60;
    legitimacy 152; principles and rights
    161–2; subsidarity 153
'checker board' solutions:
    compromises 62
Christian tradition 75, 85–8, 90
churches 63, 85–8, 90, 137
'citizenization' 54
citizenship 2, 120, 125; *see also* direct
    citizen participation; European
    citizenship; European Union citizens
citizens' initiative 134, 136–7
civil society organizations 127, 129, 133
class conflict: Europe 20; USA 10
Closa, C. 119
coercive mechanisms 18
Cohen, J. 98, 130
Cologne mandate 155
comitology 52
comity 117
Commission officials: transparency 149
Committee of Regions (COR) 125
Common Foreign and Security Policy
    117
common language 43–4
communitarians: constituents 82;
    legitimacy 78–9; objectives 83; values
    85–8, 86
competencies: centralization 73;
    division 70
compliance 177
compromises: categories of 59–64, *65*;
    Convention on the Future of Europe
    64–74; reasons for 57–9
conceptions: of liberty 103–6
conferral 116
*Considerations on Representative
    Government* (Mill) 43
constituents: First Draft (FD) 82–3, 89
Constitution: USA 11, 34
constitutional design rules 25–6
constitutionalism 5
constitutionalization: federalism 13;
    process of 178–9
'constitutional patriotism' 158
constitutional politics 7
consultative resources 109
convention method 1–2
conventionnels, les 11, 183–4
Convention on the Future of Europe:
    compromises 64–74; idealists' and

cynics' views 56–7; Laeken
    Declaration 1–4; legitimacy deficit
    75–81
Convention Praesidium: first draft (FD)
    80–2
Convention process 7
convergence: voluntary public 93
cooperation: enhanced 73
'cooperative federalism' 176
Copenhagen summit (1973) 46
COR (Committee of Regions) 125
corporatist theory 148
Coulmas, F. 46
Council of Ministers: EU 28
Craig, P. 1–4, 130, 135
criminal justice 119
cultural differences 20
cultural diversity: democratic theory
    43–5; European identity 45–9;
    integration 52–3; Nice summit 49–50;
    subsidarity 53–4; as a value 84, 89
cultural goods: trade of 68
cultural homogeneity 42–5
cultural identities 54
Curtin, D. 126, 128, 129, 130, 139
Cyprus 3
Czechoslovakia 19
Czech Republic 3

Dahl, R.A. 176, 178
DD (democratic deficit) *see* democratic
    deficit
de Búrca, G. 95, 98, 102, 123, 125, 135
decision-making: asymmetry 35
decision-making method: Convention
    67–8
defence pact 117
defence policy 33
deficits *see* democratic deficit;
    legitimacy
Dehousse, R. 100, 124, 126
de la Porte, C. 93, 96, 97, 98, 100
deliberation: public philosophy 76
deliberative democracy 129–30
deliberative theory 140–1, 143
democracy 2, 8, 19, 122–38, 181;
    deliberative 129–30; federalism 15;
    judicial role 169; Treaties 122–3
democratic deficit (DD) xii, 34, 124,
    125–6
democratic equality 181–2

democratic interculturalism 54
democratic legitimacy: OMC 97–8
democratic participation 125
Denmark 3
depillarization 118–19
De Rossa, Proinsias 86–7
De Schutter, O. 129
De-Shalit, A. 78
differences: cultural 20
direct citizen participation 128–9; *see
    also* citizenship; European
    citizenship; European Union citizens
direct democracy 128
discrimination 120
distributive bargaining 145–6
diversity: cultural *see* cultural diversity;
    of representation 3–4; as a value
    84–5, 89
Dobson, Lynn ix, 8, 180
dominium (private power) 108
'double anchoring' 94
double asymmetry 35
Dougan, M. 118, 119
draft Constitution (July 2003) 2–3, 34
Duff, Andrew 86
Dworkin, Ronald 62, 166
Dyson, K. 32

Eastern Bloc 1
Eberlein, B. 93
ECB (European Central Bank) *see*
    European Central Bank
ECHR (European Convention on
    Human Rights) 165
ECJ (European Court of Justice) *see*
    European Court of Justice
Economic and Monetary Union (EMU)
    34–7
economic governance 72
e-democracy 128–9, 129
'editorial' control 109
EESC (European Economic and Social
    Committee) 126–8
efficiency-issues: transparency 149
Egeberg, M. 177
Eichengreen, B. 37
Einem, Caspar 136
Ekengren, M. 93
Elazar, D.J 31, 35
Elgström, O. 145

Elster, J. 56, 76, 129, 139, 140, 141, 142, 146, 178
Ely, John 168
EMU (Economic and Monetary Union) 34–7
English language 44
enhanced cooperation 73
enlargement 2, 33, 49, 66
environmental sustainability 120
epistemic elitism 171
equality 84, 87, 181–2; gender 120; as a value 89
equal rights 153
equilibrium 24
Eriksen, E.O. 56, 64, 129, 158
Eskridge, W.N. 27, 166
Estonia 3
European Central Bank (ECB) 35, 36, 145
European Charter of Human Rights *see* Charter of Fundamental Human Rights
European citizenship 125; *see also* citizenship; direct citizen participation; European Union citizens
European Convention on Human Rights (ECHR) 165
European Council President 116
European Court of Human Rights 166–7
European Court of Justice (ECJ) 119, 123, 124, 152, 154, 156–7, 166, 173
European Economic and Social Committee: (EESC) 126–8
European Employment Strategy 92
European identity 81, 149; cultural diversity 45–9
Europeanization 49, 51
European Union citizens 59; *see also* citizenship; direct citizen participation; European citizenship
European Union President 29, 33
European Union Treaty (1992) *see* Maastricht Treaty
European values 5
Euro (single currency) 73
Everson, M. 130
exit clause 82; *see also* secession; withdrawal

Fabre, C. 160
Falkner, G. 124
fascism 86, 87
FD (First Draft): 1-16: 85, 88; 2: 84–5; constituents 82–3; Convention Praesidium 80–2; objectives 83–4; values 84–9
Featherstone, K. 32
federal constitutional principles 26–7
federalism xii, 6, 10–24; American 11; definition 11–12, 23–4
Ferejohn, J. 27
Ferrera, M. 96, 97
Figel, Jàn 85
Filippov, M. 24, 25, 26, 27, 28, 29, 30
Fini, Gianfranco 78, 85
Finland 1, 3
First Draft (FD) *see* FD
fiscal centralization 36
fiscal decentralization 35
Fisher, R. 146
Fiss, Owen 168–9, 170–1
Follesdal, Andreas ix, 3, 76, 77, 130, 178, 181
foreign affairs 33
foreign policy 2
formal symmetry 14–15
Fossum, J.E. 129, 158
France 3, 50, 68, 117; privacy rights 59
Franck, T.M. 31
freedom 8; autonomy 104, 113–14; conceptions of 103–6; non-domination 104–6, 108–9, 112–13, 115–16; non-interference 107–8, 111–12, 115; positive 109–11, 115; and power 106–11
Friese, H. 158
fundamental boundaries 156–7
fundamental rights 58–9, 151–63

'gag-rules': compromises 63
game and rational choice theory (RT theory) *see* RT theory
Gargarella, Roberto ix, 8
gender equality 120
German Länder 70, 125
Germany 3, 37, 44, 50, 68, 117; Bundesrat 27; privacy rights 59; Tocqueville 11
Giscard d'Estaing, Valéry 2, 66, 67, 120
global affairs: and EU 2

Goetschy, J. 97
Goldsmith, Lord Q.G. 155, 161
Goodin, R.E. 142
governance 15–16, 138
'governance debate' 131–2
governance processes: 'soft' policy co-ordination 91–2
Greece 3
Grimm, Dieter 44
Gustavsson, S. 35
Gutmann, A. 139, 140

Habermas, Jürgen 44, 56, 76, 78, 158
Habsburg monarchy 40–1
Haenel, Hubert 79, 87
Hain, P. 81
Hallstein, Walter 42, 45–6
Harlow, C. 139, 145
harmonization 93; fiscal 36
Hart, H. 165
Hayek, F.A. 107, 108
Hayes-Renshaw, F. 146
Héritier, A. 93
Hix, S. 145
Hjelm-Wallen, Lena 81
Hobbes, T. 104
Hodson, D. 92, 93, 97
Hoffmann, L. 119
Holmes, J. 28
Holmes, S. 63, 155
Hooghe, L. 41, 93
Hoskyns, C. 139
Howse, R. 23
Hughes, K. 96, 97, 116
Hüglin, T.O. 53
human dignity 180
human rights 58–9, 151, 176, 182–3; *see also* fundamental rights
Hume, David xiv
Hungary 3

identity 17, 42–5, 143, 158; European 45–9, 81, 149; national 77; partisan 19; population 14; regional 30
'identity politics' 46
ideology 31
IGC (Intergovernmental Conference): Laeken Declaration 1–2; October 2003 10
immigration 33, 68
impartiality: judicial 172–4

imperium (public power) 108
India 29
Indian Constitution 26
indivisibility 159–60
input-orientated legitimacy 139–42, 150
institutional balance 117, 123, 124, 135
integration theories 16–19
integrative bargaining 146
interculturalism 54
interest groups 129
Intergovernmental Conference (IGC) *see* IGC
Ipsen, H. P. 123
Iraq war 2
Ireland 3
Islam 86
Italy 3, 117

Jacobsson, K. 93, 97, 98, 100
Jàszi, Oscar 40–1
Jayal, N.G. 29
Joerges, C. 130
Jönsson, C. 145
Judeo-Christian tradition 85–8
judges: scope of powers 164
judicial discretion 164–74, 183; ECHR (European Convention on Human Rights) 165; impeachment 169; independence 170; institutional system 170–1; legal interpretative theories 166–7; motivation 171–4; theories 168–9
judicial motivation 171–4
justice 33
'Justice and Home Affairs' 119
justification 76; *see also* legitimacy

Karlsson, C. 144
Kaufmann, Sylvia-Yvonne 86
Keiser, R. 93, 96
Kendall, J. 127
Kerwer, D. 93
Keynes, John Maynard 175
Korsten, A.F.A. 128
Kraus, Peter A. ix, 6, 7, 42, 46, 181
Kymlicka, W. 173

labour market 68
Laeken Declaration (2001) 66, 75; IGC (Intergovernmental Conference) 1–2

Laeken European Council meeting (2001) xi, 1
Lamassoure, Alain 136
Lamfalussy Report 92
Länder 70, 125
language: common 43–4
Latvia 3
laundering effect 141–2, 150
Le Galès, P. 54
legal interpretative theories 166–7
legal norms 165
legal personality 116
legislative power 124
legitimacy 75–81, 176; democratic deficit 123–4; 'input-orientated' 139–42; normative discourses 125; open method of co-ordination 97–8; output-orientated 143–4, 147; participation 128, 131; transparency 179
Lenaerts, K. 129, 135
liberal democratic theory: cultural diversity 42–5
liberals: constituents 82; legitimacy 77–8; objectives 83–4; values 84, 86
liberty 6, 8, 103–21, 180–1; *see also* freedom
life-style differences 20
Lijphart, A. 25, 32, 63
Lindberg, L.N. 123
lingua franca 44
linguistic diversity 43–4, 84, 89
linguistic pluralism 44, 46
Linz, J.J. 5
Lisbon open co-ordination processes 91–2
Lithuania 3
lobbyists 126
local autonomy 125
Lodge, J. 126
log-rolling: compromises 60–1, *65, 69*
Lord, C. 139, 145
loyalty 117
Luxembourg 3

Maastricht Treaty 1, 32, 47, 125; democracy 122
Madison, J. 107
Magnette, P. 66, 67, 100, 119, 130
Maher, I. 92, 93, 97
Majone, G. 140, 149, 150

majority voting 118
Malta 3
Mancini, F.G. 78
Man Without Qualities, The (Musil) 40
Marks, G. 41, 93
mass media 144
Matsaganis, M. 96
Maurer, A. 71
May, K. 62
Maynor, J. 108
McKay, David x, 6, 23, 28, 35, 36, 176–7
McKersie, R.B. 145, 146
McKinnon, R. I. 36
McRoberts, K. 29
media 144
membership: of the Convention 66–7
Merrills, J. 167
Meyer, Jürgen 136
military mobilization 18
military power 19–20
Mill, John Stuart 178; *Considerations on Representative Government* (Mill) 43; cultural diversity 42–5
Ministers 149
minorities 63; contestory democracy 109; judicial protection 168–9, 170; mediation 112; representation 3–4; rights 84, 110
'mixed' sovereignty system 113
MLG (multi-level governance) 16, 41, 93
modes of representation 27–30
Modood, T. 64
monetary policy 34–7, 72
Monnet method 2, 18
Moravcsik, A. 34, 56, 125
Morriss, P. 106, 107
Mosher, J. 96, 98
multi-level governance (MLG) 16, 41, 93
multinational polity 41
Musil, Robert: *The Man Without Qualities* 40

national action plans 100
national identities 51, 77, 84
nationalism 41, 51
national parliaments 116
nationhood 21
nation-states 51
natural disasters 117

Naurin, David x, 8, 145, 179
negative freedom 104–5
'negative' integration 52–3
negotiating: compromises 60–1, *65, 69*;
  Convention 68–70
negotiation theory 145, 148
Nentwich, M. 4, 124, 128
'nested games' 147, 148
Netherlands 3
Neunreither, K. 50
Neyer, J. 64, 130
NGOs (non-governmental
  organizations) 126–8
Nice summit (2000) 49–50; *see also*
  Treaty of Nice (2000)
Nicolaidis, K. 23
non-discrimination: as a value 89
non-domination: concept of freedom
  104–6, 112–13, 115–16, 180–1
non-governmental organizations
  (NGOs) 126–8
non-interference: concept of freedom
  104–6, 111–12, 115, 180
North America: federalism 10
Nozick, R. 112

objectives: FD (First Draft) 83, 89
Obradovic, D. 124
observers 67
Offler, H.S. 23
Olsen, Tore Vincents x, 7, 137
Ombudsman 119, 125
OMC (open method of co-ordination)
  7–8, 179; constitutionalization 94,
  101–2; critics 97–8; democratic
  legitimacy 95, 97–8; differentiated
  framework directives 99–100;
  efficiency 96; ideal type 92;
  legitimacy 96–7; national action
  plans 100; normative concerns 98–9
O'Neill, O. 162
open markets 120
open method of co-ordination (OMC)
  see OMC
Ordeshook, P.C. 24, 25, 26, 29, 30
output-orientated legitimacy 143–4, 150
'overlapping consensus': Rawls 157
over-representation 18

Paciotti, Elena 86
Palombella, G. 154

Parekh, B. 45, 79
parliamentary democracy 124
Parmar, S. 154
participants: Convention 3
participation 129–30
participatory democracy 8, 122, 123,
  126–38, 181–2
particularism 151
partisan identification 19
party systems 30
Pateman, C. 128
peer review: OMC 92
Peers, S. 118
'peripheralization' 23–4
Peterson, J. 183
petition right 137
Pettit, P. 105, 108, 109
Phillips, Anne 173
PLG (poly-centric governance) 16
pluralism 84; as a value 89
pluralists 24, 37, 90; constituents 82;
  legitimacy 79–80; objectives 83;
  values 84, 87
Pochet, P. 93, 97, 100
Poland 3
policy *compétences* 14
Polish Constitution: values 85, 87
political parties 29
political rights: European citizenship
  125
political unity 42
politics of recognition 52–5
poly-centric governance (PLG) 16
'popular' sovereignty 109–10
population identity: federalism 14
Portugal 3, 71
positive freedom 106, 109–11, 113–14,
  115
Potter, G.R. 23
power 6, 8; and freedom 106–11;
  legislative 124
Praesidium 4
Prange, H. 93, 96
Preamble, the 88, 90
President of the European
  Commission: system for election 71
President of the European Council 70,
  116
price stability 120
primacy 116
privacy rights 58–9

private power *(dominium)* 108
problem-solving capacity: loss of 146–7, 150
procedural compromises 61–2, *65, 69*; Convention 70–2
procedural resources 109
property ownership 120
proportionality 116
public interest 143
publicity 139, 144; Convention deliberations 67
public philosophy 75–7
public power *(imperium)* 108

qualified majority voting (QMV) 50–1, 71, 89, 118

Rabushka, A. 37
Radaelli, C.M. 92, 93
Rae, J. xiv
ratification procedures 89, 118
Raveaud, G. 100
Rawls, J. 56, 58, 77, 152, 157, 158, 159
Raz, J. 156, 160
reasoning by analogy 61
recognition: politics of 52–5
redistributive issues: transparency 149
referendums xii, 118
reforms 49
Regh, W. 129
regional autonomy 125
regional identities 84
religion 63, 85–8, 90; as a source of legitimacy 7
religious education: compromises 63–4
religious schisms 20
representation 2, 129, 147, 148; Convention participants 3–4; modes of 27–30
representative democracy 8, 122, 123, 125–6, 131, 132–8, 181–2
revision: procedures 89; of treaties 33
rights 8, 10, 112; bills of 154; equal 153; fundamental 58–9, 151–63; human 176, 182–3; minorities 84, 110; political 125; privacy 58–9; *see also* Charter of Fundamental Human Rights; European Court of Human Rights
Riker, William 14, 23, 25, 28
'roles' 3–4

Romania 3
Rome, Treaty of *see* Treaty of Rome (1957)
Room, G. 100
Roth, G. 123
Rousseau, J.-J. 109
RT theory (game and rational choice theory): EU institutional arrangements 24–30; monetary and fiscal policy 35–7; relevance to EU 30–4
Rudolph, L.I. 26
Rudolph, S.H. 26
rule of law 123, 182–3
Russia 32; *see also* USSR (Union of Soviet Socialist Republics)

Sabel, C.F. 96, 98, 130
Sacchi, S. 96
Sartori, G. 128
Scalia, A. 166
Schaber, T. 126
Scharpf, F.W. 96, 97, 99–100, 130, 139, 140, 142, 150, 176
Schattschneider, E.E. 147
Scheingold, S.A. 123
Schimmelfennig, F. 146
Schmid, H. 100
Schmitter, Philippe C. x, 6, 24, 148, 176, 177, 178, 182
Schönlau, Justus x, 7, 58, 87, 158, 162, 178
Scott, J. 92
secession 34, 108, 118, 176–7; *see also* exit clause; withdrawal
second-best: compromises 61, *65, 69*
secularity 86
'security community' 19
security issues 18
segregation: compromises 63, *65, 69*; Convention 72–4
self-interest 139–40
SGP (Stability and Growth Pact) 35, 36–7
Shapiro, I. 109
shared competences 117
shared values 179–83
Sharman, C. 28
Shaw, J. 67, 113, 119, 189
Shepsle, K.A. 37
Shvetsova, O. 24, 25, 26, 29, 30

Simon, V. 122
single currency (Euro) 73
Single European Act (1986):
    democracy 122
Skaarup, Peter 86
Skinner, Q. 105
Slovakia 3
Slovenia 3
Smismans, Stijn x, 8, 120, 125, 127, 130,
    135
Smith, Adam xiv
Smith, G. 129
'Social 'Europe' project 120
social justice 84, 85
social security 33
'soft' policy co-ordination governance
    processes 91–2
sovereignty xii, 5, 53–4, 77, 84, 89;
    'mixed' 113; 'popular' 109–10
Spain 3, 71
special interest groups 126; *see also*
    minorities
Spruyt, H. 54
stability 24, 27, 175–6
Stability and Growth Pact (SGP) 35,
    36–7
stateness 21; federalism 13
statists: constituents 82; legitimacy 77;
    objectives 83
Stepan, A. 5, 181
Stewart, J. 129
Streeck, W. 148, 182
subsidarity 53–4, 68, 73–4, 116, 125, 130
Sunstein, Cass 169
supermajoritarianism 116, 118
supra-national secretariat 16–17
Supreme Court: USA 11
sustainability 30, 31, 120
Sweden 1, 3
Switzerland 23, 29, 30; Tocqueville 10,
    11
Szajer, J. 82, 87

Tajani, Antonio 85, 86
Tallberg, J. 149
task-orientated: Convention 67
taxation 33, 72; centralized 18
Taylor, C. 52, 78, 82, 106
Telò, M. 101
Temple Lang, J. 117
territorial boundaries 13–14

terrorism 117
Terry, M. 98
Thessaloniki (2003) 2
Thompson, D. 139, 140
Tilly, C. 54
time scale: Convention 66
Tocqueville, Alexis de 10–11, 19, 21, 177
Towers, B. 98
trade: in cultural goods 68
trading: compromises 60–1, *65, 69*
transparency 8–9, 49, 97–8, 100, 125–6,
    139–50, 179; and accountability
    144–5
Treaty of Amsterdam (1997) 1, 47, 85,
    87, 122
Treaty of Maastricht (1997) 1, 32, 47,
    125; democracy 122
Treaty of Nice (2000) 1, 20, 66, 122; *see
    also* Nice summit (2000)
Treaty of Rome (1957) 47, 122
Treaty reform 66
trimming: compromises 63, *65, 69;*
    convention 72
Tronti, L. 98
Trubek, D.M. 92, 96, 102
Trubek, L.G. 102
trust 16–17
Tsakatika, Myrto x, 7, 179
Tsebelis, G. 147
Tully, J. 54, 80, 113
Turkey 3, 86
'Two Concepts of Liberty': Isaiah
    Berlin: essay 104

UK (United Kingdom) *see* United
    Kingdom
unanimity 116, 118
un-elected elites 31–2
unilateral withdrawal 89
United Kingdom (UK) 3; subsidarity
    125
United States of America (USA) 28, 29;
    Constitution 11, 34; federalism 10,
    11; federalism model 12; Iraq war 2;
    military 20; privacy rights 59
universalism 151
unselfishness norm 143
USA (United States of America) *see*
    United States of America
USSR (Union of Soviet Socialist
    Republics) 32; disintegration of 1, 19

values 82, 179–83; European 5; of the
    European Union 75; *see also* public
    philosophy; FD (First Draft) 84–9, 89
Vandenbroucke, F. 92, 93, 94
Van Kersbergen, K. 125
Van Parijs, P. 114
Verbeek, B. 125
Verdun, A. 32
Vergés-Bausili, A. 119
Verhoeven, A. 122, 129, 135
veto power 116
Vibert, Frank 111–12
voluntary public convergence 93
voting power 117
voting procedures 118

Wagner, P. 158
Waldron, J. 158, 160, 165
Wales, C. 129
Wallace, H. 92, 146
Walton, R.E. 145, 146

war: Iraq 2
Ward, I. 125
Weale, A. 4, 115
Weatherill, S. 119
Weiler, J.H.H. 42, 128, 139, 154, 156–7
welfare state: harmonization of 20
Westlake, M. 125
Widgren, M. 116, 117
Williamson, P.J. 148
Wilson, Woodrow 140
withdrawal: unilateral 89; *see also* exit
    clause; secession
Wittich, C. 123
women: Convention participants 3
Wyplosz, C. 37

Young, I.M. 79
Yugoslavia 19, 32

Zeitlin, J. 95, 96
Zieleniec, Josef 77, 83

For Product Safety Concerns and Information please contact our EU
representative GPSR@taylorandfrancis.com
Taylor & Francis Verlag GmbH, Kaufingerstraße 24, 80331 München, Germany